GROWING UP
CHICAGO

GROWING UP
CHICAGO

EDITED BY

DAVID SCHAAFSMA,
ROXANNE PILAT, AND
LAUREN DeJULIO BELL

FOREWORD BY
LUIS ALBERTO URREA

NORTHWESTERN UNIVERSITY PRESS
EVANSTON, ILLINOIS

Northwestern University Press
www.nupress.northwestern.edu

Printed in the United States of America

10   9   8   7   6   5   4   3   2   1

Library of Congress Cataloging-in-Publication Data

Names: Schaafsma, David, 1953– editor. | Pilat, Roxanne, editor. | Bell, Lauren
    DeJulio, editor.
Title: Growing up Chicago / edited by David Schaafsma, Roxanne Pilat, and Lauren
    DeJulio Bell.
Other titles: Second to none: Chicago stories.
Description: Evanston : Northwestern University Press, 2022. | Series: Second to
    none: Chicago stories.
Identifiers: LCCN 2022002102 | ISBN 9780810143685 (paperback)
Subjects: LCSH: Short stories, American—Illinois—Chicago. | Short stories,
    American—21st century. | Chicago (Ill.)—Fiction. | LCGFT: Short stories.
Classification: LCC PS572.C5 G76 2022 | DDC 813.01083277311—dc23/eng/20220119
LC record available at https://lccn.loc.gov/2022002102

We dedicate this collection to all tellers of Chicago stories—
past, present, and future.

CONTENTS

FOREWORD

LUIS ALBERTO URREA

*It is hopeless for the occasional visitor to try to keep up with
Chicago—she outgrows his prophecies faster than he can make
them. She is always a novelty; for she is never the Chicago you
saw when you passed through the last time.*
—MARK TWAIN, *LIFE ON THE MISSISSIPPI*

TRIED TO RESIST CHICAGO, I REALLY DID. I FOUND MYSELF STAND-
ing among the Brutalist architecture of the towers of the University of
Illinois Chicago (UIC) after years of wandering the mountains and deserts
and bayous of the country. It was my first tenured job, but I didn't think I
would last. As it always does, though, Chicagoland had its own ideas.

I was lucky to land a few doors down from David Schaafsma, whose
love of the city and its writers was the springboard for this project. Our
offices are perched high enough in University Hall to have a panoramic
view. The scene is bereft of great skyscrapers or the shores of Lake
Michigan but has become dear to me for its unvarnished urban reality. I
think we usually want to roll up our sleeves and get some work done. The
view from our floor reminds us why we're teaching here.

Schaafsma and I have been faculty co-conspirators now for twenty
years or more. The other editors of this volume, Roxanne Pilat and
Lauren DeJulio Bell, have been colleagues, educators, and co-participants

in workshops for several years as well. We have all been, in one way or another, involved in the literary life of this city: as teachers, as facilitators, even helping nonprofit literary outreach programs get a footing here. All of the editors of this collection, by the way, are excellent authors themselves, each with strong ties to Chicago.

This book first made itself felt during lunch conversations between Schaafsma and fellow faculty member in the Program in English Education Tony Grosch—a scholar of Chicago novels and the creator of a Chicago literature course at UIC. The idea of a book about the writing that emerged from Chicago neighborhoods surfaced in two of those neighborhoods, Little Italy and Greektown, just blocks away from Jane Addams's Hull House. Just a shade west and across Halsted, not too far from where Mrs. O'Leary's cow kicked over that lantern and started the Great Chicago Fire. A comfortable stroll a few blocks north from Maxwell Street, home of the Blues. You couldn't get more Chicago than that.

Because the editorial team consists of serious scholars, all of whom are deeply involved in English education, they had a scholarly view. They had a plan, of course. The book was intended for a high school or college audience—it was to be a collection of works that teachers could share with students as examples of the importance of place in writing, and as a demonstration of contemporary, engaged, community-based literacy. And it's certainly met those goals. But hey—this is Chicago. This book was fated for more than its initial noble cause. Too many amazing writers had given the editors too much living prose. Mark Twain warned us: we are not going to keep up with Chicago. Chicago has its own idea and its own energy and its own narrative and its own immense mojo. And so the reach of the book has grown. It wanted to be something more.

As the book took shape, it became clear that it might reach a wider audience. As more and more writers shared their stories, the book's purpose expanded, too, to become a collection of Chicago voices, revealing and celebrating the city's varied and intensely alive neighborhoods to readers beyond the classroom, and beyond the city. Who wouldn't want to read it?

Well, how lucky are we? For here it is: *Growing Up Chicago*.

Studs Terkel, longtime guardian of Chicago's stories, would be proud of this volume's editorial team and its authors. For you lucky guests who come to our town: I hope the book becomes part of your visit. A literary guide to the soul of this great, burly place. For all you homies: celebrate these many streets you know so well—maybe you'll learn something. But I know you'll find many things that already connect you, deeply, to Chicago. And for you students: this is that book from class that you'll put on your shelves to keep.

INTRODUCTION

ROXANNE PILAT, DAVID SCHAAFSMA, AND LAUREN DeJULIO BELL

WHO ARE YOU? WHO AM I? HOW DO WE ENTER INTO THE SPACE that stands between us? How can we travel through that unknown divide, to better understand each other, and to better know ourselves? These are the kind of questions that drive us to read, and to write. And now our many divisions spark newer questions, intensified by events close to home and far away: racial reckonings, pandemics, climate change, dwindling resources, and increasing refugee crises across the world. How do our circumstances of birth limit or propel us? What choices may we need to face in the future? What does it mean to live, and especially, to come of age in such a time? These are the questions that bring our experiences—and our stories—to life.

There is a certain kind of power in storytelling. In a well-told tale, there is a voice that comes from a place, in space or time, that leaves an indelible stamp on our minds. Stories have a power that can help us negotiate our way through the worlds we inhabit. Growing-up stories can be especially powerful, as it is hard to deny that there is a lot to negotiate in the first twenty or so years of living. Our bodies and minds are in a constant state of flux and growth, as we seek to find a sense of identity and equilibrium amid persistent and turbulent forces, often outside our control. This may be how life continues for most; but when we are young, every new experience, every new struggle, every new skill, is uncharted territory. Dealing with these forces for the first time makes them feel bigger and more challenging.

Growing up in a place like Chicago offers chance after chance to come to terms with questions of identity, beginning with the city's sheer size and geographic complexity, which could easily make a person feel small, unnoticed, irrelevant. From afar, its muscular skyline—much of it rebuilt after the Great Chicago Fire, and later expanded on landfill that pushed the original shoreline out into the lake—conveys a certain Midwest practicality, coupled with a seeming determination to conquer the impossible. This is a city that had the fortitude to rebuild after the fire, the imagination to reverse the flow of the Chicago River. The reach of its skyline today frames the expanse of Lake Michigan, stretching north to south, with tall and taller buildings rising into the clouds, like arms of concrete and steel, limestone and granite, as if to say "We are here!"

The long view of Chicago is mesmerizing. Driving into the city, Chicago looks like an enormous snow globe, tinted by azure tones of the lakeshore. But enter the canyons at the foot of those skyscrapers, and there, on its sidewalks and stairwells, beats the true pulse of the city—its people. There's the Mexican pushcart vendor selling savory elotes, bucket boys drumming vibrant beats on street corners, *StreetWise* sellers hawking copies of the city's street magazine, and dancers leading Argentine tango lessons in Grant Park. Peek in the storefront windows and you might see a chef slicing gyros off the spit, or an Indian artist drawing intricate henna designs on an anonymous hand. The city hums like a hive, and people-watching comes easy here: from students and workers to lake-path runners and theatergoers; from sports fans and museum hoppers to street artists and window shoppers. Each and every person has a story to tell—if you ask them—and Chicago's literary heritage is an evolving mosaic of such stories.

Chicago is a city of writers and for writers. It is home to the internationally recognized research library, The Newberry, as well as the Poetry Foundation, the American Writers Museum, and the Chicago Humanities Festival. It is the site of the annual Printers Row literary festival, a variety of indie bookstores, and an especially vibrant theater community. It is home to Louder Than a Bomb, the world's largest youth poetry festival. The city's Beaux-Arts inspired Harold Washington Library Center with its five oversized rooftop owls is the main outpost for a library system that supports seventy-nine branches throughout the neighborhoods.

Chicago, founded in 1833, is a city of neighborhoods, often starting as ethnic enclaves, each with distinct identities of their own, evolving as their populations changed. Its potential as the future hub of the nation's industry and transportation made it the destination for countless immigrants and migrants, who came to find work in the rail yards, stockyards, print shops, and steel mills. Even today, newcomers cluster—in areas such as Bronzeville, Chinatown, Pilsen, Little Italy, Argyle Street, Greek Town, Ukrainian Village, Bridgeport, and more—where the neighbors, the places of worship, and the mom-and-pop stores are reminders of other homes left behind. Though populations have shifted and urban redevelopment has gentrified some of the older neighborhoods during the past half-century, reminders of Old World ties still exist, in statues and landmark buildings, festivals and parades, and in the stories told here. Other neighborhoods have been revitalized by newer social enclaves, such as Wicker Park and Northalsted (formerly Boystown).

Chicago is a city of contrasts, epitomized for some by the noxious odors of highway exhaust, but for others, by the sweet downdrafts of cocoa from its candy-making factories. It is a city where the laughter of children is heard at local parks that emerge unexpectedly amid stretches of three-flats and squatty brick bungalows, while the prayer-minded quietly line up at churches, temples, and mosques that anchor the neighborhoods. Across the city, you can find tagging, street art, and murals on the sides of buildings, under viaducts, or on train platforms, while the reflective glass windows of high-rise condos simply mirror what's across the street. Late in July, beachgoers stretch out blanket-to-blanket, blaring boom-box rhythms, or grill barbeque even as intrepid seagulls snatch bits of unwatched food. But even in winter's deepest freeze, the lakefront attracts a faithful cadre of runners, dog walkers, and those who seek inspiration in the visible presence of nature's force. Year-round, there's an ongoing rebirth of opportunities to connect in many parts of the city: from the Hermitage Street Community Garden in Englewood to the Evanston Art and Big Fork Festival; from the Kids and Kites Festival at Montrose Harbor to the renovation and new tours in Pullman's historic railcar-manufacturing neighborhood; from Bike the Drive on Memorial Day weekend to the Chicago Marathon in October, with jazz, rock, and other music festivals in between. All the while, the city streets crisscross and zigzag, and its elevated trains continue to screech and rumble.

Dubbed the Second City, the Windy City, Chi-Town, and other nicknames, Chicago has withstood more than a few attempts to diminish its importance as a national force, and writers have long portrayed Chicago as a place with strength, endurance, and attitude, depicted in the iconic imagery of Carl Sandburg's "Stormy, husky brawling City of the Big Shoulders" as well as Eve Ewing's concrete yet ethereal "All I ever really wanted you to know about me was Fullerton Avenue." Yet the city is more than a nickname or a location on a map. It is a place steeped in the legends of its earliest natives, the ambition of its settlers, the invention of its builders, the history of its development, and the diverse populace who came to reside within its boundaries. Chicago was named for the native garlic plants (*Checaugou*) that grew along its river. That name, popularly interpreted as "wild onion," became an apt metaphor for the city's unbridled spirit, flavor, and energy. If the city today evokes a similar attitude, then *Growing Up Chicago* is a literary expression of that point of view.

What we come to identify as the locale or setting of any story sparks a reader's expectation, and Chicago's neighborhoods, along with its surrounding suburbs and rural outposts, provide a solid foundation for the voices included in this collection. Beyond its stance bordering Lake Michigan, Chicago is known for the opulence of Buckingham Fountain, the mysteries found in the city's museums, zoos, and botanical gardens, the drawbridges that connect its neighborhoods, and a river that runs through it, one that is actually tinted green each year on Saint Patrick's Day. In recent years, the oversized shiny Millennium Park ornament titled *Cloud Gate* (what everyone calls "the Bean") has claimed its own place in Chicago's identity. But not everything about Chicago draws admiration—the city is known for its protests as much as its parades, its boarded-up buildings as much as its landscaped boulevards. Poverty, crime, and violence loom larger than all of it sometimes. As this collection of stories has come together, the city and its peoples are confronting the enduring questions of race, gender, and abuses of power and privilege with intensified focus. As Chicago continues to grapple with prejudice and bias, its stories increasingly call out for us to find answers, to do better, to be better—for the city, and for those who call it home.

There are 234 square miles in the city of Chicago proper, the core of nearly 10,000 square miles in the Chicago metropolitan area, connected by 55,000 miles of streets and highways. That includes seventy-seven city neighborhoods and fifteen counties. Chicagoland borders Lake Michigan, stretching to meet two state lines—Wisconsin and Indiana—and reaching west and south, past the Illinois River, a main tributary of the Mississippi. This location was vital to its earliest settlers, who envisioned Chicago as the gateway for the nation's expansion, for industry, and for the growth of a populace that would make for a prosperous future.

Three hundred people lived in Chicago at its founding in 1833, and by 1893, that number had grown to a million. Chicago epitomized the changes happening within the country's industrial North. The development of its canal and railroad systems made the city a locus for economic power as factories brought in immigrants, most of whom lived in overly crowded two- and three-story buildings in a working-class environment bordering on poverty, one that social activist and writer Jane Addams recognized as both vital and volatile: "In the disorder and confusion sometimes incident to growth and progress, the community may be unable to see anything but the unlovely struggle itself."

The struggle to rebuild after the Great Chicago Fire in 1871 enabled the city to re-create itself around the lakefront, and the ensuing construction of skyscrapers made the most desirable locations more profitable by fitting more people into smaller spaces. During that same decade, Mark Twain came to identify Chicago as "a city where they are always rubbing the lamp, and fetching up the genie, and contriving and achieving new impossibilities." He recognized Chicago as unique—particularly in its adaptability to change, a quality that longtime Chicagoans brag about.

More than 2.7 million people live in the city today, but nearly 7 million are found in its surrounding suburbs and outlying towns. Nearly a quarter of those residents are eighteen years old or younger.

The city is a starting place for the writers in this collection, whose stories begin in the 1950s and continue to the present day. As a textual space, Chicago voices emerge from race, gender, class, and other core aspects of identity, reflecting the city's historical and social development. Collectively, their words urge us to consider identity not as a static entity but as one that is constantly in flux, whether chosen or imposed, coherent or conflicted. We are, each of us, living spaces where multiple identities reside. Some of these spaces have been dominant forces within the city's literary canon, while others have been marginalized. In publishing this anthology, we affirm that we each hold the ability to shape the places in which we live and write and read, as much as those places shape us. The individual writers here are part of a newer collective voice of Chicago identity, and their stories make us ask new questions, and seek newer answers. Each narrative in *Growing Up Chicago* reflects the real experiences of real individuals, enabling others to enter into the city's spaces and see Chicago and its people from new perspectives.

What combination of qualities characterizes a "Chicago" author? Is that title a distinction earned by a certain pulse of the language? Or is it based on a particular tone of voice or syntactic sensibility? Is it found in the mention of specific neighborhoods or landmarks? This collection is primarily built on the work of authors who spent their growing-up years in Chicago. We also include writers who did not grow up within the city limits, but lived in nearby suburbs such as Lisle, Evanston, and Blue Island; their connections to Chicago make their words just as dynamic. The authors in this collection write from distinct narrative spaces, which help us realize the rich diversity of this city and its surroundings. Yet some universals seem to emerge in the process. We all have families, or friendships, of one kind or another. We all suffer pain, we live, we learn.

The anthology honors but does not include earlier writers whose words captured Chicago in some of its most brilliant and some of its most abrasive times, among them Jane Addams, Nelson Algren, Saul Bellow,

Edgar Rice Burroughs, Gwendolyn Brooks, Sandra Cisneros, James Far-
rell, Lorraine Hansberry, Ernest Hemingway, Harriet Monroe, Carl Sandburg, and Richard Wright—authors whose words recorded the changing
scenes of Chicago's literary and social landscapes. These authors were
writing in a time when literary realism demanded a certain objectivity of
voice and purpose. The Chicago narratives included in this volume, while
grounded in realism, are melded with a more subjective stance, reflecting our national ongoing contemporary engagement with life narratives,
essaying, and memoir. These narrative modes echo and expand upon the
symbolic statement of the city's sky-grazing architecture: "Here we are!
Pay attention!"

As editors, we have worked with a vision of building an inclusive
landscape of voices—an anthology that acknowledges and respects the
spectrum of identity, culture, life choices, class, age, and more. Previously
marginalized Chicago voices are coming to find deserved recognition in
today's stories—and this is a welcome and vital change, one that is still
under way, even as this volume is published. It is a narrative mandate
demanding that we continue to ask: Just who gets to speak for, and about,
growing up in Chicago? As editors, we sought to include authors whose
backgrounds and experiences would make the content more representa-
tive of the city. We recognize that it is easy to feel disengaged from the
literature that we read, written by authors who are faceless and distant
from our own lives and communities. So each author has penned an intro-
duction reflecting on their motivations and the relevance of their work in
today's complex times.

Though Chicago is the starting place for each of the writings that
follow, there is no single literary narrative of the city. Our goal is to empha-
size that the creation of literature and the act of writing do not belong to
a single group but are born out of a variety of experiences. We aim here to
stoke your reading curiosity and understanding, and especially to encourage you to consider the diversity of Chicago as a space where you may find
purpose and empathy in the worlds and words of others.

Such starting places can be found in the memory of something as literally concrete as George Saunders's recall of the panoramic cityscape from

a suburban sidewalk in "The View from the South Side, 1970." In "Planet Rock," Dhana-Marie Branton's impression of the giant neon Magikist lips that once perched above a city expressway becomes a touchstone for her Chicago existence. In "Dillinger," the gun that shot the notorious gangster becomes the object that links three generations of Jessie Ann Foley's family together in a quest for a bit of a better life.

In "Chicago," Daiva Markelis takes us along on her immigrant parents' field trips to the city, where they visited giant cultural landmarks such as the Art Institute, the Chicago Symphony, and the Lyric Opera. In "Growing Up in Chicago," Tony Romano invokes the streets of his childhood, where vendors sold aromatic lupini beans and the kids played nighttime games of ringolevio. But the Chicago connection can be ephemeral, too, such as a link to the city rooted in a moment of recognition that people are often not what they may be labeled, which Maxine Chernoff unpacks as she gets to know the attendant at the local gas station in "The Untouchables."

Some of the stories that follow examine identity and the challenges of stereotyping, bias, and xenophobia, while others consider concepts of gender, ethnicity, class, and power. Most of the selections detail, and sometimes celebrate, the commonplaces and complexities of coming of age. James McManus writes of his after-school angst with his own burgeoning sense of sexuality in "Detention," while David Mura finds that he has unwittingly crossed an invisible racial dividing line at his first boy-girl party, in "All-American Boy."

Narratives in this volume often intersect in a quest to better understand links to another generation, or ancestral homeland, such as Ana Castillo's revisiting her Mexican roots in "My Mother's México," Daiva Markelis's education in her Lithuanian heritage in "During the Reign of Vytautas the Great," and Rebecca Makkai's reflections on a homeland she never knew in "Children of the Fifty-Sixers: Growing Up in Hungarian Chicago." From other growing-up perspectives, Erika L. Sánchez wrestles with cultural expectations as she tries to unravel a family secret, in an excerpt from *I Am Not Your Perfect Mexican Daughter,* and Samira Ahmed seeks to take a stand against her parents' protective demands in an excerpt from *Love, Hate & Other Filters*. In "Discovering My Femininity in Menswear," M Shelly Conner remembers her discomfort in childhood ballet classes, which leads to a self-reflective essay on how the clothes you wear come to impact your identity—from the inside out.

Childhood is also complicated for Nnedi Okorafor, when she and her sisters face racist hurdles as they traverse their neighborhood, in "Running Girl"; for Charles Johnson, as he seeks to reconcile his artistic ambitions with his father's own dream for his son, in "My Father's Pillow Talk"; and for Anne Calcagno, who sifts through the complicated debris of neighborhood friendships and parental worries in "Between Boys."

Other essays wrestle with memories of intense and troubled times, such as the aftermath of Makkai's experience with sexual assault, in "The Power and Limitations of Victim-Impact Statements"; Christian Picciolini's toxic teenage foray into white supremacy in "White Power"; and in "Grave News," Saja Elshareif's reckoning with the wartime existence of faraway relatives, as viewed from the local television news reports.

For some of the tales told here, Chicago emerges not just as a stage, but as a character, too—visual and rich with emotion and dynamism. The personality of the city infuses the story with meaning beyond its geography, allowing us to see that the urbanscape, like human nature, is constantly in flux. In the dark humor of "Death of the Right Fielder," Stuart Dybek offers a semi-somber eulogy, within the confines of a city icon, the neighborhood outfield. In "Vigil," Dybek offers nostalgic humor, providing impressionistic glimpses of the city at Christmas, embellished by his Polish roots and traditions.

The anthology is wrapped in the work of cover artist Emil Ferris, whose complex images, like those depicted in her graphic work "Mothman," capture compelling memories of city dwellers, in all their strange beauties and complexities. Her artistry shows Chicago as always, ever, multifaceted. It is a diamond, rough and even dull in its natural state, waiting for an author's hand to find just the right angles, just the right words—to shape an idea, to record a memory, to retell an event, to make a point.

Growing Up Chicago reminds us that stories, too, are multifaceted, reflecting both our public and private spaces. These Chicago narratives urge us to reconsider what matters and to insist that we hold ourselves responsible for our biases, prejudices, stereotypes. In the words of Gwendolyn Brooks, "We are each other's harvest; we are each other's business; we are each other's magnitude and bond." Brooks's words remind us of our collective humanity. We are obliged to reach across the spaces that separate us and find moments in which we may learn that we are more alike than we are different.

Our overriding aim has been for this collection to offer you, its reader, stories in which your own cultural and social identity may resound, in the echo of some known and some newer Chicago voices. We believe the stories that follow have the potential to broaden readers' perspectives, to open minds to the multitude of personalities and situations we encounter in the world, and to build empathy. Some suggest that growing up happens throughout your life. We like that idea. Knowing that every day, wherever you find yourself, there are moments waiting to happen, full of possibility and challenge and even hope, moments that may transform you in ways you never thought of before. Stories remind us of that, too. Perhaps here, amid the words of others, you will find—and even be encouraged to write—your own stories, ones yet to be told, but just as valued.

GROWING UP
CHICAGO

CHICAGO

DAIVA MARKELIS

Although I loved and admired my immigrant parents, there were times I was also embarrassed by them. They mispronounced words; they didn't know who Ernie Banks was; they insisted on taking us to the Art Institute instead of Riverview amusement park. For my parents, what was great about Chicago had a lot to do with its culture. They were fans of the Lyric Opera and the Chicago Symphony Orchestra, and viewed baseball and amusement parks as unworthy substitutes for more elevating activities: visiting museums, listening to classical music. My parents' love of the arts has been a big influence on how I see the world and what I value. I do think, however, that they missed the boat on baseball, which has turned out to be one of the great passions of my life. Amusement parks, not so much.

MY PARENTS BELIEVED THAT ONE WAY TO CONTAIN THE FLOOD OF popular American culture was to construct a dam out of the lofty bricks of European civilization. If they couldn't prevent my sister and me from playing Mother-May-I in the alleys of Cicero with questionable non-Lithuanian friends, if they couldn't thwart the growing pile of comics in our bedroom, well, then, they could take us to museums and expose us to great books and magnificent architecture and classical music.

"We're going to the *meno institutas*," my mother announced one Saturday morning in July when I was ten, her voice an unconvincing whisper of excitement.

My sister and I didn't want to "visit the pictures" at the Art Institute; we

3

wanted to ride the Candy Cane Sleigh at Santa's Village Amusement Park and see the Twirling Snowballs and feed the reindeer with Diane Metrick.

"Reindeer bite," my mother explained in Lithuanian. "You'll get rabies."

"Cos too much," my father continued in English, as if the switch to the language my sister and I spoke with ease would strengthen the firmness of his message. "An too far," he added, as if Santa's Village was in another country.

"It's only an hour away," we whined.

"Vie go distan suburb? Vee explore gray seedy of Chikaago."

"It's *great city*, dad," I muttered.

"Yeah, learn to speak English," my sister added.

"No Satan's Villa for you," my father answered, repeating the phrase several times.

And so instead of piling into the Metricks' beige sedan, we boarded the Douglas El on Cicero Avenue, my mother clutching her handbag, my sister and I in prim little cotton dresses, my dad in a short-sleeved shirt. As the El climbed to the level of the treetops, rumbling slowly downtown, I felt a growing sense of excitement. Although the day was hot and there was no air-conditioning on the trains, the breeze at the open window felt good. And I liked the way the conductor called out the names of the stops, stressing one syllable over the rest: Killl-dare, Pu-laaas-ki, Central Paaa-rk.

"We're in sunny California," my sister shouted as the train stopped at Twenty-Sixth and California, near the Sheriff's Office and the Cook County Jail. A grizzled old man entered clutching a paper bag next to his chest; a group of Black teenagers smacking gum grabbed the handrail above my father's seat. My mother held her purse a little tighter. A few stops later, the El descended underground into total darkness. We stepped out at Adams holding hands, looking around to catch our bearings. We trudged up the large concrete stairs, my sister and I, *step-step-rest, step-step-rest*, emerging into the bright sunlight of day.

INSIDE THE ART INSTITUTE, room led into high-ceilinged room like a maze. We spent an hour with the Rembrandts and Vermeers, my mother reading each title aloud. She then steered us toward the Impressionists, talking all the time as if she owned the pictures, then on to modern European art. Rita, prone to nightmares, began to whimper at Dali's *Inventions of the Monsters*. My mother, worried that my sister would have a nervous breakdown right then and there, decided on a quick change of venue: "We're going to see the Africans and Greeks." She said she wanted us to envision the world as a place made beautiful by the hands of *ordinary* people. *Liaudė*, she said. The folk.

I stared at a giant warrior mask with teeth as protruding as my own while Rita shrunk away from the disembodied head of a female deity carved out of stone.

Later that week my sister and I demanded that my mother turn our apartment into a museum. We pestered her to tape our tempera-painted pictures onto the living and dining room walls, in the kitchen, even the bedrooms. My father came home from work to find the house filled with our creations: pastures full of swaying flowers and trees with apples as big as bowling balls; oceans swarming with ruby-colored fish; little girls with huge bows in their hair, girls who towered over their tiny mothers and even smaller fathers.

WE WERE SOON whining about amusement parks again.

"Can we go to Riverview? All our friends have been to Riverview."

"You'll fall off the Ferris wheel," my mother said, inculcating yet another lifelong phobia.

"No Reeferview for you," my father answered, repeating the phrase over and over with self-satisfaction.

Instead we went to the opera, the Lyric Opera production of *Boris Godunov*. We didn't understand why our parents were so thrilled to be here, listening to music in Russian—a language I thought they hated—with action that took place in the 1500s, mostly in monastery basements. The initial pleasure of peering down from on high and viewing the people at the bottom soon wore off, as did the fun in my sister's loud insistence that the opera should have been named Boris Badenov after our favorite cartoon villain, the Pottsylvanian spy whose schemes of killing "moose and squirrel" we constantly booed.

"He's the world's greatest no-goodnik," Rita announced as the curtain rose on Act I.

"Sharrup you mouth," I couldn't resist, mimicking Boris's favorite response to his sidekick Natasha.

THERE WERE MORE trips downtown, to the symphony once or twice, to the Natural History Museum, to the Chicago Public Library. We went to the unveiling of the Picasso at the Daley Plaza. The place was packed: there were men in business suits and polyester ties; women in pencil skirts and heels and crisp white blouses, coifed hair held in place by Aqua Net; old people who couldn't hear when you said "Excuse me" and had brought folding chairs as if this were a picnic. But there were also teenagers in jeans and sandals and long straight hair. A few young men and women were handing out pamphlets protesting the Vietnam War; for the most part, they were ignored.

Mayor Daley talked about the great gift the city had received from *Pick-ass-o*. "What is strange to us today will be familiar tomorrow," he read slowly from a piece of paper. He then pulled a heavy tasseled cord: the blue cloth covering of the statue collapsed to the ground to expose an enormous steel creature with giant wings and a small, odd, angular face that reminded me of the countenance of one of the nuns at school.

"What's it supposed to be?" people murmured.

"An aardvark."

"An angel."

"It's a girl. Dats what da sculpture said," a woman wearing a large orange hat and oversized sunglasses proclaimed.

I knew the difference between *sculpture* and *sculptor*, but I dared not correct the woman. I had seen what happened when my impetuous mother did this: people cast dirty looks or sometimes even told her to mind her own business. My mother shoved us away from the woman as if she were a criminal, then whispered: "It can be anything you want it to be."

"It's the god of birds," my sister shouted. "Look at the pigeons worshipping at its feet."

A man behind us wearing a suit complained: "Dey shoulda builda stat-chew ta hahnor a great poisson from Illanoiz. Like Abe Lincoln."

"Or Ernie Banks?" another man suggested.

"Who's Ernie Banks?" my mother asked.

"Ernie Banks?" The man looked outraged. "The baseball player?"

"Does he play for the Cubes?" my father asked helpfully.

I wanted to crawl away in shame. I knew almost nothing about baseball, but I knew who Ernie Banks was. Non-Lithuanian classmates whispered his name like a god's. My feelings of embarrassment were coupled with a sense of pity for the man who'd suggested the Ernie Banks statue; clearly, he lacked imagination. Still, I wished that my parents were just a little more worldly. My mother thought Wrigley Field (or Wrigley Field's as she called it) was a department store, the poorer cousin of Marshall Field's. My father refused to let us go to the Odditorium, the Ripley's Believe It or Not Museum in Old Town, even though I told him it was like the Art Institute in some ways, filled with artifacts: ossified human heads and sharks' teeth as big as chainsaws and a sculpture of JFK made entirely of gum balls.

"Seeing is believing," I told my father, mimicking the Ripley's motto.

"Living is believing," my father answered, once again taking a popular slogan and turning it upside down so it made both perfect sense and no sense at all.

AS FAR AS my parents were concerned, there was no need to venture beyond the borders of the charted landscape—the North Side offered nothing in terms of necessity or luxury. In their parochial outlook—at least when it came to the city's geography—my parents were no different than other members of the Lithuanian community, who bought their bread from Baltic Bakery and their cars from Balzekas Motors, who married off their sons and daughters at the Lithuanian Youth Center and buried their dead in St. Casimir's Cemetery.

My parents' disinterest in what lay north of the John Hancock Tower on Michigan Avenue wouldn't have bothered me so much had it not been for Old Town, home not only to Ripley's Believe It or Not but also to a store called the Bizarre Bazaar that carried ankle bells and glow-in-the-dark posters and strawberry incense and little soaps that smelled like tomatoes. I was verging on adolescence; my desire for Flower Power patches for my jeans coincided with a growing need to break away from the old-fashioned, constricting world of my parents. I wanted to listen to folk music at the Quiet Knight or the Earl of Old Town while puffing on a cigarette, perhaps talking to a member of the Chicago Seven, whose trial I had watched on television. I knew which side I was on from the very beginning: the hippie defendants were young and smart and hip and looked as if they were having fun.

THE FIRST TIME I set foot on Chicago's North Side I was fifteen. I had persuaded Cindy Zikowski to cut school and take the El to Old Town one spring afternoon.

"We can catch an afternoon concert at the Earl," I said casually, as if I'd done this many times before.

Cindy and I were friends from theater arts. We were smart and shy and well developed, though Cindy was smarter and shyer and bustier than I. Rumors circulated concerning her bra size—40 D, the boys whispered. An even greater burden was her almost supernatural intelligence; she had the highest IQ in all of Morton East, 192, higher even than Harold Smith's, president of the Chess Club.

We wore our most tattered bell-bottom jeans. I donned a red wool poncho while Cindy put on a fringed leather jacket. We piled on the makeup—orange eye shadow, frosted lipstick, globs of Maybelline mascara—and dabbed patchouli oil behind our ears.

As we sat in our seats on the El, clutching our clove cigarettes, I remembered the day my family rode downtown to the Art Institute, visitors from

Squaresville, Lithuania. I thought of how far I'd come, how unutterably cool I looked.

Strolling down Wells Street, Cindy and I struggled to maintain our facades of practiced indifference. Everything was fascinating: brass hookahs and multihued rolling papers in the windows of little shops, Hare Krishnas selling incense sticks, a young male couple walking hand-in-hand.

"Far out," Cindy would say when she saw something particularly interesting.

"Yeah, man," I'd add.

A white banner waving in the wind announced the Earl of Old Town. We entered with trepidation; it was much easier to be noticed in a cozy, storefront place where everyone seemed to know everyone else than in a bigger, more impersonal club. Cindy and I were worried that the tall, somewhat surly looking man at the cash register, who turned out to be owner Earl Pionke, would look deeply into our faces and ask in a very loud voice "Can I see some identification?"

We sighed in relief as he smiled and led us to a round table toward the back of the room. We didn't dare order alcohol, however; how embarrassing it would have been to have our cover blown surrounded by long-haired women in cottony flower dresses and leather boots and bearded men in overalls who might have been folk singers themselves. We pretended to admire the bare brick walls while secretly scanning the place for stars of the Chicago folk scene like Steve Goodman and Bonnie Koloc.

The musician that afternoon was the Autoharp player Bryan Bowers. We weren't exactly sure what an Autoharp was—it looked suspiciously like the *kanklės* played by young girls in Lithuanian costumes at somber independence day commemorations. The minute Bowers started performing, however, we relaxed, charmed by the music and Bowers's easy manner with the audience.

We clapped along to "Pick a Bale of Cotton" and listened in respectful silence to "The Battle Hymn of the Republic." We smiled at "Twinkle, Twinkle Little Star," and strained to listen to new, unfamiliar songs about love and longing. I suppose we would have preferred a more hardedged performer, one brimming with discontent, but we were glad just to be there, in Old Town, listening to folk music. Everything was going well until the end of the concert, when Bowers announced: "I'd like to conclude with 'Will the Circle Be Unbroken?' Take your neighbor's hand in yours and sing along."

There were men on both sides of us. I had never held the hand of a boy. Cindy had never held the hand of a stranger. I played with the beads on my macramé purse; Cindy fiddled with the ice cubes in her Diet 7-Up.

"Come on, everybody, hold hands," Bowers repeated and began to sing. He stopped in the middle of the song. "You two," he shouted out and pointed to us for all the audience to see. "Don't be shy. Take the hand of your brother."

"Will the circle be unbroken," we sang, our hands limp and clammy, our voices shy, humiliated echoes of our former selves.

THE RIDE ON the El back home seemed endless. We were stuck in the tunnel between Clinton and LaSalle for fifteen minutes. The train's dim indoor light did little to illuminate the passengers, who seemed like cartoon ghosts of themselves, faces tinged in gray.

"You're a little late for dinner," my father said.

"The meatloaf is cold," my mother added.

"How come you're wearing all that makeup?" Rita asked. "You look like a slut."

"Shush," my mother admonished, though I could see she was upset.

"I had to stay after school to work on a project," I lied.

"What kind of project?"

"An art project."

I wasn't even taking art that semester, but my parents didn't know that. If I'd have said history or geography or English, they would have asked questions: What period in history? What part of the world? What novel, what poem? But art was large and uncertain and imprecise. Art was anything you wanted it to be.

BETWEEN BOYS

ANNE CALCAGNO

In Chicago, I became a mother, and parenthood grew me up. I revisited childhood with a new magnifying lens. It was startling, invigorating, frightening.

I grew up in cities, always in multilevel apartment buildings, never in a one-family house. In Chicago we bought a home, so strange to be on street level! How novel to get to know the neighbors!

"Between Boys" occurs in the northwest neighborhood of Sauganash—considered quite idyllic, almost suburban—our home only short a white picket fence, though plenty of those abounded. Here, we discovered something deeply relevant for those raising families in Chicago: school choice. Children either attended Queens of All Saints, a private Catholic school, or the Sauganash public school, which bussed in affirmative action kids (no longer true), or were themselves bussed to CPS selective enrollment and magnet schools scattered throughout the city. Their dispersal created small pockets of inclusion and rivalry up and down our blocks. But this generation of millennial kids, more than ever before, got parental involvement. We showed up at sports practices, parades, school and summer camp functions. It was the neighborhood norm, although we gathered more as semi-strangers than as a conjoined community. Mistrustful and ignorant of each other, we intensified our investment in our children as extensions of ourselves. We were entering dangerous territory. Territory in which, I came to believe, we parents felt our children's struggles as demanding parental assertions of leadership. We impeded our children's important negotiations with each other, critical rites and lessons in growing up. This is not solely a Chicago phenomenon, but it was through living in Chicago that I witnessed parental jockeying for position and the fracturing of young souls.

JULIAN NEEDED OTHER BOYS, AND FOR THAT HE PAID A PRICE. He'd be caught in a promising game of Fish or a magnificent confrontation of Battleship, his ships in victorious alignment, his adrenaline pumping, his face a jack-o'-lantern grin, and know there was nothing more he wanted in life. Then a parent would come along and shut things down.

How Julian disliked solitude. He liked people. Alex, his best friend, could turn a soggy Sunday into mad joy, tossing the best action-adventure pillow fight in the Midwest. It rarely worked out as well with girls. Julian was eight, and avoiding girls.

Just last month some eleven-year-olds, dashing across the front lawns tossing a football, had stopped to laugh. At him. Julian had been speeding up and down the sidewalk on his scooter, fast as the wind, swooping into his turns, Karen in hot pursuit, totally unable to vanquish him, when Tom, chief bully, had shouted, "Julian has a girlfriend! Kissy! Kissy!" The others joined in, "Julian has a girlfriend, Julian has a *girrrrrrl*friend."

Julian felt his face on fire. He screeched to a stop. Karen smiled sweetly, vaguely. Then Julian was slamming his scooter to the ground, the weight of his whole body on Tom, pummeling Tom's back. He screamed, "Shut your pie-hole! Don't you *ever* say that!" Tom's tiny wrinkled grandma rushed out onto their front porch, her hands shrunken tambourines shaking around her ears. She yanked on Julian's pants. She was yelling, "Help! Heeeelp!" The other boys, now called to action by an adult, tore Tom and Julian apart.

"He crazy! You lunatic! You terrible boy, lunatic—" the grandma shook her crooked finger at Julian. "Don't you steps on this lawn again!" Tom sneered. He raised two rabbit's ears above her head, flipping Julian the finger with his other hand.

The grandma had spoken sharply to Julian's mom. Julian's dad had shrugged. Julian decided girls were the risk. Danger came with liking girl stuff, and Julian didn't. He had a teenaged sister, Angie, eight years older, woman-looking, and she was plain mean. She called him "runty scum," screaming with fury if he entered her room. His mom was OK, mostly nice, but tired all the time. By late afternoon, her hair stuck out like a Tinkertoy construction, her eyes heavy-lidded, saying, "Jules, go play. Mommy's got to nap." By evening, she woke up. She wandered about the house sweaty and hunched, sponging the tables, the counters, the walls, forgetting to make supper. After Dad microwaved hot dogs, Mom tromped back to bed, too weary even for TV. Dad shrugged. Julian disliked the leaden weight that clung to him in his house. But if a friend came over, he could always forget.

Julian thought hard about how he played. If it was kickball at school, he always got picked, because he could nail that ball. But his best thing was basketball. Julian was fast on his feet, with nervy legs, a quick turn-around, and a good eye for the hoop. He loved how his hands and feet pounded, alive; how the team needed positions: guards, defense, forwards, and anyone making assists. It was one of the few games that, if a friend couldn't be found, he played alone, rushing full tilt up his driveway, trash-talking to the hoop hanging over his garage. Third grade had no school team, but in gym or after school on the playground, the boys dumped their backpacks on the sidelines, and got going. That big orange ball would fly, orbiting through the air, and Julian's heart would soar, waiting for the release, the gravitational pull, hands up, his eyes shining. Then down! He had it bouncing, snap, snap, snap, pounding, before he threw it to live wire Alex, his best friend.

Alex had an older sister, too. Marie. But she had a different mom than Alex and his little brother Zachary, and Marie detested them both, hissing in Alex's ear, "I never had my own room. I slept on the living room couch. All the time my dad was with you, he should have been with me. You got everything." Marie had things to say to her dad and Alex's mom, too. She knew how to make everyone miserable and, even after her dad slapped her hard in the face one morning, she didn't stop.

Alex studied defensive moves like kung fu, preparing for life's battlefield. And, even more essential, he and Julian made sure to have a blast together; it was the best, best way to alienate all the forces of opposition. This was such important work, survival work, that it worried Julian how parents could step in the way, in a mood, simply tearing down everything *because*.

They lived a block apart, on Greenfield Avenue in a part of Chicago with old brick houses with lawns that parents called a good area for raising kids. Alex went to St. Mary's Catholic school, while Julian went to the

Lowell Public, but after school they always met up. They built fortresses out of boxes and pillows or traded Gameboys, watching each other play, rooting for wins. Alex particularly liked imagination games in which, maybe with reflecting foil-covered buckets on their heads, yelling into walkie-talkies, they fought aliens from the Red Planet with squirt guns, getting soaked. Julian liked any game he played with Alex.

Alex was so cool, had all the best Pokémon and Yu-Gi-Oh! cards always before Julian. Alex's parents liked technology and all the latest gadgets, his dad being a computer analyst. Julian's parents tended toward the outdoorsy and wanted him to make cities out of wood blocks or practice wilderness camping in a tent in the backyard.

Which was how, on that Wednesday afternoon, Julian had been in the yard swinging a stick-sword at Alex who cleverly grabbed the handy patio glass-topped table as a shield, lifting it to his chest, except he lost his balance, falling hard against the picket fence, whereupon Julian was suddenly aware that the table was shattering, and Alex was looking up at Julian in shock, his right arm, all at once, studded, and pierced with glass shards. Alex wasn't crying but his face was blotchy in a weird way, getting redder, and his eyes were huger than ping-pong balls. He breathed funny, too, kind of: "Hah, ah, ah, hah! Ah, ah!" Julian ran hysterical into his parents' bedroom, yanking his mom awake, screaming so she jumped up instantly, running wide-eyed behind him, grabbing dishtowels on the way. Julian's mom flung herself down next to Alex on the grass, clasping his arm, steadying herself. Alex's arm sprang blood in tiny fountains. His eyes swiveled as he blurted, "Hah, ah, ah!"

"Julian, call Alex's house! Now!" His mom pointed vehemently toward the kitchen phone. As Julian ran, he could hear her saying behind him, "Alex, honey, breathe deep. It looks worse than it is. Cuts is all. It's just cuts. I'm going to start pulling out some glass. I'll be very fast. Breathe deep." But Alex had started sobbing.

Julian's mom cooed unconvincingly, "Honey, honey, your mommy's coming."

It was Alex's dad who picked up the phone. He appeared almost instantly through the back gate off the alley, huffing and puffing, his tub of a belly straining against the buttons of his business shirt, "How the fuck did this happen!? Buddy, Alex, hang in there."

"Julian? Yes! What happened?" His mother pointed the story at him; why didn't she just beat on him on the skull with a hammer? She plucked and dabbed at Alex's leaking arm, one rag cloth clasping extricated glass shards, another staunching the blood.

Julian squeaked, "We were warriors. He tripped, and the shield fell—"

"Did you knock him down?" Alex's dad yelled into Julian's face. "You're out of control! Aren't you?" He swung around to Julian's mom, "He needs stitches! I'll get him to the emergency room!"

"Yes!" his mom said. "To be safe, that'd be good. Good, yes. Shall I come?" Julian noticed her face seemed pressed in, as if she were battling hurricane winds that squinted her eyes and crumpled her mouth.

"I'll be better alone. Call Sylvia for me, though." Alex's dad ran to get his car. He drove back like sixty miles an hour, screeching. Julian's mom guided Alex to the passenger seat.

Julian was saying, "I'm so sorry. Sorry, Alex." Alex looked like he couldn't understand.

Julian's mom buckled Alex's seatbelt. Alex's dad tore onto the main road.

Back in the yard, Mom surveyed the mess of glass. She rubbed her forehead. "What happened, Julian?"

"I didn't spear him. He was already falling!" Tears seared his eyes, plonking out in quick succession. Alex's arm rose, flailing in his mind's eye.

"Go inside and think about this." Mom cleaned up alone, while Julian watched from the kitchen window. One hour ago, everything had been tremendous. Would Alex remember Julian hadn't knocked him down? That was the thing about accidents; not everybody remembered them the same. He saw Alex's ghost sitting, legs splayed out in front of him while his arm turned into a sprinkler, spluttering on his T-shirt and pants. At first he had just looked startled, then terrified. When you loved someone and saw something terrible happen to them, you wanted to vomit or claw your insides out. Julian was clutching his stomach, watching his mom bend over the piles of sparkly glass that had shattered this day.

WHEN ALEX REMOVED the bandage to show Julian, his arm looked like a crazy patchwork. From his wrist to his shoulder, tiny black threads ran like railroad tracks, their knots stiff-ended. "Man, you're like Frankenstein!" Julian was impressed.

"I know." Alex grinned. Alex was the bomb. Everyone found out his arm had been cut like pieces in a kaleidoscope. Other boys looked at their own white or brown arms, suddenly finding them boring. Alex couldn't play during gym or after school, especially not basketball. He wasn't supposed to yank his arm around. No one thought any less of him. And because Julian had been there when it all happened, he gained a secondary status: storyteller, eyewitness. Both he and Alex remembered that Alex had tripped, that Julian wasn't at all to blame.

But that wasn't how Alex's mom and dad saw it. They came over to Julian's house five evenings later. Alex's dad again looked ready to explode, the buttons of his shirt strained, his neck and face pulsing with veins. Alex's mom, Sylvia, was tiny. She had huge blue eyes probably meant for a larger face that roved around the room like zap lasers. Julian sat still, feeling small and awkward surrounded by the adults. "We want to pay any medical bills," Julian's dad said. "Hand over everything."

"This isn't about money." Alex's mom had a shrill voice. "We all know that."

Julian's mom repeatedly wiped her forehead, as if some kind of genie might spring from her head to guide them. She and Dad apologized repeatedly. "I can't get that picture of Alex out of my mind," Julian's mom whimpered.

"Brenda, Julian needs psychiatry. He needs anger management. Therapy. Face it. He assaulted Tom last month. Now Alex."

"He had nothing to do with Alex's injury," Julian's mom cried. Julian again thought he might vomit. "Alex admits it!"

"Alex is a very loyal child, Brenda. He doesn't want to hurt Julian. That doesn't mean we adults won't step up to the plate." Alex's dad jumped up, jutting his chin, like he was king of the room. "Julian is no longer allowed near Alex."

Julian watched Alex's dad in horror. How could a man get things so wrong and still be so convinced? He had that bad first wife, right? And then miserable Marie? He should know he didn't get *every*thing right. Did Alex know this would happen? He hadn't said anything. What were they going to do?

The parent fortress was impenetrable, one Great Wall of China. And, when parents were out, the Sisters guarded the Wall. Alex and Julian were blockaded. Julian felt all carved out, like a hollow bowl. He stayed after school with some kids, climbing the playground's jungle gyms, running down the slides. The kids from Alex's school no longer stopped by to join them. They walked past Julian, a phalanx of Catholic uniforms, faces averted, especially Alex's. The separation had grown so much bigger than just the two of them. All Julian *really* cared about was Alex, who was the best of them, a friend of more than you could say with words, the way he knew how to keep a game going and going, and always came up with the coolest ideas. Julian was a swing with no one in it, a bench crapped with bird poop. Grown-ups had judged the incident, and now there was no way of explaining that what they thought *was* in fact *wasn't*.

Sure, he still had his classmates and all, but he thought they acted cautious around him, like he could undo people's limbs right and left. He was even nice to Karen when she came over, asking him to play, but he felt mixed-up, knowing she wasn't really what he wanted, looking over his shoulder the whole time she talked.

Julian thought about the way an upside-down cake was right side up first, and every night followed after the sunshine. He tried to believe that the slow movement of the earth could resettle things, like old scores, floods, accidents. If things just kept moving, the bad would rotate away, and new roads would be revealed. Time carried change, and might drop new parcels at your doorstep. He'd survive if all he had to do was wait a bit more. For Alex. But it wasn't easy.

HE PHONED ALEX a couple of weeks later. He'd seen Marie outside, and guessed the house was clear. "Alex! You think your parents will ever let up?"

"Hey man, this sucks. I got a new Gameboy, you should see it."

"Oh man," Julian groaned.

A shrill female voice blasted through the line, "We have caller ID Julian Metsos, jerk off. Get off the line, or my parents are going to sue your ass big time." Julian clicked the line dead as fast as he could. The phone lay heavy in his hand. The room around him felt like a gaping hole. Dad was at work. Mom was resting. Angie was upstairs blasting Metallica. She'd already told him she didn't give a crap about this whole mess; she hated whining. Julian walked into his bedroom, everything in position, his old toys staring at him as if they were amused. He lay down on his stomach and cried until he fell asleep soaked in the pillow.

WHICH IS WHY, another month later, he sat paralyzed on the front steps, seeing Alex, Zachary, and their dad moving down the sidewalk, about to pass his house. Julian stayed glued, mute. But Alex glanced at his dad and darted over. He poked Julian in the arm and said, "What's up?"

"Nothing."

Alex's dad had stopped. He stared at the sky as if waiting for a revelation. Alex ran back, tugging on his dad's arm, gesticulating. Julian didn't move, conscious that anything he did could haunt him.

Then Alex was at his side, shouting, "You can, you can! Dad said you can play basketball with us. At the park. Come on."

Julian ran in to tell his mom, who smiled. Out front on the sidewalk, Alex's dad looked hard at Julian. "No craziness from you." Julian nodded somberly, stricken. But step by step, nearing the court, his mood lightened, with Alex chattering, "I got some new moves, man. You'll never catch me."

"Right, right," Julian said. "We'll see, Mr. Big Mouth." He was grinning, didn't even care who won. It was just so fantastic to be with Alex, here, now.

At the court, Alex's dad decided, "Me and Zachary against you two losers." It was odd how he was in a good mood, wearing a big old gray

T-shirt, less red in the face than Julian had ever seen him. Though it didn't take long, as they played, for his face to turn from pink to scarlet to a mottled purple. Julian worried about this, but then again adults were hard to understand. Anyhow, as the game pressed forward, Julian forgot to study Alex's dad. He was again remembering and doing what he and Alex did best, which was play. Alex threw the ball over Zachary's head to Julian, who pedaled it to the hoop fast as he could, the ball smack, smacking, leading him like an elastic he snapped back, and soar! He got a basket. He and Alex high-fived it, doing their celebration dance, singing, "Oh yeah baby we did it, we did it, we diiiiid it!" Zachary laughed.

"Our ball." Alex's dad swiftly took over. "Zak, my boy, we've got challengers." All at once, he stormed past them all, fat as a thundercloud, and zonked the basketball in. "Number One, that's us!" He cheered, swatting Zachary on the back. Suddenly, he grabbed the ball again and tossed it in the hoop. "Another two points!" he shouted.

"Dad, that was ours," Alex complained, stomping his foot on the asphalt for emphasis.

"But you were too slow. Hah! Hah! Don't be pissy."

Alex quickly grabbed the ball from his dad, shouting, "You old fart!" And went charging to the other end, Julian close by, Alex doing a lay-up, netting them two more points, when suddenly Julian realized that with the new rules, he should go for two more. He rushed to swoop up the ball, but heard, loud in his ear, "Oh no you don't!"

He felt the power of the man's body lifting him off his feet and backward. Then he was slammed to the ground. Everything went black. Maybe for a second or two or ten. Julian's eyes suddenly flipped open to a harsh burning up and down his back, his eyes watering involuntarily, his breathing thick and weird. His mind swirled, trying to grasp the fireworks that continued in his head and back. "Thought you could beat me, didn't you?" Alex's dad stared down at him.

Julian struggled to sit up, choking, forcing out words, "You pushed me!" He saw Alex watching, wide-eyed.

Then Julian was being lifted to his feet by a fist clasping his T-shirt. "You can dish it out but you can't take it, huh? I knew this was a bad idea.

You don't deserve a second chance. We're taking you home. We won't ever do this again, you get me?" Julian couldn't even nod.

As they walked home, Julian fighting hard not to cry, he whispered to his friend, "He pushed me."

"I know," Alex murmured. "I saw."

Julian's mom must have seen them out the window because she opened the door, smiling at Alex's dad. Julian rushed past her, flinging himself up the stairs. He heard Alex's dad say, "Don't even start, Brenda. I'm done listening—"

Julian filled the bath. He climbed in to drown his sorrows. Or at least to find the balance between the sobs that heaved tears down his face and the bathwater. And it was only as he dried himself, blood appearing in streaks on the towel, that he caught his reflection in the mirror, his back a bright ugly smear scraped raw, shoulder to butt. He had been flung full weight on asphalt by a large man. Body slammed like professional wrestling. It really hurt. He would tell. He must. He stung and burned. It frightened him. But the more it grew and scorched like a poison, blood seeping into the towel, the more he grasped that it would be much better to hide. Adults just made things worse. And worse. That he really knew. He hurriedly put on his darkest pajamas and closed himself in his bedroom. He didn't know how he was going to live without Alex.

That night his parents quietly entered his room. They shook their heads like jack-in-the-boxes, full of chagrin. They would comfort him. Dad said, "We heard you called Alex's dad an old fart. We know you threw a tantrum."

The backs of Julian's eyes stung and pulsated. "I did not! It was him—"

"Oh honey, please," his mother interrupted, "Stop it. We're here to protect you, to teach you. You're going to be left alone, with no one to play with. How will you like that?"

They needed to ask? Julian had done everything he could so it would never be so, had been so careful, more careful than anybody. The sky didn't hear his serious need. Those heavens were no best friend. And the ears stuck on the heads of adults heard you as well as thumbtacks, pinning you to a bulletin board. You were their reminder of everything still to be done. All that could ruin your whole life.

Julian's parents left with a back pat—he would not let them see it hurt—and shuffled tiredly into the hall. There Julian was, his back a growing fire whipping up and down his spine. He must fall asleep on his side. A neighbor's dog barked, seeking something mysterious in the dark. It was everything parents did not imagine that separated them from you.

RUNNING GIRL

NNEDI OKORAFOR

Nnedi Okorafor, Nigerian American, primarily an African-based science fiction and fantasy writer, grew up on the outskirts of Chicago. Early on she wanted to be an entomologist, and she was a terrific athlete—track and field, tennis—close to breaking through to the professional level in her late teens, when the scoliosis she had been inflicted with at thirteen finally required surgery. In that surgery, she became paralyzed from the waist down for several months, helping her turn toward writing as a career.

Her story can be read in *Broken Places & Outer Spaces: Finding Creativity in the Unexpected*. In that book she admits that the theme and trajectory of the suffering-to-success story is not a new one, likening her own story to others such as Frida Kahlo's and the monster's in Mary Shelley's *Frankenstein*, but she makes the point that she would never have become a writer had she not faced this adversity.

Okorafor connects this time in her life to the stories she has now written of girls who overcome challenges, not only to walk but to fly, travel in space, and excel in science and magic. And who very often love weird bugs and creatures. She also tells of visiting Nigeria and being inspired by her ancestors and family members, who have supported her along the way in various ways.

WHEN I WAS A CHILD, I WAS ALWAYS RUNNING. AND SO THIS Wednesday, in the Chicago South Suburbs of South Holland, Illinois, 1982, was much like any other day back then.

I was running fast, close at the heels of my two older sisters, Ngozi and Ifeoma. I was breathing harder than normal because I was terrified. I passed uniform homes as I ran. Red brown white bricks, wire and white-painted wood fences that were recently placed around houses and back-yards, and white Ford Mustangs and Datsuns with black speed stripes, and once in a while a weedy, empty lot. During more peaceful moments, when I wasn't being chased by a group of young racists, I would traipse around in these places looking for what I could find.

The light-green bulbous spittlebugs were easy to find. They lived in a dollop of saliva-like fluid. When they grew up, they became green- and sometimes rainbow-colored leafhoppers. Lovely. My favorite creatures were the chunky yellow, black, and red fat-butted grasshoppers and vibrant green katydids. These were always a treasure because they were hard to spot, let alone catch. There were also bumbling ladybugs, wrig-gling caterpillars, busy butterflies and moths, tunneling earthworms, and sometimes pinching crayfish, grumpy toads, and slippery frogs. I avoided the sneaky spiders. My father always liked to hear about my day's catch. He too liked to witness nature. Unfortunately, because he was always on call at the hospital, he'd often hear about my day's catch late at night, long after the creatures had been freed.

However, at the moment, I wasn't at peace. I wasn't where I wanted to be at all. It was the middle of summer, eighty-five degrees, not a cloud in the sky. The sun shone brightly on exactly what was happening under it. I wore pink shorts, a rose-colored shirt and black Chuck Taylors. My legs and arms were long and lanky, and people at school called me Palm Tree, Nnedi Spaghetti, and Daddy Long Legs, among other less savory things.

"We're gonna get you, niggeeeeeers!"

Ifeoma was ten, Ngozi was nine, and I was eight. All of the kids chas-ing us were high schoolers. The three of us had rounded a corner, on our way home from the park, when we met the group of white kids. My sisters and I had frozen as we stared back at the seven, eight kids. The moment was a stalemate of realization. All of our schedules were about to be very modified.

The white kids were no longer going to talk shit to each other for the next fifteen minutes about why the Scorpions rocked harder than Ratt, and my sisters and I were no longer going to take the short way home. Without a word, the three of us took off. Ifeoma leading, then Ngozi and then me. Our shiny Jheri curls dripped oil and sweat into our eyes. I was sure in my stride, so I snuck a glance back. We would outrun them, though we were much younger. Speed ran in our family.

Our father had competed nationally in the hurdles in college. Once in a while I went with him to the track and marveled at how fast he could run run run, leap, run run run, leap. Our mother had made the Nigerian Olympic Team by throwing the javelin, and I liked to speculate that we had warrior blood in our veins. If only I'd had a spear this particular Wednesday.

We ran down the Chicago South Suburban sidewalks of 1982, like those relatives before us who ran down the dirt roads of Isiekenesi and Arondizuogu, Nigeria, like those of my stolen relatives who ran down the dirt roads of Jackson, Mississippi, and so the cycle continues.

My family was one of the first Black families to move into the neighborhood, and there was a heavy price to pay for this. They threw paint into our swimming pool, forwarded hate letters to our mailbox, shouted "Niggers go home!" as they passed in their cars. Constant harassment.

Nevertheless, neither my sisters nor I thought much about it. It was all a part of the territory. And being the daughters of confident immigrant doctors from Nigeria, we were taught that all ailments—physical and otherwise—could be worked with, if not cured, to always walk with our heads up and to look a scary thing in its many eyes. My parents were essentially healers, their jobs were to make people feel OK, and their kids were not exceptions. Their words were like vitamins to us.

"Just because someone thinks something, does not make it true," my mother always said. My parents knew this well, for they came to the United States in 1969, during a time when Black people were still believed to be essentially lazy, unambitious, and slow-minded. They came with nothing, ignored these words and sentiments and did their thing, which included earning PhDs and MDs and bringing four children into the world. No, my parents knew better than to go by old American "truths."

As we ran, something told Ifeoma to make a sharp left between two houses, and Ngozi and I quickly followed. It turned out to be a dead end. We stopped and turned around to face the group. I felt adrenaline surging up my legs to my head. I was alive and damn ready to fight. I was lanky but that didn't matter. I'd just about had enough of this bullshit. It was like this almost every day. We were always running. The minute we got off the bus, we were running from white folk. We'd be walking around the block and the next minute we'd be running from white folk. On the playground. Everywhere. Something had to give.

I remembered weeks ago, sitting near the front of the bus and looking back when I heard someone say "nigger." It couldn't have been aimed at anyone else, since my sisters and I were the only Blacks at the Holy Ghost Elementary School.

I turned around and looked down the aisle to see Cermak, the fattest kid in school, standing in front of Ifeoma. He had a doughy head that reminded me of the fufu we ate at home with egusi soup. But I loved fu fu and greatly detested Cermak. The bus had come to a halt; it was our stop, but Cermak was standing in Ifeoma's way. Ngozi was sitting right behind me, and we both stood up.

"What are you going to do, you African nigger bitch?" he said to Ifeoma in a singsong voice. "You're just a dirty monkey and we're gonna take you to jail. Where you belong."

I gasped. Jail! Oh my God, I thought. At the time, I believed him. I knew he was wrong but I was so scared that I believed him. My ten-year-old sister was going to jail! Such a terrible place. Just because she was Black. In that moment, it really hit me what it meant to be Black.

To be Black and female. Ugly. Helpless. A victim. Even back then, I knew this wasn't me. I listened to and agreed with my parents' sentiment about the power and limitation of words and ideas. Still I felt sad and disturbed that people perceived me in this way when I'd done nothing to deserve it. And none of us could fight that evil fat boy who had been evilfied by his parents, brainwashed, confused, and then initiated so early into the white man's role as king of the world. I made eye contact with Ifeoma. She was the tallest and the oldest and the most stoic. She could be very mean when she wanted to be, but she was also very protective. I could tell by the look in her eye that she wasn't scared at all. She was glad that he had chosen to pick on her instead of Ngozi or me.

"Leave her alone!" Ngozi said in her high voice. She was beefier than both Ifeoma and me, but she was not as imposing as Ifeoma.

"Shut up," Cermak said. He turned back to Ifeoma, drew back his hand and slapped Ifeoma across the face. Ngozi lunged forward but a boy held her back. I looked back at the bus driver, who only watched in the rearview mirror. I turned frantically back to my sister, my legs frozen. I was too skinny and small to fight him. And his several friends were too big.

"Where is my daughter?" a voice bellowed loudly enough to shake the bus. Everyone froze.

"Mom?!" I screeched, realizing for the first time that tears were in my eyes.

My mother moved forward quickly past me.

"Go get in the car," she said as she passed. Ngozi and I obeyed.

I never saw how my mother diffused the situation, but for the next month my mother waited for us at the bus stop to make sure all was well. And for a while, we didn't have to run as much.

This incident must have surprised my mother a bit. We didn't have the habit of complaining to our parents about the kids from school or the neighborhood. Once again, dealing with such things was an assumption of the territory; it was part of being who we were, where we were. Our parents had raised us well, and for that reason we didn't walk with hunched shoulders or feel ashamed of our dark skin or our names or anything else that made us girls of African descent. Still our mother had a sixth sense. And that day, she appeared.

But a mother cannot always patrol the world of a child. The minute she stopped waiting at the bus stop, the harassment commenced. And now, in that dead end we'd been chased into, as the three of us stood facing the enemy, it was the moment of truth. I balled up a fist.

"Where're you monkeys gonna run now?" Michelle Ryan sang. The rest of the kids grinned uneasily. They had never caught their prey and they weren't sure what to do now that they had. But I saw their hands, which were clenched and shaking. And I saw the look in their eyes that broadcasted group violence. This was not a good situation. My sisters and I were significantly outnumbered, outweighed, out-aged, and most of them were boys. There was only a moment to decide what to do. I noted a tall, leggy blond boy to the left.

We hadn't been raised to give up. Our parents had come to the United States with little and made much. They knew of the racism that would attempt to hold them back and they maneuvered their way around it. Where there was a will, there was a way. In this case, a way out.

The three of us acted at the same time. I moved forward and my sisters moved backward. I lunged and dove, right through the blond boy's legs, jumped to my feet, and took off. Behind me, Ngozi and Ifeoma easily scaled the fence and were gone. The group stood indecisive about whom to chase and then instantly gave up.

I ran and ran. Past houses, empty lots, cars, and driveways. Rounded the corner and ran some more. As fast as my legs would take me. And when I got home, I ran through the door my sisters had left open for me and ran inside.

VIGIL

STUART DYBEK

"Vigil" is one of the stories that pretty much happened. It is part of a book of such stories, stories set on the southwest side of Chicago as I was growing up that "pretty much happened." It was published as fiction but could just as easily have been published as memoir. I'm attracted to pieces that inhabit borderlines or no-man's-land between genres, such as the prose poem, and that figured in the writing of this piece. It is also a Christmas story, a subgenre I've always had a fondness for as frequently it comes with snow, which I also have a fondness for. I loved the way it transforms a city night, and that physical transformation hopefully signals, and maybe even facilitates, other transformations as well.

IT WAS THE HOLY NIGHT VIGIL, WIGILIA, WHICH MEANS IN POLISH "TO watch," as the Three Kings from Orient watched the rising of the Star, as the shepherds, gathered in the cold, watched and waited the birth of a babe in a manger, a birth from which the world and time would begin anew.

And I watched and waited, too. My empty stocking dangled above the space heater from a clothesline shimmering with silver icicles. The colors of the bubble lights on our tree boiled across the steamy window-panes, while outside, a snowfall that seemed conjured up by my father's spirited reading of "The Night Before Christmas" settled on a deserted Eighteenth Street. I was in my flannel pajamas, ready for bed, when a knock came at the door. Although our holiday decorations included an extra plate set at the straw-strewn dining-room table for any stranger who might arrive, my parents weren't expecting company. My father glanced at my mother and shrugged, but for once he didn't ask who before unchaining the safety latch.

The door opened on the bespectacled face of the grizzled, spooky old Bohemian from the taxidermy shop downstairs. He stood cradling what looked to be an enormous, misshapen gift. It was wrapped in newspaper bound with green plastic clothesline, and my father's first instinct was to politely refuse it.

"Stashu, tell him to come in and have some eggnog," my mother said.

But the old Bohemian wouldn't step from the hall. He hadn't come to disturb us with a visit, only to deliver his package, which he finally managed to press into my father's arms.

"Pan, come in and join us and break oplatki for health in the New Year," my mother called.

Traditionaly on Wigilia a white wafer of oplatki was passed around the table, as we had earlier that evening, and each person broke off a piece and made a wish for the coming year. Oplatki—Angel Bread—melted like a wheaty snowflake on the tongue. I was told it tasted like the Host did at Mass, something I was too young to know, as I was still a year away from my First Communion. My mother always addressed the old man as Pan—"Mister," in Polish. I don't think she knew his name. His taxidermy shop was nameless too. Earlier that day, when she'd taken me with her to drop off a paper plate of Russian tea balls at his shop because he was alone at Christmas, I'd told her that kids said he'd escaped from the booby hatch.

"He came from the Old Country during the War," my mother said. "He came alone because they left him nothing. We can't imagine what he's lived through. Never forget how blessed we are."

Now that he'd delivered the gift he'd lugged up four dim-lit flights of stairs, the old man refused any further obligation. "No, no, enough, Missus, dekuji, dekuji," he said, bowing with thanks while edging away from our door.

My parents bowed back, wishing him Wesolych Swiat, and he wished us Merry Christmas in Czech in return. His spectacles flashed a last gleam before he disappeared into the cavernous hallway.

My father shouldered the door shut and carried the gift to our kitchen table. "Oh, my God," my mother said.

She snipped the knotted line with her sewing shears and they began to unwrap the newspaper. The top sheets peeled off easily, but each layer of newspaper was increasingly damp. When the wet, pulpy sheets shredded in his hands, my father resorted to the spatula he used for flipping pancakes. By then the pinkish-bronze tail fin and the gray thick-lipped snout with its white mustachios that looked like parasites were exposed. A fishy odor insinuated itself into the scents of fir, baked cookies, and homemade eggnog that filled our flat. As my father scraped off clots of newspaper, a confetti of what looked like thumbnails stuck to the table, the walls, and the floor. At last the giant fish lay exposed, glistening in its own slime. Shreds of newsprint and the muddy colors from the funnies section adhered to the iridescent scales that remained along its bloated belly. Its cold, bulging eyes appraised us reproachfully.

My parents would never be so nosy as to ask the old man where he'd come up with such a monster on Christmas Eve. I thought that perhaps it was related to the trinity of piranhas whose desiccated heads with ice-pick teeth and empty eye sockets served as a welcome sign above his jangling shop door. Or maybe it was a trophy catch that some night fisherman had yanked through the ice on the Sanitary Canal just blocks away, and that, instead of mounting, the old Bohemian had brought to us.

His shop was on the street level, and not a day went by that I didn't stare into its dusty display window. No matter how wintry the weather, that window emanated the vaporous green of a prehistoric jungle of ferns. A fierce menagerie poked from the foliage: a horned owl with golden irises spread its great wings to lift the terrified hare pinned in its talons; ermines with ebony pupils reared upright to hiss; a blood-eyed red fox dragged off a cock pheasant; an arched lynx, its emerald eyes seething with fury, bared yellowed fangs. I might owe my impression to the magnifying effect of the taxidermist's thick, rimless spectacles, but the pitiless glass eyes of the beasts in his window seemed modeled on his own. His gaze frightened me, but I was fascinated by the ferocity of the creatures he'd preserved, and regarded them as my secret pets. I wouldn't encounter a similar wildness until a day in my twenties when, diving in the Caribbean, a school that seemed more like a herd of aptly named bigeye tuna surged past. Eighty feet underwater, their myriad eyes, simultaneously those of predator and prey, recalled the window on Eighteenth.

"Do you have any idea how to clean it?" my mother asked.

"Do you have any idea how to cook it?" my father replied.

As a boy he butchered and sold pigeons that he hunted on the roofs of churches, one of his several enterprises that kept the family going after his drunken, immigrant father was committed to Dunning, the state mental hospital. But fish confounded him. The only fishing he'd ever mentioned doing as a kid was jigging with a string and chicken livers for mudbugs from the Douglas Park Lagoon. That night was the first time I heard about him catching carp.

"I never had to clean one, but my kid brother Vic and I sold carp one year along with Christmas trees in front of Lujak's butcher shop on Cermak," he began. "A taco place is there now, but back then it was all Poles and Bohunks. Lujak set a couple oil drums half-full with water and carp out on the street. Selling live fish means you have to catch them. Lujak's net was too small, so my job was to spear them with a pitchfork. Lujak called me Neptune. He collected the money; Vic's job was to keep the water in the drums from freezing. We were freezing, especially our feet, from the water splashing every time I jabbed out a fish. Vic wouldn't watch that part. We'd wrap it, still flopping, in wet newspaper. They'd stay alive and fresh a long time. We sold out except for a fish that got off the pitchfork and sank to the bottom, and Lujak tried to give us that one instead of the money we'd earned. He said the carp was a better deal, but it had been speared in the gut and didn't look too appetizing. Vic wanted no part of it, so we took the buck twenty-five and never told our mother we turned down a Christmas carp. That's as close as I ever got to eating one."

"My Aunt Helene baked carp in aspic," my mother said. "Helene was noted for her cooking, and for keeping tradition. She called Christmas Eve Gwiazdka—"the Feast of the Little Star." You fasted and waited until you saw the first star and then lit the candles before sitting down to dinner: pickled herring, smoked whiting with horseradish, shrimp

31

cocktail, salmon caviar on blinis—seven fish courses, I'm forgetting some. The carp came last, the pièce de résistance, Helene called it, but to tell the truth, I don't remember liking it. One Christmas Eve, just as we lit the candles, a stray gray kitten showed up—"

"Probably smelled all that fish from miles away," my father said.

"It perched on the sill outside the dining room, yowling in the cold. Helene said it was caroling and took it in, because it would be bad luck not to. She named it Gwiazdka. That cat, Gwiazdka, was with her till the night Helene died, and on that night the cat, who never left the house, got out. We heard her in the alley caroling as she had when she first showed up, and then she disappeared. Stanley," my mother said, "what are we going to do with this thing? I got a turkey defrosting in the fridge. We don't have room for it."

The dilemma was so extraordinary, they forgot about my bedtime. I listened as they discussed what to do, and all the while I watched the carp. My father had said that wrapped in wet newspaper, a carp could live a long time out of water. I watched its eye to see if it moved, and the longer I watched, the more I felt as if the carp was watching me. My father tried to think of someone they might give it to. My mother made a joke, wishing the fish had arrived a day earlier so she could have passed it off in the Secret Santa exchange of gifts during the holiday party at the truck-dispatching depot where she worked part-time. Neither of them could think of anyone who would want a giant carp at 11 P.M. on Christmas Eve.

"If this ain't the screwiest G-damned thing," my father said.

"He meant well," my mother said. He'd brought the fish, not because it was something a person who belonged in the booby hatch would do, but because carp on Christmas was a tradition for Poles and Czechs alike. It had something, she couldn't remember what exactly, to do with the early Christians using a fish as a secret symbol for Christ. In a way, the carp was sacred. To dishonor his gift could bring bad fortune. Whatever happens on Wigilia influences the new year. If people quarrel on that night, the entire year will be troubled. If food is wasted, especially in a world where people are starving, one might find himself hungry.

Even on other nights, waste in an immigrant household was a cardinal sin. Food was sacred any time of year. I knew that from painful experience.

One of the tortures of my childhood was having to sit alone at the table long after supper was officially over, until my plate was clean. I was forced to devise desperate methods for disposing of my dinner. Into the paper napkin I politely daubed against my lips, I'd spit mouthfuls of liver; I'd line my trouser cuffs with peas, boiled carrots, and canned lima beans; the Brussels sprouts cooked to mush were slipped into my socks—all to be disposed of later behind the hooked door of the shared bathroom down the hall. It had a high-tank toilet, and jerking the pull chain was like a gesture of good riddance that nonetheless left me with the taste of guilt as I watched the remains of my dinner swirl off to the Sanitary Canal.

That visceral connection between meals and growing up gives food the power to summon back childhood. In college, one autumn afternoon, the all but forgotten memory of the snowy night of our Christmas carp returned in a rush. I was at Loyola's lakefront campus, sitting with a girl I hadn't seen since the end of the previous school year. I'd been the first American boy she'd brought home to meet her Ukrainian parents. They called me the American Boy; that wasn't a compliment. I hadn't been in touch with her all summer, and we were arguing about broken promises. When she threw the sandwich from the bag lunch her mother packed for her into the lake, I knew I'd just witnessed a sacrilege.

"I can't eat," she said. "Satisfied?" The gesture was beyond bursting into tears, and her accent made it sound all the more dramatic. We watched the lettuce, cheese, and rye bread slathered with butter float off. Gulls swooped down but failed to pluck anything out. I recalled my family's misgivings about wasting food, and the carp suddenly rose so vividly to mind that I had the urge to tell her the story. The memory came accompanied by an absurd vision of the fish surfacing, its barbeled maw opening to gulp her bobbing lunch. She wouldn't be amused. She held an apple as if it might be next to hit the water. "I'm sorry," I said. Her eyes, an ultramarine all the more striking for her black hair, searched mine to determine whether I was sincere. I had never been able to read her eyes in return. Finally, she took a bite of the apple and then offered it to me. I bit from the spot on the fruit where her mouth had just been. Sexual details, no matter how minute, never escaped her. She smiled. "Take a walk with me," she said.

My father was attempting to wrap the carp back in the damp newspaper. He seemed more like someone concealing a body than wrapping a gift. It looked like a fish mummy. My mother dug out a Goldblatt's shopping bag from the drawer where we saved bags.

"Better double-bag it," my father said.

He tried to stuff the carp in headfirst and the shopping bag toppled to its side. The fish was too large for it, but my father tied the green line to the handles of the bag in a way that would let him sling it over a shoulder. He changed from his house slippers into his galoshes, zipped on his woolen cardigan, buttoned on his overcoat, and gathered his scarf, hat, and gloves. I watched him dress.

"It's way past your bedtime, sweetheart," my mother told me.

"What are you going to do with the fish, Dad?" I asked.

"I don't know, sonny boy," he said, and then, I think, surprised everyone, himself included, by asking, "You up for a walk in the snow?"

"Stashu!" my mother said, followed by something in Polish that I couldn't understand exactly, but knew translated to: "Stanley, are you crazy or what?"

"I thought for a special Wigilia treat," my father said.

"Cookies and eggnog are a special treat," my mother said. "I don't know what you'd call this. He better not come back with pneumonia. You bundle up," she told me.

"Leave your pajamas on underneath," my father said, "they'll be like long johns."

The idea seemed strange, as if I'd be walking around secretly dressed for sleep, but I wanted to be out in the snow with my father and that mustachioed, monstrous fish that had stared me down before my father newspapered its accusing eye. I hurriedly pulled my clothes on over my pajamas, then buckled on my galoshes. My winter jacket with the mittens clipped to its cuffs had a hood under which I clamped the white earmuffs that I pretended conveyed secret transmissions from the league of superheroes. My mother wound a plaid woolen scarf across my face like a mask. My father hoisted the shopping bag, with the carp's mermaid tail protruding, and unlocked our door.

"Go down the back way," my mother whispered. She didn't want us going by the old man's shop. "Hold on to the banister in the dark."

The flights of winding back stairs had no hall lights, so my father, prepared as always for emergencies, shined the penlight from the pen, pencil, and tire-pressure-gauge set clipped to his shirt pocket. My father wore tools as part of his daily dress as naturally as women wear earrings. At the bottom, by penlight beam, he unlatched the rusty metal door, which groaned as he forced against its powerful spring, and we stepped into the white silence of the frozen alley. Flakes floated from the height of a streetlamp. I'd never been out this late, and the world seemed newly made. I looked up into the snowfall for the Holy Star, but couldn't even see a night sky. I thought of the Magi mounted on camels that stopped for neither water nor sleep, bearing gifts of gold, frankincense, and myrrh, following a Star they never lost sight of, and of the huddled lambs and shepherds—the pastuszkowie, a Polish word with "pasture" in it. And here I was with my father, as if we had stepped into their vigil on a night when an ancient world held its breath.

I wasn't aware until I wanted to tell Alyona the story, years later beside the lake, that the carp had survived in memory as an emissary from a magical, ancient world, one that existed in an alternate dimension overlapping the ordinary landscape of my childhood. This was my sophomore year in college, a crossroads in my life. I had challenged my father's faith in practicality, and elected to dare a life of financial doom by switching my major to English. We didn't refer to it as "switching majors," but as "dropping out of premed." Aly, with her foreign accent and parents who didn't speak English, was an English major too. Her favorite books were *Lolita* and *The Diary of Anaïs Nin*. If she hadn't just thrown her lunch into Lake Michigan, she might have been impressed by the literary echo between the Wise Men bearing gifts and my father lugging the shopping bag with the carp down an alley on Christmas Eve, wondering where to dispose of a gift he couldn't accept. I might have made a joke about Christ as Carp, and Aly would have turned the phrase to a carping Christ.

The snow, undisturbed, rose yeast-like from the lids of trash cans. It crunched like crystal beneath our rubber treads. Freshly powdered ruts stretched ahead as if a sleigh had preceded us. We tramped, each in his own rut. My scarf covered my mouth, so I couldn't ask where we were going, but my father obviously had no intention of dumping the fish close to home. As we approached the end of the alley, I could hear voices on the street. People on their way to midnight Mass passed beneath the street-light, looking dressed for Sunday despite being bundled up for winter. They were followed by a small procession of older kids, caroling and holding sticks topped with foil stars.

"They're Gwiazdory," my father said. "Star carriers." In church, candles affixed to their sticks would be lit. He promised that when I was older and had made my First Communion, he'd take me to midnight Mass, and maybe I could join the Gwiazdory.

We paused in the shadow of a garage doorway until they passed, then we crossed Eighteenth into an alley that traveled along the backside of Blue Island Avenue. Ice crusted where my scarf chafed my runny nose. I slid the scarf down and my breath chuffed before me, visible like my father's, in a stillness that made audible the friction of snow sifting off the edges of roofs. Then the dog attacked. Barking furiously, it stabbed its snapping muzzle through the slats of a fence, and I jumped away, tried to run, and fell down in the snow. My father picked me up, brushed me off, and took my mittened hand. When my father was a boy, their land-lady's chow attacked him. He still had the teeth marks on his arms. The landlady refused to have her dog quarantined for rabies; she said that if my grandmother Victoria reported the dog, she'd throw the family out on the street. So my father was forced to take rabies shots. Treatment then required twenty-one shots in the stomach. He was ten years old. The pain was such that he had to take repeated baths to be able to endure the next day's round of shots. He loved dogs, though, even watchdogs. My fear of them should have been his; it seemed as if I was feeling it for him.

The dog continued to bark behind us. I was afraid he'd chew through the fence and chase us down. My father told me to forget the dog and listen for when the bells from all the churches in the neighborhood—St. Proco-pious, St. Pius, St. Ann's—would chime the first bars of "Silent Night" as a summons to midnight Mass. "Listen," he told me. "Bells always sound most beautiful in the snow." The reason for this had to be practical: maybe the cold made the metal contract, tuning the dull clang of iron to a silvery chime, or maybe the sound waves resonated through the crystalline snow-flakes, affecting their gravity so that the chiming hovered; he didn't know why exactly, but bells sounded more beautiful in the snow.

I slipped my earmuffs off to better hear, and my ears turned cold. I wanted to watch and see if the sound of bells was visible in the gravity of snowflakes. We stopped in the middle of the alley to listen. The dog was no longer barking; maybe he was listening too. My father set the shop-ping bag down. It looked as if its weight, impressed in the fresh snow, would keep it upright, but it flopped over, tearing, and the fish, which had dissolved its soggy wrappings, slipped halfway out into a rut. My father didn't bother to right it. He knelt at the center of the alley before a discol-ored, circular depression I hadn't noticed. With gloved hands he dug and brushed away snow until the black sewer cover, exhaling wisps of fog, was exposed. He tried to lift the cover by hooking a finger into a slot at its edge, but it wouldn't budge.

"Frozen," he said. "Jump on it, sonny boy."

I jumped up and down, and the hollow thump of my galoshes reso-nated beneath the alley while "Silent Night" began to chime above the roofs. My father tried again to raise the cover, but couldn't. "Keep jump-ing," he said. "It'll keep you warm."

He removed a glove, dug out his keys, detached the multitooled jackknife he kept on his key ring, and pried out the can-opener blade. I stopped jumping and he knelt and ran the blade around the sewer cover. He cut the green line attached to the handles of the shopping bag, and tied a knot he noosed around the center of his knife. Carefully, he worked the knife down through the slot of the sewer cover and pulled the string taut so that the knife was drawn against the underside of the cover. He rose, planted his feet, and with both hands exerted a steady tug. With the carp lying on the snow beside him, he looked like an ice fisherman who had already caught a jumbo and had another monster on the line. The sewer cover grunted and gave slowly, as if the fog trapped below was lifting it.

"Grab it, sonny boy," he said. "But watch your fingers."

We slid off the cover and stared into the foggy, seemingly bottomless hole.

"Hear it?" my father asked. "An underground river down there flows all the way to the lake."

What I heard sounded more like wind than water moving under the alley. My father put his glove back on and freed the fish from what remained of the newspaper. He passed the fishy newspapers to me and I stuffed them into the torn Goldblatt's bag.

"Probably revive him when he hits the water," he said.

That caught me by surprise. Despite his earlier remark about carp being able to survive out of water, I hadn't considered that my father thought this particular fish might still be alive. He'd seemed oblivious to the possibility, as he'd scraped newspaper from the carp on our kitchen table and sent scales flying. In the kitchen, when I'd realized the carp was staring back accusingly at me, I'd regarded that as a secret between the fish and me. Its eyes looked filmed over now, like those of an old person with cataracts.

"It's dead, right?"

"You never know, especially if it's kept cold. Trash fish are tough. They live on the bottom, in muck where other fish can't. Wouldn't be a miracle if it swam off," my father said. "How about a hand giving it the old heave-ho."

Fog clouded from the sewer and smoldered over the surface of the snow. We knelt beside the fish. "A-one," my father counted. "A-two." He'd never hooked so much as a perch, nothing but mudbugs out of the Douglas Park Lagoon, and now he was giving the old heave-ho to what might have been a record catch, the second time in his life he was passing up his chance for carp on Christmas. How many chances could one expect? "A-three!" and we slid it rasping along the snow. I couldn't feel, through my mittens, whether the fish was still alive, but I would smell that bottom fish in their wool until my hands outgrew them. Its fin caught for a moment on the lip of the sewer. "Holy cripes! See its gills move?" my father exclaimed, and before I could look, the fish nosedived, slithering through our hands and disappearing without a plop. I imagined it stunned, swimming away in the darkness, a little woozy until it realized it was free, with miles of tunnel to go before it reached the lake.

"You see that?" my father asked, facing away from me as he set the sewer cover back over the hole, smothering the fog.

"I think so," I said.

He unhitched the line from his knife and stuffed the line and the Goldblatt's bag in a trash can. My ears were freezing numb. I fit my earmuffs back on and raised the bandanna of my scarf and we started back. We had to pass the watchdog again, but at least I'd be ready for him this time. The bells had stopped chiming.

"It's midnight, sonny boy," my father said. "Merry Christmas."

ALL-AMERICAN BOY

DAVID MURA

As I reread this selection from *Where the Body Meets Memory*, I'm struck by how precise and particular the memories are, how historical. I also think of how, in my childhood, the internment camps were unknown to me, a vague unspecified presence that no one in my family talked about—well, except for the question that occasionally came up: What camp were they in? No one ever explained to us children what camps the adults were referring to. We Sansei, the third generation, lived in a zone of historical silence we did not know existed and yet which shaped how we thought of ourselves and who our parents wanted us to become.

These days, when I speak about the internment of 120,000 Japanese Americans during World War II, I invoke the anti-Muslim, anti-Arab xenophobia so prevalent after 9/11. I have students, colleagues, and friends who must deal with this enmity. For instance, this past summer, a Muslim Indian American friend talked to me of exploring his own story growing up near San Jose, the fallout he experienced after the first Gulf War and 9/11. In so many ways, our backgrounds are so different, and yet, the parallels are there too.

But beyond the anti-Muslim sentiment of 2016 or the anti-Japanese prejudice of World War II, my friend Zahir and I share something else: we know what it's like to be brown boys coming into adolescence in America—a culture that told us there was something wrong with our bodies, that our bodies somehow repelled others. For me, all this is captured in what I call the Spin the Bottle section of this excerpt. Whether the reactions of others to me were prompted by my own clumsy and pressing attempts to garner attention or were reactions to my brown body or both, I still do not know for certain. But in my first boy-and-girl party, I came away with a distinct sense that there were other lines, racial lines I didn't know existed until sexuality appeared within my social circle. My subsequent experience and the sexual stereotypes of Asian males that persist till the present have only confirmed this.

Beneath the surface of this whole excerpt lies what is now called "internalized racism," hatred of the racial self. It's there in the way my younger self avoided a fellow Japanese American student who was unathletic and seemed odd because of his quirky behaviors—behaviors that eerily echoed the silenced history of the Japanese American community.

When I speak to young people these days about the internment camps, I point out that Japanese Americans were not imprisoned during World War II for anything they did: No Japanese American was ever convicted of an act of espionage or fifth column activity. Instead, the Japanese Americans were imprisoned for their race and ethnicity.

Now if you shoplift and are imprisoned for it, when you get out, to show you're reformed, you don't shoplift anymore. But what are you to do if your crime is your race and ethnicity? You try not to call attention to it, you try to blend in, you try to forget your imprisonment. That is part of the psychological mindset of my parents and their generation, and that is part of the climate I grew up in. And all this is part of the background a reader should consider in this excerpt about an ordinary Japanese American boy growing up in Chicago in the fifties and sixties.

I AM WAITING, STANDING AT THE CORNER OF THE SCHOOLYARD, WAIT-*ing for the boy there to become a man.*

He bites his nails, his body slouches as if he were carrying heavy luggage. He is round, rotund, with the face of a fat boy. Perhaps he is eating a hot dog, marveling at the taste of mustard. He loves fossils, baseball, the names of the planets. He'll never be taken prisoner of war. He dies so gallantly, so dramatically, like John Wayne's buddy at Iwo Jima. He believes in the flag, the anthem of the Marines.

Every Sunday he goes to church, there are parables, and terrible stories of a sad, sad death. The boy doesn't really understand these parables and stories.

He loves throwing noodles from the Sunday school luncheon out of the window in the Reverend Nakano's study. He and the others are never caught doing this. Amid the holy books, drafts of sermons, and the old hymnals, they giggle uproariously. He isn't terrified of God or sin or the reverend. It's his father who terrifies him, who teaches him sums and letters and quizzes him daily, who will not let him go out to play until he has done his lessons, many lessons, many more than any other boy he knows. When the two of them sit at his father's desk and go over his sums, there are only the answers, the terrifying truth, the mistakes at hand. Learning is hard, it takes work, the world takes work, you must buckle down, this is what his father says. The boy doesn't think of running to his mother. That's out of the question. He's not a mama's boy, though Michael Ogata calls him that. His mother is beautiful, the woman at the stove, stirring a bubbling vat. His mother is absent somehow at night, a voice in the dark, whispering, chastising.

At night there are horses rippling beside his bed, great herds of buffalo glide through his room, robbers in masks. His Davy Crockett rifle hangs on the door, his cowboy hat and six-guns guard the foot of his bed. Cattle stampede in the gully between his bed and his sister's. He hears murmurs, perhaps raised voices, his parents arguing down the hall, then only the muffled TV, Shane stepping out into the dusty street. Suddenly, his younger sister begins to taunt, "You can't hurt me, you can't hurt me."

Who can explain where this chant began? Or why the brother then hit his sister? Or how the sister's cries brought forth their father, who then hits his son to silence the cries, the chaos that had erupted in his house?

I think there was a song for us that none of us could sing, a hymn or dirge or lullaby that traveled many years and miles to arrive, so faint no one ever heard it, not even my mother and father, though it contained their voices; it ranged across the years in the dark, swampy regions of Arkansas, in the cold, high mountain plains of Idaho, in the smoky rooms where they waited and waited for the war to end, so much safer than others all around the world, perhaps they grew to believe it was for their own protection.

It is another night, after the night of the spanking. His father sits on the edge of the bed. He is telling us the story of Popeye and the three monkeys, how the three monkeys threw coconuts and conked Popeye on the head. Katonk!

Katonk! The boy and his sister giggle with laughter. They never want to go to bed.

I hear my father's voice now in the stories I tell my daughter, the lullabies I sing to my son.

I don't hear the Japanese ones, I will have to learn them. No, I will never learn them, they are too far past, I am too lazy, too distant a son.

I see my parents once, twice a year now. I sometimes live my life as if I've almost forgotten them. And yet, they cleave through this story, like the smell of smoke. I write my life as if they were present each moment, every hour of the day.

God, said a poet, is a furnace that keeps talking with his mouth of teeth, his mouth filled with feasts, smells of gasoline and airplanes, train rides, long journeys, and human ash, a clear, cold river bottomed with dark round stones. God loves us like fire, he destroys us like fire, he consumes us all.

God, I would say, is my parents, their aging flesh and love, what I cannot see, what feels so distant and palpable, I keep trying to hold it back.

God, I would say, is my wife, who sleeps beside me each night, who listens to this song. Is the journey through which we would destroy and lose and still find at the end a boldness, a common tune: each other.

How did that boy disappear? When did he become a man?

CHICAGO IN THE fifties. The great years of Ernie Banks, slapping line-drive homers into the bleachers at Wrigley Field, his lean, whiplike arms and ever-ready smile. Years of the brief ascent of the White Sox, who climb to the World Series, win the first game, which my father takes me to see, and then lose four straight to the Dodgers, Larry Sherry and his untouchable sinker. Years of Mayor Daley, when the city was still "safe" and, as in Mussolini's Italy, "things worked." The city of broad shoulders and clean winds off the clear surf of Lake Michigan, city of the stock-yards and the El and the Magnificent Mile, of quiet ethnic neighbor-hoods where people know their place and the garbage is cleared like clockwork. Picnics at Wilson Beach or Foster Avenue Beach. School trips to the Museum of Natural History with its mysterious mummies in the basement, sealed from air and natural light. Trips to the great lions that guarded the art museum, confrontations with Seurat, the abstractions of modernism; trips to the planetarium, where the planets and stars reeled above us and I whispered to my maiden aunt Miwako so many names of planets and constellations she marveled at my memory. The train ride at Lincoln Park Zoo and the great cages of gorillas and tigers. Corned-beef hash and brownies at the cafeteria of Marshall Field's. Just a few years before the suburbs drained the city's whites and wealth (and our family too).

Their small diaspora of the war and the internment over, my family lived in an apartment on Broadway, about a mile from Wrigley Field, one block off of Lake Shore Drive, with its luxury high-rises. These towers loomed above the traffic with views of the lake we could only imagine. In their lobbies gleamed gold chandeliers, a doorman. The traffic streamed by, glinting in sunlight.

The building we lived in was an ugly brown three-story structure. Out back was a dirt courtyard, an alley entryway of shadows and cinder. The building was owned by my Uncle Lou's family, the Hirakawas; his wife, Aunt Ruby, was my father's sister. With the exception of one Jewish family, we were all *Nihonjin* (Japanese)—the Hirakawas, the Ogatas, the Fukuyamas, and the Uyemuras.

Uyemura was our family name until I was seven, when my father shortened it. "For better bylines," he said. He worked at INS, the International News Service. Everyone was always mispronouncing the "Uye." "You-ee stir-ee bowl-ee up," Michael Ogata used to say. He was the oldest among us, the best athlete, rivaled only by Jimmy Paris, who was Chinese and whose parents ran Paris' Hand Laundry just down Broadway. "Ooey, ooey"—rhyming with "gooey"—the others would chant. Whites would sometimes pronounce it "Oi-yea," which always reminded me of the phrase "Hear ye, hear ye . . ." called out by clerks of the court on television.

Everyone spoke English except for a few choice phrases and the names of food. Among themselves, the Nisei spoke English. Those who spoke Japanese spoke it to their parents, the Issei, and there weren't many Issei around. My mother's mother died shortly after the war, my father's mother died when I was four. Later, both my grandfathers returned to Japan and remarried. Usually, it was the older Nisei, the eldest children, who spoke the best Japanese; neither of my parents were as skilled in Japanese as Aunt Ruth or Auntie Sachie. Would my parents have spoken Japanese to us if they were fluent? Probably not. What purpose would it have served? And those Japanese Americans who settled in the Midwest probably had less of a desire to return to the past or nurture their cultural roots than those who went back to the West Coast after the internment camps.

Surrounded by relatives and other Japanese Americans, going to the Japanese American Congregationalist Church, marching as a bugler in the Nisei Drum and Bugle Corps, which practiced at the Uptown Buddhist Church, I lived in our little ethnic enclave cozily unconscious of race. Whenever the name of a new person came up in conversations, one of my relatives would always ask, *"Nihonjin* or *hakujin?"* ("Japanese or white?"), though even this simple bifurcation slipped hazily by me, because of my lack of Japanese. I sensed what these words meant, but I was never quite sure. Perhaps I just simply wasn't attentive enough.

Years later, I would be embarrassed when, in my first book of poems, I wrote the word for Japanese pickle as *"utskemono"* rather than *"tsukemono"* and some critic took this as a mark of my own ignorance and distance from my ethnic background. Which, of course, it was.

AT THE AGE of five, in every picture of me, I've got a pair of six-guns cinched around my waist. Or else I'm pointing them at the camera, my black cowboy hat pushed back, my mouth snarling with a bravado and toughness I evinced only as a pose or when alone, walking down the dark steps of our apartment building out to the street. At each step I'd wave to the fans at the rodeo, shouting, "Howdy, folks," the way I imagined Roy Rogers stepping into the arena and mounting Trigger, the Wonder Horse. Before I went on to collect baseball cards, I collected cowboy cards, with the heroes from various television series, together with a slice of chewing gum for a nickel. *Have Gun—Will Travel, Sugarfoot, Maverick, The Gene Autry Show, The Lone Ranger, Cheyenne, The Rebel,* classic American icons of the fifties.

In one of my poems, I picture myself riding in the back of our Bel-Air, shooting at the glass, bouncing up and down in gunfight delirium, wearing the black cowboy hat and cold, cocked steely gaze of Paladin, who'd leave his calling card, "Have Gun Will Travel," everywhere he went. When a Japanese Canadian playwright, Rick Shiomi, read the poem, he remarked, "Do you remember what happened at the beginning of that show? This Chinese guy with a pigtail would come running into the hotel lobby shouting, 'Teragram for Mista Paradin, teregram for Mista Paradin'?"

I don't remember this Chinese messenger at all, whose name, Rick informs me, was Hey Boy. All I see is Richard Boone striding down the stairs, the epitome of cowboy cool, his pencil-thin mustache and tight glinting gaze.

ONE AFTERNOON, IN second grade, I return home from school, toss a note on the kitchen table before my mother, and run to my room. I know I'm to wait there until my father comes home. My teacher, Mrs. Berman, has kept me after school. I have been talking in class, have been disrespectful. I can't quite recall the specifics of my crime. Perhaps in the spelling bee I yelled too loudly and blurted the answer out of turn. Or perhaps it was during the filmstrip which talked about the whites and the red man, when I bellowed, "What about the pink men?" Or perhaps it's when Dolores Garcia is sent to the corner in the back, and I'm sent there too, for talking, and I twitter, "Good, I get to see my girlfriend," and jump into her lap.

Though I've forgotten what has prompted the note from Mrs. Berman, I do remember waiting for my father to come home, the endless, torturous waiting. Through the screen I hear the shouts of Michael Ogata and Jimmy Hirakawa, my cousins Marianne and Sharon. I slip onto my saddle chair and ride a bit through the range, but my horse won't quite come alive today. I fiddle with my six-guns. I feel this sinking in the pit of my stomach, a whole set of butterflies and the fervent wish that today were yesterday or the day before. If only the note from Mrs. Berman did not exist, if only I were anywhere but here waiting for my father . . .

The afternoon shadows lengthen in the room.

In the corner, unnoticed, is my Zorro whip. Zorro, who rides through the night when the full moon is bright; Zorro, the black-clad, masked horseman, whose sword leaves a dark and slashing Z wherever he goes, who escapes through the shadowy trees, whipping his horse to gallop, rearing at the crest of a hill, saluting the night. It is this whip which will become the instrument of my punishment. I will remember it in my father's hand more vividly than any of my misdeeds.

I know there's an unfairness in my obsession with this whipping. I have a far greater recollection of punishments I received as a child than of whatever I did to drum them forth. Those memories take on a force, a disproportionate weight, as if to prevent the surfacing of positive memories. The moments of happiness I do recall make me feel uneasy, they're too discomfiting.

Perhaps it's not the events of the past which shaped my character, but the way my memory shapes my life, the unsettling way it keeps returning me to my body.

I AM STANDING in the sunken courtyard which leads to the basement, the washing machines and the furnace of our apartment building. It's late afternoon. I'm five years old. There's no one about. In the dark under the porch are the rusted garbage cans, large industrial canisters, where Jimmy Hirakawa once saw a rat scurrying. I'm wearing corduroy pants, a T-shirt, a cowboy hat, and Keds.

I look up at the windows above me. Is anyone looking?

Slowly, deliberately, I begin to pull down my pants, exposing myself, hoping for what, frightened of what, thrilled with what, who knows, but the feeling that returns now in memory seems so familiar, echoed often in other experiences as I grow older. No one leans out the window and shouts, no one sees me; the crime, the secret goes undetected.

Two years later, I'm in the bushes, near the berry tree, in the vacant lot next door we call simply the Empty. Michael Ogata, the oldest kid in the group, is shooing out the younger kids; only he and Jimmy Paris and a fourth-grade girl are allowed to look. Flies buzz, zapping about in the heat;

a cabbage white flutters by my face. I feel their gaze behind me; I'm riveted, confused by their attention, by what I've agreed to do, and again, this time under the watchful gaze of others, I pull down my pants and expose my buttocks. Why are they watching like this? Why am I doing this?

It is over in a few seconds. I walk out of the bushes, back into the sunlight.

PERHAPS IT WAS always too late. Perhaps it was never my parents or the world around me. Perhaps there was something in my nature which accelerated me in the direction I was going without my knowing it.

There's a fleshiness to my photos as a child, I have the face of indolence, indulgence. I was always too eager to raise my hand, to shout out the answer. It's a face I've never lost, really, unpenetrated by experience, by weathering or scars. It's the face of a child who's never known poverty, knows he will never know it. A face capable of ingenuousness and shame.

Every day during those years my father was planning the future, his and mine. For several years he worked two jobs, one at INS as a reporter, one at the camera store owned by the Ogatas. Every afternoon, when I was in second grade, before I could go out to play, I had to work two pages in a fifth-grade math book. He wanted me always to be several years ahead, out in front of the pack. There's some tremendous drive churning inside him. Perhaps fear too. Fear he will not be able to keep rising toward the future, the promises he's made to himself, his wife and children. (When they were first married, he offered my mother a choice—money or his time. She chose money.) He is not yet thirty, older than I sometimes think I'll ever be.

I wanted what all little boys wanted. To be a hero. To ride horses and hit home runs and kill the enemy and never die.

BY THE TIME I was in first grade, both my grandfathers had moved back to Japan. By the time we left the city in third grade, I didn't think about them much. I was hardly aware they were alive. I can't remember when either of them died.

I do remember going to Buddhist ceremonies to commemorate my father's parents. We'd meet my Aunt Ruby and Uncle Lou and my cousins at the apartment of a Buddhist priest on the far North Side. In the living room there was a black shrine with gleaming brass bowls, sticks of incense, flowers, and bowls of fruit. Dressed in a suit, the priest would greet us all, go back down the hall, and return in his flowing black Buddhist robes. He directed us to the two rows of folding chairs, then he knelt in front of the altar, and lit a stick of incense. He picked up his prayer beads, rolled them around in his hands, and began to chant.

At first, the droning voice seems strange, half foghorn, half human. The syllables are nonsense, like no language at all. Na-na-na-na, na-na-na-na. A four-beat rhythm, as monotonous as the ocean, incessant as waves. Our parents bow their heads, their faces quiet and steady. A guttural sound, like someone gargling deep inside his throat.

My cousin Marianne is the first to break. I hear it. The priest drones on. Now it's in me. A small giggle. I feel it coming, gurgling up in my throat too. I can't help it. I hear my sister Susan begin to giggle. The priest drones on. Then my cousins Sharon and Debby. My brother John. I keep waiting for my father or mother to say something. Finally my mother says, "Shhh." But it's too late. The priest drones on. All of us kids are now in fits of laughter. My mother gives up. The priest drones on, never looking back, never stopping, never acknowledging the uproarious Sansei children behind him, his eyes closed tight, his mind centered on the prayers of Buddha, colorless and deep.

On the altar, Tatsue and Jinnosuke, my grandparents, stare out from the pictures at their daughter and son and their families, the uncontrollable grandchildren who find some unbridled mirth in these ceremonies for the dead. This is what they have bequeathed to the future, another strain of American song.

And so it goes, by now all of us kids are rolling on the floor, clutching our stomachs, laughing so hard, our sides ache, laughing so hard, we're out of breath.

THE SUMMER AFTER third grade, we move out of the city and into our own house. Each week that spring before, we make the drive to Morton Grove, taking Lake Shore Drive, stopping at the McDonald's near Loyola. The house seems to signify the flush of luxury, though it's only a standard cookie-cutter bi-level. The boys in the neighborhood play softball in the street, talk to me of exploring our house when the workers are gone. My father stands before the house in its last stages and feels a thrill of accomplishment. He's made it to the middle class, the All-American dream—a house in the suburbs. He's working for the American Medical Association in their Communications Division. In his lectures to me about schoolwork, he'll tell me how he and his boss, Joe Stetler, stay long after everyone has gone, how Mr. Stetler teaches him what he needs to move up the corporate ladder. My father takes up golf, and we all go with him to the driving range at night, watching his drives lope upward into the lights. Soon, he'll trade in his Bel-Air for a Buick LeSabre, a machine smelling of new money, with its black vinyl interior and solid wide frame.

Oddly, our block in Morton Grove is mainly blue-collar—Herbie Thompson's father drives a truck for Brach's candy, Terry Steinberg's father sells plastic slip coverings, the Walters' father is a mechanic. The Hoshizakis, Bob and Doug, live on the next block and their father is an engineer. They're the only Japanese Americans in the neighborhood.

In school, I'm a member of the elite in class. I get good grades, but more importantly, I'm the third-best athlete, behind Greg Jacubik and Gary Hancher. When we play softball or football, I tip the scales; whichever side I'm on usually wins. In basketball, Gary and I vie for the top slot. Back around my house, I'm a Little League All-Star, the quarterback whenever we play football.

Aside from my continuing check marks for unruly behavior in school, everything seems fine. Certainly, the issues of race don't trouble me. My sense of how my experience compared with other Japanese Americans' wasn't a question I ever asked. I never talked about such things with the Hoshizaki boys; all we ever talked about was sports, when today's ball game was going to begin, if we were playing marbles or football.

In fifth grade, though, there's another Japanese American boy in my class, David Nakayama. Extremely short, with bottle-bottom glasses and a crew cut, he's not like me at all physically. I'm one of the larger boys, at times running to husky, but also tall and a good athlete. David Nakayama is not a good athlete. He earns good grades, but gets into trouble frequently. I may make wisecracks in class, I may speak out of turn, but David Nakayama's behavior is truly bizarre.

He proclaims, for instance, that the area in front of his desk is his sovereign nation.

"You must have a pass if you are to cross here," he shouts. The pass must be issued by him. It must possess his official stamp.

Inadvertently, Tony Desalvo crosses David Nakayama's desk to reach the pencil sharpener. David springs up from his desk, shakes his fist at Tony, and shouts, "I declare war. You are now my enemy."

Tony laughs, sharpens his pencil, and goes back to his seat. At his desk, David madly scribbles a declaration of war.

Most of us think David Nakayama is crazy and avoid going by his desk. But Steven Cartwell is different. He can't resist goading David Nakayama. At least once a day, he rises from his desk and deliberately walks towards David's desk.

"Don't you dare, Steven Cartwell," David barks out.

"I'm going to trespass," Steven taunts, "I'm going to cross into your country without a pass."

David eyes him like a hawk, like a gunner waiting for the target to get in range.

"I don't have a pa—asss, I don't have a pa—asss," Steven sings out. Now he's crossing right in front of David Nakayama. David cannot believe it. His face scrunches up, livid with rage.

"Steven Cartwell, you are a traitorous spy." David raises his fist, brandishing a pencil—sometimes it's a compass—and starts to chase after Steven, yelling, "I declare war," at the top of his lungs. They run around and around the room, chasing each other like Sylvester and Tweetie Pie, until Miss Phillips finally gets hold of both of them and sits them in the corner. On those times when David draws blood, she sends him to the principal's office.

From time to time David shows up at our desks offering a newsletter which spews spirited attacks against the scurrilous Steven Cartwell. There are articles about his spy activities, about how he's an agent for a foreign government, betraying secrets, conducting clandestine fifth-column activities. There are pictures of him with devil's horns on his head. There are headlines, of course, declaring war on Steven Cartwell, blasting his sneak attacks.

I tend to steer clear of David Nakayama and Steven Cartwell. To me, they are spazzes; neither of them is good at sports. When we play baseball or football at recess, neither of them takes part. No one would pick them for their team even if they tried to play.

By junior high, David Nakayama became less of a wildly eccentric figure and more a figure of mild ridicule. He was someone people picked on or laughed at from time to time, but wasn't quite noticeable enough to be the constant brunt of bad attention. The other boys called him "Nak-nak" (pronounced "knock-knock"). I don't think the girls noticed him at all. Occasionally, he still put out his newsletter, but he had ceased backing it up with his grade school antics.

He was most conspicuous in gym class, where his short stature and slightly plump body marshaled him to the margins. Indeed, his lack of physical prowess seemed almost astonishing. The shortess of his long jump was improbable to us, a joke. The rest of us could have jumped that far on one leg.

Of course, I continued to avoid any association with David Nakayama like the plague. He and I weren't even in the same league. I don't think anyone took particular notice that we were both Japanese American, but if I'd been confronted with this connection, I would have spilled forth a list of our differences—from his glasses and crew-cut hair to his tiny, unathletic body to his nondescript clothes to the stories of his wild exploits in grade school and his obsessions with secret pacts and trespasses which continued to propel his self-published newsletter. If, by junior high, I wasn't exactly in with the "in crowd," I still had hope of being invited to its parties.

And then, one day in the locker room, Mike Wrangel starts to yell at David Nakayama.

"You moron, you can't even catch a ball."

David says nothing. He's naked, still dripping from the showers. He's putting on his T-shirt.

"Look at his underpants. They're all brown."

I look across the bench to where Wrangel and David are standing. I don't want to say anything. Wrangel has just transferred to our school last month. He smokes, wears a leather jacket, sports sideburns; he's flunked once, which means he's a year older than the rest of us. Not someone to be messed with.

"God, you're a spaz," Wrangel continues.

David tries to turn toward his locker, away from Wrangel. He gropes for his thick glasses. His body is that of a little kid really, and Wrangel towers over him. In my mind, I suddenly see the image of a huge polar bear descending on a penguin, a strange mixture of terror and absurdity. I hesitate. It's not my fight. Why should I do anything? Maybe Wrangel's going to stop. No, he's not. I can't stand it any longer.

"Leave him alone, Wrangel."

"What's it to you?'

"Just leave him alone."

Wrangel strides down the bench to me.

"What are you going to make of it?"

"Nothing. Just leave him alone." I try to laugh it off. "He's not worth the bother."

Wrangel looks at me for a moment. We're about the same size. I could probably take him on the wrestling mats, but in a street fight, no way. My stomach gurgles. My skin takes on a malarial heat, tingling all over, my arms feel leaden and limp.

"Oh, so he's one of your buddies," he sneers.

"No way, man. . . . Just let him go."

The bell rings. Wrangel takes a look at me, at David Nakayama, then turns and walks away.

Neither David Nakayama nor I look at each other as we dress in silence. We're still in two separate worlds.

IN EIGHTH GRADE, I was captain of the intramural basketball champions. Every year, the champion team played a team of all-stars from the other teams. The odds were generally in favor of the all-stars. But that didn't faze me. I knew we were going to win.

It wasn't just that I was the leading scorer in intramurals. I studied the game, checking strategy and plays in the sports books from the library. I read through Bob Cousy's biography, his book on playing in the NBA finals against the Lakers, books with titles like *Full Court Press* and *All-Star Forward*. I understood the chemistry needed to make a winner, how each player fit like a cog in a machine, from the rebounding role player to the playmaker to the defensive specialist to the scorer.

The night before the big game I sat outside the school with Steve Fine, the second leading scorer on our team, waiting for the bus. Fine was quiet, intelligent, and better-looking than I. He had this small hint of a pompadour that seemed to curl just right and which I envied. His jump shot was smooth and accurate. He said he hoped he played well in the game, because on Saturday everyone would be talking about it at Marla Friedman's boy-girl party. I nodded; I felt the same way. Our breaths came out in clouds in the chilly evening air. In my mind I ran through the last few pages of *Full Court Press*, the description of the nail-biting title game, the gritty guard who made it all happen. Lost in reverie, I was jolted by Fine's voice.

"Hey, man. The bus." He looked at me and laughed. "You better be more awake tomorrow night."

The game was close throughout. But Rick Gordon, who was guarding me, constantly overplayed his hand, and I ripped past him for several layups. Although I usually looked for assists first, spotting Fine in the corner, the flow of the game was pulling me more and more to look for my shot. Every time it looked like the all-stars might pull away, someone would make a key basket, often me. In the fourth quarter huddle, I kept shouting to everyone about defense. "No zone. Just good man-to-man. Just stick to your man."

When the clock had wound down to the last seconds, the game was tied; the all-stars had the ball. I saw Allan Rosenbloom glance at Rick

Gordon and I pounced into the passing lane, intercepted the pass, and before they knew it, in a long floating drive I remember to this day, I made the winning layup. I'd scored over half of my team's points.

I dressed for the party on Saturday night carefully, with the proper Levi's and paisley shirt and brown penny loafers, the style of dress that the kids from Skokie called "collegiate." Its opposite was "greaser," and if you were in neither of these categories, you were simply unworthy of mention. I spent several minutes before the mirror, patiently grooming my pompadour. I walked the three blocks to Marla Friedman's house, still warmed by the memory of my last-second basket, immune to the brisk November wind that buffeted about me. I recalled how Laura Bennett seemed startled at how good I was, better than Allan Rosenbloom or Rick Gordon or any of the other guys from Skokie, the ones she'd gone to grade school with. Laura Bennett, the prettiest girl in the class, whom I had a secret crush on and who, through the luck of the draw, was my science partner. I'd feel this soft caving inside me whenever I was near her, whenever I thought of her, and I kept envisioning some time when she would see I was not like the other guys, that what I felt for her was deeper, purer. Week after week I'd been helping her with her write-ups, wishing there was some way we could talk about something else. Here was my chance.

But when I got to the party, no one talked about the game.

At first, everybody talked about what records to play. There were arguments about the Beatles versus the Rolling Stones; everyone wanted to hear the new Beach Boy album Marla had just bought. We were in the basement rec room, and from time to time, Marla's mother would call down. It seemed clear she wasn't going to interrupt us. I kept waiting for someone to mention the game, but somehow the center of things always seemed to be whatever Rick Gordon or Jeff Lappins was talking about, even though Lappins hadn't even played in the game. Gordon was a year older than the rest of us, wore a leather jacket, and regaled everyone with tales of the fights he'd been in on with his older brothers. He pulled out his switchblade, flicked it open and showed it to everyone. Laura laughed and pretended to shy away from him, as if she were frightened. Lappins had hair just like the Beatles, and it was rumored several girls in the room had crushes on him. He talked about how fast the girls were from Crandall, a junior high just across town in Evanston.

"You can't believe what they're like. They even give hand jobs."

"That's disgusting," said Marla. Lappins laughed. It was just the response he was looking for. The other girls giggled.

Watching all this, I wanted to jump into the conversation, but there never seemed a spot to slide in. I made a show of looking at Marla's records, reading the album covers. I tried to talk to Fine about the game, but he didn't seem interested. And then, Marla came out of her utility room carrying an empty Coke bottle, and several girls started giggling. Riki Leavitt took the bottle and shouted, "It's time for Spin the Bottle."

What was that? I didn't know, but of course wasn't going to ask. Fortunately, Riki explained, then ordered everyone into a circle. Rick Gordon grabbed the bottle to spin first, and it landed on Riki. Everyone oohed. There was a rumor Riki and Gordon had a crush on each other.

I began to feel this flush of excitement. When was it going to land on me? I wanted it to happen and I didn't. What would I do? I'd never kissed a girl before. How was I supposed to do that?

Then, as the Searchers sang "Needles and Pins" on the stereo, Andi Levine spun the bottle, and it slowed to a halt, pointing at me. I scrambled across the center of the circle. She sat up, leaning forward slightly. I think she expected just a simple peck on the lips, like everyone else was giving. I don't know what I expected, but when I pressed my lips to hers, something seemed to pull me toward her, pressing my lips tighter, and I kept them there, thinking I should let go now, feeling I didn't want to let go, I couldn't. And then I heard people around us cheer, and this spurred me on, until she finally pulled herself away, as if trying to grab her breath. The calls erupted louder then, and my face reddened with the attention. Suddenly people were talking about me. So I did the same thing on the next spin. And the next.

Finally, the bottle I'd spun pointed to Laura Bennett. I turned to look at her dark face, her long dark hair, her almost Italian-looking eyes, her full mouth, all vaguely reminiscent of Sophia Loren, of someone several years older. But what I saw in her eyes was a mixture of mock horror and a real, though slight, repulsion, as she made a show of backing up and putting her hands up before her face, fluttering them there as if waving away a stream of gnats. She ran to the other side of the room and refused to kiss me. Everyone laughed.

The next Monday at school I was labeled "Lover Lips." I tried to wear this moniker as a mark of distinction, though I sensed that wasn't quite the case. All I knew was, the rules had changed.

FROM
LOVE, HATE &
OTHER FILTERS

SAMIRA AHMED

American-born seventeen-year-old Maya Aziz is torn between worlds. There's the proper one her parents expect for their good Indian daughter: attending a college close to their suburban Chicago home, pursuing an acceptable career, and, eventually, marrying a suitable boy. And then there is the world of her dreams: going to film school and living in New York City—and maybe pursuing a boy she's known from afar since grade school, a boy who's finally falling into her orbit at school.

There's also the real world, beyond Maya's control. In the aftermath of a horrific crime perpetrated hundreds of miles away, her life is turned upside down. The community she's known since birth becomes unrecognizable; neighbors and classmates alike are consumed with fear, bigotry, and hatred. Ultimately, Maya must find the strength within to determine where she truly belongs.

While Maya faces many difficult situations, she is also a girl like all the other girls—one who is excited for her prospects beyond high school and who wants to have the best senior year ever, hanging out with her friends, going swimming at a secret pond with a secret crush, and sharing her first kiss with a boy who might not be "the one" but is wonderful nevertheless.

In this excerpt, Maya goes on her first date with Kareem—really her first date ever. Like many kids growing up in the suburbs, Maya is drawn to Chicago, with its promise of a vibrancy and energy and infinite variety that makes it a truly singular place. I also wanted to highlight the quiet magic of Chicago—the moments when the city feels like it exists just for you. For Maya's first date with the worldlier Kareem I chose a walk through Old Town and dinner at Geja's Café—a fondue place that has been around since the mid-1960s and is often considered one of the most romantic spots in the city. Maya is a young woman facing a difficult future, but I wanted to give her one perfect kiss on a lovely spring evening, with the city and her future blossoming before her.

H INA MEETS ME AT THE TRAIN STATION, A SQUAT GREEN GLASS behemoth that looks too big for a city block. My pocket camcorder raised to my eye, I film the Saturday afternoon crowd entering and leaving. I love how inconspicuous this camera is; it fits in the palm of my hand. As we exit, I turn my lens to the pink banners fluttering from the lampposts— ads for a fund-raising walk for breast cancer in a few weeks. I make sure to capture them on film.

Hina designed them. They're all over the city. I'm in awe of her again, as always.

I pan down the line of taxis, right up until Hina and I enter one. She squeezes my shoulder as I adjust my belt. "So glad you're going on a date and doing teenagery things. Try to get into at least a little bit of trouble, OK? And where is the young, dashing Kareem taking you?"

"A fondue place not far from your apartment."

"Geja's Café? He must want to wow you."

"Don't worry. He's not going to pop the question or anything," I reply coolly, though my pulse quickens.

"Well, my wry little niece, he's definitely trying to make an impression. And he asked your parents for permission to see you, right? A very suitable boy, indeed."

The driver pulls over in front of Hina's place. I love my aunt's condo—a two-flat walk-up in Chicago's Old Town neighborhood. To me, it is freedom.

"Go ahead and get settled in your room. I'll get lunch together." Hina steps into the kitchen while I head down the hall.

The comfy bed is piled high with Indian patchwork pillows in rich hues of chocolate, burgundy, and emerald embellished with tiny mirrors and gold tassels. The raw silk duvet cover is a deep bronze color. A wooden partition carved with intricate floral designs serves as the headboard. It belonged to my grandparents and smells like the sandalwood incense my *nani* used to burn day and night.

I unpack my dark skinny jeans, the slightly wrinkled black silk camisole I borrowed from Violet. I hang them in the closet. Then I fold my cherry-colored cashmere sweater and place it on a chair. After that I kick off my beat-up, round-toed black flats and flop onto the bed, turning to stare at the ceiling. Kareem is picking me up at seven. That leaves five hours for nervous anticipation. I need to get all the blushing out of my system now.

It's been two weeks since we met at the wedding, and weirdly, it feels like a million years ago, but also yesterday. We've texted or messaged each other lots. But that also means my contact with Kareem has been virtual, and my contact with Phil has been real. But for years—literally *years*—Phil was neither real nor virtual; he was a faraway dream. Until now. Only I'm about to go on a date with a guy who is actually available, infinitely more suitable, and definitely interested.

This is why they invented drugs for heartburn.

The guest room door is half open, but Hina knocks anyway before coming in. I sit up on the edge of the bed as she perches next to me. "How about we eat a quick lunch and go to a movie before your big date? Or we can on-demand something. Have you seen *Roman Holiday*? You know, about a princess who feels trapped in her life?"

I smile. "Yeah, that sounds about right."

"Trust me: Gregory Peck and Audrey Hepburn are pretty much Saturday afternoon perfection," Hina says, giving my hand a squeeze.

My mom picks *Bride and Prejudice*. Hina picks *Roman Holiday*. Somehow their movie choices totally define my relationships with them. They both try. One misses the mark. The other nails it.

AFTER THE MOVIE, we sit on the couch, sipping cups of creamy spiced chai.

"Did I ever tell you about Anand?" Hina asks out of the blue. She rarely talks about the guys she dates; it must be some tacit agreement she has with my mother. So I immediately perk up.

"Ummm, no. But I am all ears."

Hina smiles. "It was India, before I left to study in England. He was such a beautiful boy. You know I went to the same Catholic girls' school as your mom, in Hyderabad? Well, there was a brother school run by priests. We shared the same athletic fields. That's how I met Anand. I was at field hockey practice, and he was playing cricket."

"Awww. And it was love at first sight?"

"Not exactly. Maybe? I don't know. I never really thought about it in those terms. Anand just started showing up to my field hockey practices and our games, and one day I finally asked him if he was going to talk to me."

"Bold move, Hina."

Hina chuckles. "My friends were so scandalized. But you know, I've always been a straight shooter."

It's one of the things I love best about my aunt.

"Well, he started bringing tiffins, and we would have little picnics of *samosas* and *chaat* and *pakoras* with mango juice in glass bottles."

"So he would cook for you? How adorable."

"Oh, no. He had his cook do it, and then his driver would bring it to the fields so it would be warm after practice."

"Must be nice."

"It was. Of course, we could never really go anywhere, so the entire fleeting romance took place on school grounds."

"I'm guessing from his name he was Hindu?"

"Exactly. But honestly, we barely even talked about that. We both knew nothing more could come of it. So we spent that spring talking and eating and laughing, and then he went to Bombay to study architecture at university."

"That's it? That's the whole story? You never saw each other again?"

"We saw each other once more, when he came home for holiday. I went to see him at Nampally Railway Station just when he was leaving to go back to school."

"And . . ."

"And that was my first kiss. A little peck in a dark corner of a bustling train station."

"That is so cinematic," I say.

Hina laughs. "From you, that is high praise, indeed."

"So were you heartbroken? Did you regret it?"

"Heartbroken? A little. Regret? No. What was there to regret? I wasn't going to Bombay with him. We were both young and different religions, and I had no desire to elope and bring down the entire wrath of both our families on our heads. So now it's simply a sweet memory. That's all it was ever going to be."

I sit back and stare into my half-empty teacup.

"Something on your mind?" Hina asks. "First kisses, perhaps?"

"Yes. No. Maybe, but not necessarily with Kareem . . ."

Hina raises an eyebrow at me and gives me a warm smile and settles into the couch.

I hadn't planned to, but I end up telling her about Phil and the tutoring sessions and how my stomach roller-coasters every time I'm around him and about how he has a girlfriend. Then I talk to her about Kareem, who is the parental dream of suitability. But he's a lot more than just his biodata.

"The thing is," I say, after my breathless debrief, "the timing is all so bizarre, I mean why now? Why me?"

She stares at me as if I'm totally clueless. "Why *not* you?"

Even Hina can make me blush. It really is a disorder.

"What *is*, in fact, bizarre, my dear," she continues, "is that you don't see what a beautiful, brilliant young woman you are. You still think of yourself as that gawky, flat-chested seventh grader with braces and two braids."

I'm not sure how to respond. I wouldn't admit this to anyone, not even Hina; I can barely even think it when I'm alone, but there are moments when I catch a glimpse of myself in the mirror and I'm happily surprised at the reflection—it's me but not me. I can see the shiny black hair that falls below my shoulders, the woman's body that looks good in a fitted sweater and tight jeans. Plus I can see I've been upping my lipstick game.

Hina clearly wants more juicy details, wants to know which boy I prefer, but even getting near that thought makes my stomach lurch. I don't know who the Gregory Peck is to my Audrey Hepburn; I have no idea if *either* boy is or isn't. I check my watch. "Crap. Kareem will be here in an hour. I need to get ready."

I hear Hina chuckling to herself as I bolt off the couch and run into the guest room.

FORTY-FIVE MINUTES LATER, freshly showered and changed into Violet-approved denim and silk, I slip into my black satin shoes. I put on a pair of dangly silver chandelier earrings and grab my sweater, then study my reflection. There is a lot of skin. My skin. I chew on my lip, hoping it's not too much. For my final task, I dab on a bit of bronzer and a claret lipstick like I promised my mom. My word is my bond—at least about lipstick. Finally, I decide to go big and add eyeliner and mascara.

The bell rings. He's five minutes early. How un-Indian of him.

Hina buzzes in Kareem and then disappears into her bedroom. I'm glad I'm not home. My parents would linger, inquire after Kareem's parents, demand that we stay and chat over a cup of chai while insisting that the restaurant would hold our reservation.

I open the door.

Kareem is taller than I remember. Maybe cuter, too? I try not to stare into those sparkly dark eyes. He's dressed in indigo jeans, a navy blazer, and a light blue collared shirt, the top two buttons unbuttoned.

"Hey." God, I hope I'm not trying too hard, because that's the exact opposite of cool. Eau de desperation.

He steps in and bends down. I think he's coming in for a hug, so I move forward. Our heads bump as he tries to give me a kiss on the cheek.

Awkward. I step back, cheeks already aflame.

Kareem laughs. "Ah, there's the blush. That took, what, fifteen seconds?"

"Ha, ha. Come on in." At least I've provided the icebreaker.

"You look amazing, by the way," Kareem adds casually. He steps forward and puts his hand on my forearm. If he's trying to keep me blushing, he's doing an excellent job.

"Uh, thanks . . ."

Thankfully Hina chooses this moment to appear from the back.

"*As-salaam-alaikum*, Auntie," Kareem says. His respectful nod oozes *tameez*, proper Hyderabadi-boy etiquette.

Hina laughs. "Please, Kareem, call me Hina. No need to stand on ceremony with me." Then she raises an eyebrow. "So, Geja's? Going for dark, romantic, and sophisticated, are we?"

I'm going to die.

"Uh, yeah," Kareem smiles. "I . . . we . . . uh . . . have a seven-thirty reservation, so we should probably get going." He turns to me. "Are you up for a stroll? Nice evening for a walk."

I nod and snatch my purse. I've already double-checked it for my mini-cam. I couldn't leave home without it—in case I want to record any part of the evening, or, more likely, hide behind my lens if things go from awkward to painfully bad. "I'm set."

"*Khudafis*, Auntie—I mean, Hina. Thanks again for letting me pick up Maya here. Does she have a curfew?"

Hina shakes her head. "Not at my house. Have fun." She kisses me on the cheek and winks as she closes the door behind us.

"ONE OF US has to say something soon. Ideally a witty or brilliant observation," Kareem says. We've been walking silently for almost ten minutes. I keep trying to think of something to say, but apparently I've lost the connection between my brain and mouth.

And that's my cue. We haven't even made it to the restaurant yet, but it's time to draw on my trusty shield. I reach into my purse and pull out my tiny camcorder, switch it on, and focus on Kareem. Roll camera. I adopt my documentary voice-over tone. And action. "Kareem, where are you taking Maya tonight?"

"You're referring to yourself in the third person now?"

I pull back to meet his gaze. "I'm the director. Kareem and Maya are the subjects in the movie. Go with it."

"Fine."

We're both smiling and trying not to at the same time.

I pick up where I left off. "So what are your plans for tonight?'

Kareem straightens an imaginary tie. I love that he plays along; I also love that he can't see how delighted I am. "I want to show Maya a good time, and so I chose Geja's Café. It's terribly romantic, but I fear that it might also be terribly messy—all that melted cheese." He pauses with exaggerated drama and strikes a ridiculous pose. "I'm willing to take that risk because I'm the kind of guy that lives on the edge. You know, carpe diem. Suck the marrow out of life."

"So you're a Thoreau fan?"

"Nah, just pretentious."

I stifle a laugh. "So besides tempting fate with melted cheese and literary airs of pretention, what else is in your risk-taking repertoire?"

"The usual: skydiving, Formula One, feeding sharks . . ." He pauses, either pretending to remember or remembering to pretend. "My mom does say I was an adventurous kid. A troublemaker. Mainly I was curious. Oh, and I loved pirates. Anything on the high seas that involved danger and swashbuckling—you know, big swells, treasure, damsels in distress. My mom loved it, too. She provided the pirate booty. She would put her banged-up jewelry and broken bangles in a small box and bury the treasure chest. I'd have to find it and dig it up. It was pretty awesome, actually."

I envision a skinny, buck-toothed version of Kareem, running around with his mom, shrieking with laughter. "Arrh, matey!" they shout at each other. I'm smiling, but I feel a twinge of sadness. I don't have those Kodachrome images of my own childhood escapades. It's just not how I grew up.

"And now?" I ask, determined to bring us back to the present. "Do you still live a life of adventure?"

"My high-seas days are over, but I'd say tonight has the potential for excitement." He looks directly into the camera. "Don't you agree?"

"I'm documenting, I can't interfere—it's not my story." I'm blushing behind the camera. This time, I'm sure he notices.

And I'm right, because he approaches and gently pushes the camera away from my face. "This is totally your story."

I look into his brown eyes. Out here on the street, they're less dazzling, but more gentle and warm and inviting. They embody him. We continue walking.

Suddenly, he stops short. "This is it . . ."

Our arrival catches both of us by surprise.

Kareem pushes open the door, holding it for me. I step into a dark labyrinth of fluttering candles, shadowy nooks. A flamenco band plays somewhere. Wine bottles line the walls and create partitions between tables. I put my camera back in my purse and let myself breathe it all in; there's no point in trying to film because there isn't enough light. A host shows us to our table—a booth toward the back, partially hidden by velvet curtains that can be undone to shroud the space entirely. A waiter quickly arrives, explains the three-course fondue meal, and leaves.

"I guess this place is kind of over the top, huh?" Kareem asks.

I smile back. "It's very film noir. All we need is a fog machine and a dame with a gun and checkered past."

Kareem laughs. "Wait. That's not you?"

"You never can tell."

His eyes narrow; he strokes his goatee. "So you're not actually this sweet girl who lives in the suburbs. You have a whole double life where you're carrying on in a nefarious way . . ."

I totally get into the act. I love that I feel comfortable enough to do it. "I'm not as simple as you might think."

Kareem shakes his head. "*Simple* is never a word I'd use to describe you." He smiles, then reaches across the table and takes my hand in his.

I'm frozen. But I don't want to move. I stare at the candle between us, feeling as if the flame has leapt inside me. I know I'm blushing, but I don't care about that, either. Kareem holds my hand tighter. I bite the inside of my lower lip.

When the waiter arrives to take our order, I reluctantly pull my hand away.

"Let's go for the works," Kareem suggests, leaning back.

"Sounds good."

Then Kareem asks me what I want to drink. "A glass of red, maybe? I'll have a glass of the house Bordeaux." He's talking about wine, studying the wine list as if this is something he always does. This is . . . unexpected. I've only tried a drop of alcohol once in my life at Violet's house, but the guilt left a bitter taste in my mouth that lasts to this day. Then I remember: he's twenty-one. He's *allowed* to do this. But that still leaves the question: *Why* is he doing it?

"I never . . . I don't . . . really drink," I sputter. "There was one time . . . Also, you may be twenty-one, but I'm not . . ."

Kareem smiles. "You're right. I shouldn't be corrupting you on our first date. Seriously, no worries. And no pressure. I enjoy a glass of wine with dinner once in a while, that's all."

I'm still at a loss. "But . . ."

"Why am I drinking in the first place?" Kareem raises his eyebrows.

I nod several times. "Does your mom know?"

"Of course. I had my first sip with my parents."

My mouth drops open. The stars are misaligned. This is not normal, not for a desi Muslim kid. "But aren't your parents . . . ? I mean, I heard your mom talking to my mom about going to the mosque and—"

His laugh stops me. "They're not sitting around getting wasted, denying the existence of God or anything. My dad considers himself a believer. But he also believes in enjoying a glass of wine now and again."

I'm too dumbstruck to think of anything else to say. My own parents aren't exactly the fire-and-brimstone types, but they've never had a drink. Of that I'm certain. Guilt plows into me. They always take me to the mosque on important holidays; they fast during Ramadan; they sometimes close their office to attend Friday afternoon prayers. I'm wracked with guilt as the waiter sets a wineglass in front of Kareem, then pours a small splash from the bottle.

Kareem lifts the glass by the stem, swirling the dark purplish-red liquid into a little tempest. He tilts the rim to his nose and inhales deeply, then puts the glass back down on the table.

"It needs to open up a bit," he says to the waiter, who seems to understand whatever this means. The waiter leaves us.

I am staring at him, not sure what to make of his expertise, but envious of it. I want to be worldly and sophisticated.

"Maya, relax. It's not like I eat pork."

We both crack up, because we know it's the one line even most lapsed Muslims won't cross.

The appetizer arrives—a steaming Crock-Pot of bubbling cheese fondue with three types of breads and apples with tiny dipping forks. I move the candles around on the table in hopes that the addition of canned heat under the pot will maybe give me enough light to get a decent shot. I take my camera and film as Kareem dips a piece of bread into the cheese, spinning the melted strands around the end of his fork. He plops it into his mouth. "H-h-h-o-o-t-t!" he yells.

"Water," I suggest, but continue to record Kareem's open-mouthed struggle with the piping hot cheese—total culinary drama.

He downs a full glass of water. "I can't believe you didn't stop filming. What if that cheese had burned off the roof of my mouth and it was the last morsel of food I would ever enjoy?"

"All the more reason to preserve the moment," I reply. "Priceless." I put the camera down because I don't need a shield anymore and because I'm hungry.

We dip and eat and talk about our parents and being Indian and the pressure to be a doctor and the Indian aunties who always think you are a little too skinny or a little too chubby and never perfect. We rate our favorite Indian foods and joke that how the first thing we want when we fly back from India is an actual Big Mac.

"I wish getting a Big Mac was still my biggest concern when I pass through customs these days," Kareem mutters.

"What is it, fries?" I joke.

"More like hoping I don't get chosen for the special Secondary Security Screening lottery."

My smile fades. He's not joking.

"Crap. That's happened to you?" I sigh. Not sure why I am at all surprised.

"Twice, coming back home. The first time they took me into this back room. I waited for, like, two hours with all these other brown dudes before being called into a separate room and being asked these basic questions like is this really my name and what was I doing in India and do I have relatives in Pakistan. Whatever."

"That's horrible."

He flashes a bitter smirk. "Hey, at least I wasn't handcuffed to a wall, right?"

"Don't even joke about that."

"It's not a joke."

"I'm sorry," I say and lightly touch his arm.

He places his hand on mine. "Don't be. You have nothing to apologize for."

WHEN WE'RE A block away from Hina's apartment, I realize it's drizzling. Maybe it's been drizzling since we left the restaurant; I'm not even sure. Kareem clutches my hand, and we run to take cover under a crab apple tree. It's April, so everything is in bloom. Pink petals fall on us, clinging to our wet faces. I glance up through the branches, backlit by the streetlamps. I breathe in the sweet, delicate scent. It lasts only a few weeks each spring. If I'd dreamed up this mise-en-scène, I would have thought it a cliché. But in real life, it is perfect.

"What are you thinking?" Kareem whispers.

I look at him. "If this were one of my parents' retro-Bollywood faves, I'd run behind that tree right now and come out singing and in a different outfit."

Kareem gently hooks a finger under my chin and draws my face toward his. "But if this were an old Indian movie, I couldn't do this." He bends down and gently brushes his lips against mine. The earth stops moving. I am frozen in this spot of time.

Turns out, I'm fond of kissing. Extremely. I close my eyes, losing myself in the falling petals, the light rain, the strength of his arms, his breath on my lips. I revel in the moment, the echo of his skin against mine.

Kareem pauses, strokes my cheek with his finger. "Your lips are so soft."

I blush even as the rain cools my face. Kareem's lips taste of wine and chocolate. He puts his left hand around my waist and pulls me closer so that our bodies touch. Thunder rumbles in the distance.

I pull away because I feel myself being overtaken. "I should be getting inside. I'm soaking wet, and—"

"OK, OK," Kareem nods. "You're a good Indian girl. I shouldn't move too fast."

I cringe a little, but he's speaking the truth. "No, I'm not . . . I mean, I am, but it's that, you know, we're in front of my aunt's place."

Kareem laughs. "Then please allow me to escort you to the door in a gentleman-like fashion. But first . . ." He grabs me and kisses me again, longer and harder. I let myself sink into the kiss—wild, reckless, until it's suddenly too intense. I pull away, breathless.

Kareem takes my hand and leads me to Hina's front door. He's not merely being polite; my feet are wobbly.

"I want to see you again, Maya," he says, softly. "But next time, I'll make sure there are no Indian relatives around."

"Thanks for dinner," I gasp. "I had a great time. Have a safe trip back to school . . ."

Kareem sneaks in one last quick kiss. I gape at him as the rain falls harder. Then he slips into his car. I unlock the front door, turning to wave good-bye before he speeds off.

Once his engine fades to silence, I shut the door and take a deep breath. I'm dizzy as I walk up the stairs to my aunt's place. I can still feel the tickle of Kareem's goatee on my face. I walk into the apartment and see the clock on the microwave flashing 12:05 A.M. and laugh out loud. If this were my house, my parents would have called the police by now. And there wouldn't have been any kissing or hand-holding; I would've been too afraid of withering under their interrogation.

I slip out of my shoes, tiptoe quietly into the guest bathroom to slip off my wet clothes, and hang them over the shower rod. Wrapped in a fluffy white towel, I examine myself in the mirror. I run an index finger over my lips and notice a few flower petals in my hair. After brushing out the long, wet strands, I wash off what little makeup is left on my face.

I savor the memory of the moment under the trees.

But when I relive it in my mind, the lips I'm kissing are Phil's.

PLANET ROCK

DHANA-MARIE BRANTON

"Planet Rock" grew out of an essay I wrote as a teenager called "The Silence." It was a feel-good piece about the morning after Harold Washington's groundbreaking election as Chicago's first Black mayor.

Twenty-six years later, I was completing an MFA program in Minnesota when Barack Obama was elected president. It was a stunning moment in history, which led an adviser, Patricia Hampl, to suggest I write an essay for my thesis. She seemed excited about the election and the things I might have to say. I was thrilled as well. But my feelings during those first dizzying days ran from elation to terror. What if Obama sucked? Worse, what if he got killed?

These questions led me to my files. I reread "The Silence" and thought, who is this? The writer—me—was guilty of the very thing she leveled at her community, being compliant and silent.

"Planet Rock" remains the hardest writing I've ever done—emotional, impossible, and terrifying. Amid a media storm lauding America's courage, I was flooded with memories of Harold Washington and 1980s Chicago. I was, in effect, chasing my own voice. I had to prove, if only to myself, that not only did I admire people who stood in their truth, I had become such a person myself.

The title, and its connection to our ongoing state of political affairs, is one of those pretty accidents that sometimes happens in creative work. Ultimately, "Planet Rock" is about the journey to individual voice, forever the bedrock of collective and historical change.

IN THE OLD DAYS, I WAS FASCINATED BY A PAIR OF NEON LIPS THAT towered above a Chicago expressway. Magikist sold rugs and the giant lips were filled with red movie lights. The sign was a local landmark, more Vegas than Midwest, and every time we passed it, I got out the box with my mother.

"Calm down," she'd say. I'd get on my knees and gawk out the rear window, counting one-two-three-four-five-six as the lips went from black to red.

"You're too old to be acting like that," my mother said when I whined about Magikist closing and the massive lips coming down. I can't say what she meant by "too old." But in our South Side community, you got you one ticket between two emotional stations: you could be mad as hell or just sit in the middle, being the stoic support that held everything together.

There was scant discussion of the other end. You left yourself open by indulging in displays of vulnerability and softness. You didn't have clearance to cry, and certainly not over some damn sign. When you did melt down, it had better be alone and never in front of *others*.

It also didn't pay to be too damn happy. If you walked around grinning, people might ask, *What are you smiling about and just what were you planning to say?*

I was a largish, dark girl with a gene that kept me buoyant and cheerful, so I had to watch my size 11 step. I could be myself at home, whatever that meant.

I used to think my mother was understanding and generous about my eccentricities. Now I realize she kept me on a long leash from plain old concern. As a preschooler, I had nearly died after running into the path of a school bus. The doctor's warning about possible latent brain damage made for a childhood that was both wild free country and a series of small dark rooms.

Nobody said it out loud, but when you left the South Side you were the informal ambassador for a people. I snapped the Oddball in when I left the house, then set my face to stone before boarding the Seventy-Ninth Street bus. I navigated the gang-riddled minefield of Calumet High School (where it didn't pay to be too damn smart), then exhaled downtown at *New Expression*.

New Expression was a part of Youth Communication, a nonprofit that published newspapers written for and by high school journalists. It was a real weekly paper presided over by a stern lesbian nun named Ann. Students were paid and mentored by the professional media. Teen reporters wrote, solicited ads, took photos, and did layout and copy.

We covered the stories high school newspapers couldn't—sex, gangs, parents, and drugs. We were also determined, in early 1983, to support the mayoral candidacy of a man named Harold Washington. He was not just a dark horse, but African American. I still hear the slogan of his trumped-up competitor, Bernard Epton . . . "Before It's Too Late."

I wasn't a joiner, but I sought out and joined Students for Washington. Epton's slogan didn't just make me angry; the truth was it cut deeply. Here was further proof that people who looked like me could never be trusted to run anything.

My mother was pissed off too. I was supposed to be downtown writing for the newspaper, not passing out buttons for some man who had didn't have a snowball's chance.

"Harold Washington is not going to win," she told my sister Pam and me time and again. A Black man would never be elected mayor, not in a syndicate-deep city like Chicago. If by some miracle he did win, the world was what it was and nothing was ever going to change. *One day*, she'd said, while spooning out something for our dinner, *you all are going to learn that*.

Still, several days a week I left *New Expression* to hand out blue "Washington for Chicago" buttons. I pinned them on students and passed them out to morning commuters on the Seventy-Ninth Street bus. Downtown, I tended to float near State and Madison where another Students for Washington rep worked. Jeffrey vented his anger by intimidating whites.

"Washington for Chicago?" If they moved, he moved. "Washington for Chicago?"

"I'm a junior at Robeson," he lied, but I would soon learn he had dropped out the previous year. He had to say something after I bragged about being editor of my high school paper and a *New Expression* reporter. I remember liking him like a boyfriend at first, before I realized he wasn't into girls.

"Do you really think Harold Washington can win?" I'd ask.

"Yes!" he'd groan, looking at me like I was daft. Jeffrey was always looking at me like that. I told him what my mother said.

"Mary, your mama is wrong."

Jeffrey called me that early, way before I gave him permission and long after I mumbled that he stop.

"My name is Donna," I'd say. "D-o-n-n-a."

"I know what your name is. Mary."

On election night, my sister Pam was invited to a victory party at Foster Walker's. Foster was an only child who lived by Dawes Park in a house with a pool table in the basement. I wanted to go downtown and cheer for Harold Washington, but my mother had other plans.

No way, she said, giving us her New Year's Eve speech, were we going out on this night when niggers was going to be mad and acting crazy. We would fix some popcorn and watch the returns together in our cold, unfinished basement.

Pam scowled and went to bed. I settled down to watch the numbers alone. At eight or nine, Washington began to surge ahead. It was past midnight when Epton conceded and Washington gave his acceptance speech. I remember standing in our cold basement feeling like the house had caught fire.

I ran upstairs to wake my mother, yelling for my sister.

"He won, Mama! Harold Washington won!" In the blue glow of the screen, I watched as an almost-smile played with her lips. She sat like a stone, saying *I don't believe it.* I strained my eyes at the cheering crowd. Somehow, I knew Jeffrey was there.

The next morning, we donned our blue Harold Washington T-shirts with tight Sergio Valente jeans. I pinned my "Washington for Chicago" button on and offered to do the same for my sister. *You're so obvious*, she said or something Virgo-driven like that. Normally, that would have started a round of bickering, but that day nothing could dampen my spirits.

When we boarded the bus, the first thing I noticed was the silence. You could have heard a pin. As I walked down the aisle I noticed that smile on the faces of the grown people. It was the crooked half-hopeful smile

I'd seen on my mother's face the night before. But why was everyone so quiet? Had they not heard? Harold Washington had won!

I cracked the cheese-eating grin I reserved for downtown and *New Expression*. They had heard. There were newspapers which people turned, beaming into the pages quietly. I can say there was a unity and pride. Still, the silence made me uncomfortable. Something about it seemed unnatural or wrong.

History was made and Harold Washington was sworn in, but my world would never return to a normal shape. One day, Jeffrey was there, waiting under the Adams and Wabash El tracks. I walked out the door, and he rushed toward me yelling.

I told you, Mary! Didn't I tell you?! We were our own bright sign for a minute. In the midst of a stony, fractured landscape sharing a Students for Washington hug. Maybe I gave him my phone number or he gave me his, but that was the beginning of that.

I FORGET MOST days we live on a rock. Or perhaps we live in it, which makes us take on its makeup—impenetrable and resistant to energy and light. To rock is to soothe, but it also signals upset. We all know rock music, played on amplified instruments and marked by a heavy beat, repetition of simple phrases that fuse a variety of elements. You can be rocked to your core or be the one on which everything must depend. There was Rocky jouncing on the steps, or the girls at Calumet who kept swallowing rocks, or whatever made their stomachs puff out. You could feel the Rock of Ages, be the hand that rocks the cradle, or off one's rocker.

That may have been the source of my confusion that morning on the bus. We came from the same place but were wired to react in different ways. I was ready to shout and dance, and all the adults wanted was to stare ahead in shock and be still.

Those early days with Jeffrey were all rapid-fire movement. One of the first things he did was drag me down the footpath where the *Sun-Times* used to meet the Chicago River. We stood outside the Billy Goat Tavern, where legendary newspaper columnist Mike Royko was known to hang out.

"Would you just go?!" Jeffrey insisted. But I stood away from the door, staring at the slogan painted on the ancient door. My palms were sweating. If Royko had walked out that door, I would have screamed. I don't care what you say—Mike Royko loved me. When I read his columns, I felt like he was standing on Sixty-Third and Ashland yelling, "Hey! This is the world, too!"

Being around Jeffrey was a constant litmus test. Every time, the stakes got higher. What could we do away from the fear and rules? How high could we fly? How fast, how far? Jeffrey had been after me to go explore the North Side. He wanted me to ride to the El stop at Belmont, when I had promised my mother I would never leave downtown.

"I only have an hour!" I whined, standing at the bottom of the El train steps. Jeffrey was an almond-colored, good-looking boy with slightly slanted eyes and a cleft in his chin. He stood at the bottom of the stairs, a boy trying to get a girl to go all the way.

"Just come on, Mary," he begged. "You'll be back in time!"

At Belmont, we ran down the steps and walked to Halsted. The North Side was its own world, with tattoo parlors and jewelry shops. I saw a lot of Beat It jackets and neon-streaked hair.

But I remember that walk down Belmont for different reasons. Away from downtown I could see Jeffrey change the way I did when I got on the Seventy-Ninth Street bus. His movements, particularly when we were on the Soul Train, seemed orchestrated and controlled to mimic the next brother's. On Belmont, he seemed as light as a feather. I grabbed his hand like he needed my heft to keep him down.

I was not impressed with Jeffrey's North Side. It made me feel weird and out of my element. Jeffrey bragged about the houses he had been in, like the three-flat where two floors had been removed and the windows showed a piece of the lake.

"I've been over here before, only it was farther," I said, or something like that. We were always in a kind of competition. It was important to impress him, but little about me did. He raised an eyebrow at my JCPenney clothes and pooh-poohed the curfew imposed by my mother. He rolled his eyes at my story of spending three weeks at Northwestern

77

University's National High School Institute. In fact, I made no impression on Jeffrey at all—not with my editor job at *New Expression*, or the novels I carried around.

"You act like a white girl," he complained.

I reminded him that the man he went to see on the North Side, the one he hid photos of in his room, the one he whined was scared to drive him home, was white. That made Jeffrey mad. He looked at me as if I were a stranger, like I didn't understand a damn thing, and said, "No, Mary. He's not."

Jeffrey could be cruel and impatient, and sometimes acted as if he didn't approve of me. His disdain escalated after I told him about the Stacey-Jackson-thing-that-happened-with-Planet Rock.

He seemed impressed by Stacey or Spacey, as the white kids that previous summer at Northwestern had come to call her. It was clear from the story I told that she did not act like a white girl. He wouldn't have had to beg her to ride the El to Belmont. He perked up whenever I talked about her.

"Call her and invite her to come here," he said, even offering to let her sleep at his house.

I said I would, but never did. I wanted my boyfriend all to myself and for a while I had him.

We stayed in the old Rock Records near Wells and Washington. They had the best selection of long-playing vinyl and tapes in the city, but rude salespeople with whom Jeffrey loved to get into little skirmishes. He did something there I never saw him do anywhere else: when he wanted to be a snot or make a point he would loudly snap his fingers.

My new friend taught me much about appearance and reality. We might be eating or riding the train. A man would get on. He looked like an average old man to me, but Jeffrey would whisper in my ear *he's one of us*. Sure enough, after a few moments the man's eyes would drift to Jeffrey's, and I'd be shut out completely. From Jeffrey I learned to be sneaky with my shit; appearing to be one thing, while turning into another.

I can't say why we became friends. I wore my house key on a black cotton shoelace tied around my neck. He elevated his to the level of fashion by positioning his keys through the tines of a metal Slinky and hanging it from his belt loop. He was an only child, while I was fourth of five. His mother worked an off-shift, while mine wanted to know my every move.

I had never met a kid like him. Jeffrey did whatever he wanted, which was make tapes of house music, scheme about how grand life would be once he got into the Warehouse or New York. He roamed the city, using the CTA like a personal limousine. Maybe his mother had told him what mine once told my brother: that once he'd left the house in the morning, it was always best to keep moving.

AS A LITTLE girl, I wanted to be Superbad. I liked to jump on my big sister's bed and stand on my mother's brown freezer. I wanted to be Stevie Wonder and James Brown or that girl on *Get Christie Love!* She stayed revved up and Superbad. She could kick a dude's tail, flip another one over, and still not have to fix her lipstick and round hair. I longed to aim my gun at the screen and say, *Hold it, sucker.*

I wanted to be Stacey Jackson of St. Paul, Minnesota, the first person I looked up when I moved to the Twin Cities. I didn't really expect to find her. There were a lot of Jacksons, and her name had likely changed. I was certain she had left the Midwest behind, since she remains the baddest person I've ever met.

The Stacey Jackson thing with Planet Rock happened the summer before Harold Washington was elected. The National High School Institute is a storied, star alumni-dotted program that still takes over Evanston each summer. The program attracts some of the country's brightest high school juniors, who are affectionately known as Cherubs, to broaden their horizons on the unbroken shores of Lake Michigan.

This was no summer camp or kids' play. Acceptance was competitive. The price was high, the training intense. Cherubs still descend on Northwestern each summer—theater kids, music kids, filmmaker kids. For nearly a century, professors and staff have been applying heat and pressure in hopes of creating diamonds.

That summer, we filled out the thin summer campus, each discipline floating in its own bubble and sometimes bumping softly against the next. All two- to three-hundred kids in the J-school had the same goals—to uncover the next Watergate, be awarded the Pulitzer Prize, and impress *Chicago Daily News* veteran George Harmon.

Professor Harmon looked like Superman, or rather Clark Kent, in his black-rimmed glasses, cardigan sweater, and oxford shoes. He floated in and out of the Medill classrooms, peering over our shoulders while we banged out leads on IBM Selectrics. I was there courtesy of the Chicago Press Club, having accepted a scholarship at a fancy lunch in a cushy private club downtown. My mother dressed me in one of her suits. I teetered on her high heels into the board room.

"Why do you want to be a journalist?" the group around the table asked. I mumbled something, but mostly I looked at the dark-paneled wood and paintings on the wall and wondered how this sparkling world managed to hide itself amid the grime of the Loop.

The class photo from the 1982 NHSI journalism division shows four dark spots dotting the hemisphere: The wings of my pressed hair stick out in the top row. Not far from me stands Sam, a gentle, brown boy from Georgia. I don't remember his last name. Third was Tananarive Due (Tah-nah-nah-reev-doo) of Florida, whose parents were prominent civil rights activists.

Today, Tananarive is an acclaimed novelist and screenwriter, but in 1982 she was a serious, bespectacled girl whose quiet confidence unnerved the whites. *She's not on scholarship*, they whispered to each other.

That summer, the four of us were pieces of one single, floating body. If Sam and I were the embracing arms and flopping legs, Tananarive was the probing eyes, and Stacey Jackson the mouth. She was a beautiful chocolate girl with deep dimples and a gap in her teeth. I found her lively and outspoken, but from the start Stacey Jackson rubbed people the wrong way. Sam and I were not immune from her perusal.

"Why are y'all taking care of them?" she'd say, or something to that effect. I didn't know what she meant and somehow, I did. She meant I should stop acting like Kizzy from *Roots*. She meant she was disappointed when my roommate Melissa told me she had a Black maid and I didn't demand another room.

"You do be acting like a white girl," Jeffrey said when I told him about Melissa.

Determined, I started following him to his house. I wasn't supposed to be getting off the train at Forty-Seventh Street either, but I was afraid Jeffrey was going to do or say something on the North Side that would get me in big, white trouble. I saw it all clearly; me and him in jail and my mother getting the call.

Once, I went to Jeffrey's house after leaving *New Expression* early. We were always wrapped up on his bed, and that time we fell asleep. I woke after the time my mother would have picked me up at the bus barn. I rushed into the living room to call. His mother was in her room. I remember seeing the light under the door, but even as I shouted on the phone, she did not come out.

"Where are you?" my mother demanded. I told Mama I was at the paper, but Mama had called the paper. The nun said I had left and not returned. She always called Ann "the nun." I think it made her feel like I was in Catholic school rather than taking the El everyday downtown. I lied and said I had just got back. I'm at the paper, Mama, and I'm leaving right now! Behind me, Jeffrey began balling up newspapers and magazines, slamming drawers and saying things like, *You got that picture, yet?* I was trying hard not to laugh, but it was funny.

I hung up and we busted a gut. It took a long time, that laughter. We laughed about it the rest of the year. From that point forward, all either of us had to do to make the other laugh was frantically ball up some paper, the way writers do when they don't like what they've just written. Perhaps that's why when I need to dispose of paper now, I don't like the sound of pages being balled up. I rip whole things neatly in half or close the sheet with a quick silent fold.

PAM HAD A boyfriend named Rock who belonged to the Black P. Stone Rangers. I am not making things up. I did not change dude's name to Rock, create my own gang called the Stones, thereby neatly merging theme with title and story. Besides, it strikes me that the neighborhood he lived in means he was much more likely a Gangsta Disciple.

Rock was a short, stocky boy whose permed hairstyle must have required he wear curlers at night or bump his hair with an iron. If you looked at the creases in his curls you could not be frightened by the scar on his face. *All is well*, I often saw him greeting his brethren at Calumet High School. The slogan was accompanied by a rapid-fire movement of the hands that seemed to be choreographed with a cool pimp-walk.

But he was also sweet, a gentle lamb basking in the presence of my high yellow sister. Her beauty seemed to soften him and shift the molecules in his body.

"Hey, Miss Reporter," he'd call out whenever I saw him. He'd assure me that what I was doing was OK. I hadn't asked his permission, but he seemed to need to tell me.

"That journalism stuff you doing? That's all right."

No one was going to fuck with me for doing that either. Rock never said that, but I knew. It was what he meant by *All is well*. I liked that about Rock, that though he was mired in one world, he knew there were others.

Jeffrey searched for the horizon on a regular basis but never seemed to find it. The trouble, he felt, was *old damn Chicago*.

"In New York, people don't live like this," he liked to say. People didn't just eat mashed potatoes and rice. It might be crowded, but you got to live the way you wanted. You could dance, paint, or just sit all day in the park. New York sounded grand, but that wasn't going to help us then, riding the Soul Train through the South Side of Chicago.

We called it "Soul Train" because of the way the demographic above and below it changed as it shot through the dark tunnels and creaked around the antiquated rails. You had left the Soul Train the minute it cleared Thirty-Fifth and Sox Park. Chinatown was self explanatory, and Harrison was Bears Country.

The middle was for everyone—it held the Loop, Michigan Avenue,

Grant Park, and Navy Pier, but it became the White Line when it emerged from the tunnel at Fullerton. After the second ballpark at Addison, the White Line gave way to the Weird Line as the train pressed through the multicultural stew of the North Side. These demarcations may have since melted or altered, but then they stood hard and fast.

Sox games brought the lines into sharp, temporary focus. Lured by the speed and price of public transportation, white people crammed the El, enduring an uncomfortable tension that ensued from the moment the train left the Loop until it emerged at Thirty-Fifth Street and Sox Park.

During that ride, the train was thick with silence, a combination of white fear and discomfort and Black resentment and impatience. The white people left and it morphed to the Soul Train again, filled with nothing but Black faces except for a few students who shunned the express bus from Michigan Avenue to ride the El. They got on and off at Fifty-Fifth, which, I would notice during the years I worked there, the University of Chicago gently discouraged them from doing.

"I can't stand them," Jeffrey muttered about whites walking beside us in the Loop and living in the world in general.

That summer provided my first glimpse into the reasons why. A week or so into NHSI, Melissa received a letter from her sister mentioning that she "understood her roommate had a darker than average tan." She recited these exact words to me and added that her maid (who made really good cookies) had scribbled at the bottom that Melissa should watch her things.

She was a tallish blond girl who wore a silk dress to our first gathering: an NHSI-wide pizza party. I remember telling her it would be OK to wear, and how uncomfortable she looked at the event. Maybe that was when she showed me how the tags in all her clothes had been carefully removed and replaced with ones that bore her first and last name.

Her father owned a company in Tulsa. I thought we were getting along fine, but Melissa suddenly moved down the hall. Word got around. Sam stood with his hands in his pockets and Stacey stomped her foot on the ground. That I remember clearly. That was Stacey Jackson of St. Paul, Minnesota. Sixteen years old, dark as night, mad as hell, and not gonna take it anymore.

"You're gonna let her get away with that?" she moaned.

I didn't know what to say. It wasn't like Melissa meant to offend me. She did have a Black maid. I stammered and looked at my shoes. Sam kept quiet and Tananarive worked her stare. Girlfriend didn't have to say a word, I knew what she was thinking. I knew the way Black people read each other's faces, because they are their mother's and father's—their very own.

Tananarive's response, had she chosen to voice one, would have been more measured and elegant. She studied me, thinking what a shame I couldn't find the courage to speak up. That I just wanted to fit in, to melt like the s'mores the white kids taught me to make at night on the shores of Lake Michigan. The combination of her quiet intellect and family background made me feel as if Dr. King himself were standing behind her, shaking his finger at me, too.

THE WORST THING I have ever done is also the best: I sobbed openly on a Red Line train going north to Howard. No one had died. I wasn't pining for a terrible boyfriend or reading a Dear John letter. I burst into tears after reading a poem.

It was in a book by my undergraduate poetry professor, who was enjoying the first waves of critical acclaim. I had always liked his work, but really gave him his props when he spent a half hour of an advanced workshop lambasting a conservative student for his politics.

Some of my classmates were angry. The poet had wasted a half hour of their time. They were paying to have his big light affixed to their poetry. Somehow, I felt different. I could learn iambics and pentameters on my own, but when he gave that kid his head on a platter, I felt as if he'd passed me a gift. I felt like I did when I used to read Mike Royko. They might be few and far between, but there were people who looked like him who would stick their neck out for people who looked like me.

I happily flipped to the poem, having no idea that the way he'd arranged a couple of hundred words would break my heart into a thousand pieces. Certain dynamics were in the right place. Something about my writing was unsettling to me.

My heart said one thing, but my hand wrote another. The moment I read the poem, the El was hurtling from the North and Clybourn station and pulling into Fullerton. I would have strangled those tears had I been riding the Soul Train.

It happened without warning. At the last line, the dam burst and something deep in me sat down and howled. I wrote to the poet and told him what had happened. His response was a mixture of delight and mild embarrassment. People squirmed and got scared. They hugged their cute shopping bags and moved their seat. One man shot glares at me that said get a room. I couldn't say why I was so upset, because at the time I didn't really know.

But hindsight is not just 20/20. It has Webcam and digital boom. In the back seat of your mother's car looking out the rearview mirror the bright sign looks pretty and dazzling. But when they took the sign down, disconnected the power and clipped the wires, you didn't think about it being dusty and bug-filled.

My meltdown on the Weird Line wasn't just about the poem. It was about my dissatisfaction with my writing, that I had heard through the grapevine about what had finally become of Jeffrey. It was all of it, from the beginning, the whole thing. It was being a pebble and following a rock, being a rock and becoming a stone, then rolling into a boulder that stopped to notice a landscape made by blood, sweat, and finally, tears.

I AM A serial friender. I have a history of attracting bright, startling friend-ships that mimic the stirrings of romantic love only to fizzle out suddenly to nothing. Much of this is my fault. Friendship is a heavy mirror that you can't forget you are holding.

Jeffrey and I were inseparable for five or six months and then he was busy or going out whenever I called. Soon, I was startled to hear from him at all. When we agreed to meet, he would be late or stand me up. I wanted him to know I was going to the navy.

I'd heard things. He was homeless on the North Side. Smoking crack and standing on park benches, talking out of his head. I wanted him to know that I had tried to reach him, by phone and mail. I was worried when his mother said Jeff didn't live there anymore. No, she didn't know where he was and she would appreciate it if I stopped calling.

I thought of Jeffrey years later, when Harold Washington had suffered a fatal heart attack while seated at his desk in City Hall. My mother did not cry when I called from San Diego, but I heard the sorrow in her voice.

"They always kill them," she'd said, or something to that effect. I reminded her the mayor had died of a heart attack. On the end of the line: silence. I watched coverage of Washington's funeral and wondered what the mood was like on the South Side buses and the train as people made their way to the viewing. Somehow, I knew Jeffrey was there.

It wasn't like he had anywhere else to go. I'd heard through a mutual friend—another boy who finally got Jeffrey into the Warehouse—that he was working the North Side, that things were troubled. There were things I longed to tell him. How I was applying to NYU. How I had gone away to Japan only to replace him with a closeted Black marine from Houston. He changed my name to Fish, but sometimes when he beat my face, trying to make my eyebrows look all Alexis Carrington, he'd say, "Mary, you need to be still." I longed to tell Jeff I'd had enough of the West Coast, where I'd learned white people had their own problems.

At a small mansion in La Jolla, I watched as the friend's little brother poured a bowl of cereal, then laid into his mother for failing to get milk. *Oh shit*, she'd said. The woman admitted to forgetting, shrugging her bony shoulders as her attorney husband stood nearby. The boy, all of twelve or thirteen, stood in the light of the refrigerator. Perhaps this lent drama to his response.

"Aw, Mom! Jesus fucking Christ," the boy said. My friend kept chewing her gum. The mother didn't aim her shoe at his head and the father didn't bum-rush the show. It was like the boy had said *Pass the pepper*. I smiled and tried to act normal, but I felt as if I were on fire.

It was the same way I felt the night of the journalism school party. I don't remember if Tananarive, who by that time was being called "Tangerine Dew," was there. But Sam and Stacey were there and so was I, watching kids dance to rock music on the open floor.

The music was not my thing, but Northwestern was not the South Side of Chicago. This was their world, so I did my best to sway to the beat. Stacey was having none of it. She marched up to the deejay.

"The only thing you're playing is rock!" she said. There was a moment of silence, some words exchanged. When the deejay took the rock music off, it made a loud scratching sound. The song she got for her effort was Afrika Bambaataa's pulsing rap-like hit "Planet Rock." The opening bars elicited jeers from the crowd.

My face was burning. Beautiful Sam of Georgia looked like he wanted to fall through the floor. But Stacey smiled, the dimples marking her cheek, the gap visible in her smile. Not only did she demand a change in the music, but when she got one, she got on the floor and danced.

She danced alone with defiance and passion. I stood there, feeling like I should help by joining in, but I was transfixed. I was also smiling, probably that half-crooked grin I saw on my mother's face and the passengers that morning on the bus.

The tension in the room was high. I looked at the faces of the white boys from Winnetka and Wilmette in their Izod shirts and leather shoes. They stood in an arc on the dance floor, their faces red with fury. The girls narrowed their eyes and pursed their lips. Stacey kept dancing. She danced to the entire long-playing song, smiling all the time.

As "Planet Rock" played, I watched Stacey Jackson dance and saw a bright sign on my distant horizon. That was who I would be the day I grew up. I would have the spine of Stacey Jackson and the gaze of Tananarive Due. Trials and tribulations would free the best pieces of my fierce mother and the unexplored rooms in my defeated father, a house painter fired from a job when the foreman found him painting circles on the wall.

"Why did you do that?" I remember my angry mother asking when he'd come home. When I was Superbad, I would be the person my father was that night, a woman who leaned in and sneered, *Because I felt like it.*

I was en route the last time I saw Jeffrey—traversing two worlds— boarding the Red Line on the North Side at Loyola University, then riding until it turned into the Soul Train and Seventy-Ninth Street. That day, the westbound bus stopped at Seventy-Ninth and Halsted. I was not getting off, but the woman beside me was. When I moved to let her by, I looked out the window and saw Jeffrey.

There was that minute when you don't know what to do. The driver pulled away and I stared at the cord, then watched as my hand pulled it. I could feel people looking at me. Figuring he was my brother or cousin. Putting two and two together and getting five. I got off and trudged two blocks back.

"Boo-yaaa!" He kept saying that like a mantra. I couldn't tell if he was on crack, heroin, or some gentle combination of both. His eyes were swilling around in his head. I said his name again and again, trying to get his attention, and though he addressed me with more *Boo-yaa*'s he didn't seem to know me. I said it over and over, "Jeffrey, it's Donna. Jeffrey? Donna?"

Jeffrey as I knew him was gone, circling the stratosphere. Yeah, I judged him for the hustling and drugs, but a little part of me was jealous. He might have taken an express train to get there, but at least he wasn't hiding. My boyfriend glowed in full view, working it out.

Had he known me, he might have said *All is not well.* He would have looked over my backpack and twinset, then snapped, "Mary, your ass is only getting worse!" He never had much use for me anyway—all over-impressed with the world and the ding-dongs with whom we tried to share it. Hadn't he told me that all he wanted was to get the fuck off this immovable planet? One day, when I came to my senses, I'd fight an urge to do the same.

Another bus was coming. I knew one day everything would be different. But the last time I saw Jeffrey was not that day, so I climbed aboard and paid my fare, then held my tears until long after I'd reached home.

WHITE POWER

CHRISTIAN PICCIOLINI

From as early as I can recall, I wanted to be the game-winning athlete who was carried off the field on my team's shoulders; to be the hero who tackled the gun-toting hijacker; to have a national holiday named after me for my contributions to the human race. I didn't always care how I achieved greatness, but that hunger for glory was what made me tick.

I went to great lengths to try to fulfill that dream, and some of the actions I took still fill me with dread and regret. For more than half my life I have searched my soul, wondering how I could have strayed so far off-track during my youth, committed such vile acts of hatred, and advocated for the annihilation of people based solely on the color of their skin, who they loved, or the god to whom they prayed.

In trying to reconcile my actions, I have come to believe that at the root of my motivations lies a basic human necessity. Far stronger than my overwhelming desire to achieve prominence was the essential human need to belong—a force which propelled me to actions both good and bad, harmless and treacherous, self-fulfilling and self-destructive. This profound need, coupled with my tendency toward ambition, defined my actions and led me down a troubled and dark path to prejudice, racism, and violence.

It is with this understanding that I present the following chapter from my book with renewed optimism that others may learn from my mistakes. We need to search for identity and purpose in healthy, inclusive communities and have the strength to listen to those who encourage us to be compassionate—instead of finding a place among those who prey on the insecure, exploiting their loneliness, fear, confusion, and feelings of worthlessness.

I also hope that by exposing racism, hate will have fewer places to hide.

CARMINE PATERNO HAD BEEN ONE OF MY IDOLS SINCE I WAS OLD enough to have one. His father was Nonno's best friend, so Carmine had been at least a small part of my life in Blue Island for as long as I could remember. He was brash and boisterous and stood proud at not much more than five-and-a-half feet. Stocky. Built like an American bulldog, his demeanor was no less fierce. He played the drums and drove a muscle car. He was six years older than me, and if I could have had a big brother, I would have picked Carmine.

Carmine always thought to pay attention to me when he and his father visited with my grandfather over beers in the garage that served as Nonno's workshop. He never treated me like I was beneath him simply because I was younger. He swore when I thought swearing was a sin, and smoked and drank openly in front of adults when I was still buying candy cigarettes and root beer from the corner store on High Street.

"Is that a tattoo, Carmine?" I asked when I saw the fresh ink on his arm.

The new design was a burning torch wrapped with a banner and some words I couldn't make out. "Yeah, I just got it last week," he replied after draining his Old Style can of its last drops of beer.

"What does it say?" I asked wide-eyed, trying to get a closer look.

He lifted his sleeve to show me the full design. "It says, 'The Power and the Glory.' It's the name of a song by a band from England called Cockney Rejects."

I thought the band's name was funny but I didn't dare laugh at Carmine. "That's sweet!" For the rest of the afternoon I hung out behind the garage singing to myself what I thought the chorus might be for a song with that name.

By the time I was thirteen, Carmine had firmly established himself as one of the coolest guys on the whole East Side of Blue Island.

MY PAL SCULLY lived directly across the alley from Carmine, and was mentored by him into ever-deepening levels of defiance. With his finger firmly on the pulse of underground music, Carmine would make Scully bootleg cassette copies of albums from the best punk bands the moment they hit the Chicago scene—The Effigies, Naked Raygun, Bhopal Stiffs, Big Black, Articles of Faith.

Those dubbed mixtapes got Scully and me hooked on punk rock music, and we began to collect vinyl albums of any punk bands we could get our hands on, local or otherwise, competing to buy every new release and imported record we were lucky enough to come across. Scully seemed to find out about those bands first, thanks primarily to Carmine. Anybody he thought was worth listening to won our immediate respect. Cockney Rejects. The Clash. Ramones. The Pogues. Stray Cats. Joan Jett and the Blackhearts. Angelic Upstarts. X. Sham 69. Combat 84. The 4-Skins. The Business. Cock Sparrer. Bad Religion. Social Distortion.

Scully and I drew the bands' names and their logos all over our ripped jeans, white tees, and Chuck Taylor high-tops. When my mom found my marked-up clothes she threw them out, sure they would turn me into a delinquent. So I hid them. Before I left the house, I tossed them out my bedroom window and changed in the alley before going anywhere.

Punk rock became a part of our lives in a way that outsiders, especially adults, never understood. It spoke to us and allowed us to speak when we didn't feel we had a voice. It was uncensored and raw and proved it was OK to be lonely or angry or confused about being a teenager in the world. Music was the common link allowing us all to see we were not lost and alone. In it we found each other, and through it we collectively directed our teen angst at a grown-up society we saw as intolerant of us.

The punk scene provided us with an alternative to lame, manufactured, popular culture and it promoted individual creativity and personal action, albeit through rebellion. Through punk lyrics we found release from the pressures of growing up. Watching our parents, we caught depressing glimpses of who we were sentenced to become someday. Slam dancing— moshing—to the driving rhythms was an outlet for our pent-up energy, anger, frustration, and insecurities. We were just kids looking to belong.

To something. To be accepted, despite the bitter promise of the boring world our parents had built for us.

It was exciting to be a part of something in the mid-1980s that wasn't characterized by mass conformity, Top-Siders, neon popped collars, and endless brown corduroy everything. Punk rebellion felt natural—right—important. It was alluring.

Naked Raygun concerts were our go-to reprieve from the ordinary. Hailing from Chicago, the band performed in clubs and rented halls, and Scully and I attended every concert we could. It hardly mattered where they were playing, we'd hop on a train to the North Side of the city and go to a five-dollar all-ages show at Cabaret Metro or sneak our way past the bouncers into an adults-only gig at Club Dreamerz or Cubby Bear.

The concerts were exhilarating. Colorful mohawks, combat boots, and ratty clothes riddled with safety pins were the fashion mainstay for the hundreds of embittered punks that crammed the venues they played. The energy in the band's songs was electric and the crowd swayed as if the surge of power lit a fuse and ignited our collective aggression. Our sweaty bodies, driven into each other by razor-sharp guitars and wild drumbeats, pulsed and swirled in unison, packed like sardines in front of the stage. A never-ending stream of willful youths clad in bullet belts and studded denim jackets dove from the edge of the stage into our eager arms in the pit where we awaited their tumbling, sweat-slippery frames. The electric energy in the room was profound and we felt alive with every distorted power chord.

Along with Naked Raygun, Carmine also blasted music from a group called Skrewdriver all over the neighborhood, and I fell hard for the edgy British punk band the moment I heard them—their tunes and beats, the slick way they dressed, and the raspy voice of Ian Stuart, their gruff lead singer. His songs were different than those of other punk bands, unlike anything I'd ever heard. They brought life to a different and wildly more exciting level. They had something to say, and Ian Stuart voiced it with unmatched intensity. But that was inconsequential. I became too engrossed in the energy of the music itself, and I barely registered their lyrics.

I stand and watch my country
Going down the drain
We are all at fault
We are all to blame
We're letting them take over
We just let 'em come
Once we had an empire
And now we've got a slum
Are we going to sit and let them come?
Have they got the white man on the run?

My benign appreciation of Skrewdriver's music screeched to an abrupt halt the night I met Clark Martell.

Early one evening, Scully and I stood zoning out, high on weed, staring at a squawking ebony crow perched atop one of the twisted lightposts that lined the alley behind his house. We passed a joint back and forth, giggling like little girls.

The garages on either side of the narrow dead-end alley were crammed with myriad pieces of old furniture, stacked boxes of orphaned Mason jar lids, piles of plastic nativity sets, and unraveling lawn chairs. With no space left inside for even half a Yugo to squeeze in, we weren't worried about anybody pulling up on us. As far as we were concerned, these deserted backstreets existed solely as a gathering place for us kids—and chatty, odd black birds.

"Hey, Scully," I said, face pointed to the sky as I studied the winged intruder looking down on us from atop the flickering streetlight. "Do you think that old crow knows what we're doing?"

He laughed. "I don't know, man. But that's a seriously dumb question."

As Scully craned his neck to look up at the watchful bird, the shotgun roar of a car bursting up the alley broke the calm.

"Shit!" He tossed the joint.

I retrieved it. "Chill out, man. It's only Carmine."

But as it turned out, I was wrong.

Carmine's primer-black 1969 Pontiac Firebird screeched to a skidding halt in the gravel beside us. I gawked at the stark contrast of the white death's-head skull freshly spray-painted on the corner of the matte hood. *Damn.* Could anyone be cooler than Carmine?

With the intermittent amber glow of the streetlamp lighting the car from above, the passenger door snapped open, and this older dude with a shaved head and black combat boots headed straight toward us. He wasn't unnaturally tall or imposing physically, but his closely cropped hair and shiny boots smacked of authority. Over a crisp white T-shirt, thin scarlet suspenders held up his bleach-spotted jeans.

He stepped across the beam of headlights and swiftly closed the distance between us. You'd have thought he'd turned in that alley specifically to hunt us down. I pulled back, wondering what the hell we'd done to piss this guy off.

Inches from me, he stopped and leaned in close, his beady, ashen eyes holding mine. The whites surrounding his granite pupils looked old, timeworn. Intense. Barely opening his mouth, he spoke softly, with a listen-closely-now attitude. "Don't you know that's *exactly* what the capitalists and Jews want you to do, so they can keep you docile?"

Not knowing exactly what the hell a capitalist was, or what "docile" meant, my nervous instinct was to take a swift draw from the joint and involuntarily cough smoke straight into his face.

With stunning, ninja-like speed, this guy with the penetrating gray eyes smacked the back of my head with one hand and simultaneously snatched the joint from my lips with the other, crushing it with his shiny black boot.

I was speechless. Frozen. I turned to Scully, but he'd vanished.

Blood retreated like flowing ice water through my veins and pooled in my heavy, tingling extremities. Shaking my head to regain my composure, I mustered enough confidence and tried to save face in front of Carmine. "What . . . what do you know . . . and who the hell are you, anyway? You're not my father," I sputtered. My voice sounded weak in my ears.

The stubbly, sharp-jawed man straightened up and gripped my shoulder firmly, drawing me in toward him. "What's your name, son?" His voice was steady and earnest.

I stammered nervously into lukewarm, broken pieces. "Christian . . . Chris . . . Picciolini."

"That's a fine Italian name," he said, his voice suddenly sounding kind. I braced myself for the inevitable knockout punchline. Sensing my nervousness, he leaned in and said, "Your ancestors were quite exquisite warriors. Leaders of men. You should be proud of your name." From my experience in Oak Forest, I wasn't, though. "Did you know the Roman army, the Centurion commanders specifically, are considered among the greatest white European warriors in the history of mankind?" I didn't. He took out a folded piece of paper and a pen from his jeans pocket and scribbled the word "Centurion" on it. "And Roman women are divine goddesses," he added with a sly smile. That much I knew. I cracked a slight grin as he thrust the paper into my hand. "Go to the library and look it up. Then come find me and tell me what you've learned about yourself and your glorious people."

In the background, Carmine was leaning against his rumbling Firebird, glossed boots with white straight-laces covering his crossed ankles. He looked different. Focused. Pinching his cigarette and exhaling a thick, steely plume of smoke, he could have been James Dean. "The kid's cool, Clark. They're waiting for us. We should go."

"Well, Christian Picciolini," he said, grasping my clammy hand, "I'm Clark Martell, and I'm going to save your fucking life."

With that, he nodded to Carmine, who jumped into his car and pulled it up alongside us. As quickly as he'd arrived, this guy climbed back inside the roaring beast, and he and Carmine tore off down the alley like a burning phoenix, leaving me surrounded by a cloud of exhaust and confusion.

CLARK MARTELL. I'D heard his name around the neighborhood before—most likely from Carmine—but I hadn't paid much attention. Now I made it my business to find out everything I could.

I started with the piece of paper he'd handed me. Scrawled on the back was the word "Centurion," but the front side revealed a photocopied flyer for a mail-order service called "Romantic Violence" that sold Skrewdriver tapes and other music for "white people with guts" through a post office box in Blue Island. The typed handbill described Skrewdriver's tunes as "marching music, fighting music, spirit-scaring white power rock and roll music from the finest white nationalist skinhead band in the West." That was the first time I ever heard the term "white power."

Martell's clothes marked him as a skinhead. Skrewdriver was a skinhead band and I'd seen what they looked like on the back of Carmine's albums; I'd even seen a couple of skinheads at Naked Raygun shows, so I knew enough to recognize one when I saw one. Carmine told me they were a spin-off from the London punk rock and hooligan subcultures and that some skinheads were about more than just music and causing a ruckus at soccer matches. But I didn't particularly care. I didn't feel called to action by the lyrics dominating their songs, words that spoke about politics, police oppression, war and history, and British unemployment. I didn't relate.

Skinheads dressed sharp. Tough. They looked intimidating and were rowdier than punk rockers. They wore British Dr. Martens work boots like their factory-worker fathers, slim denim jeans or tailored Sta-Prest work trousers, and thin suspenders they referred to as "braces." They shaved their heads and got tattoos and lived in England and a few other places in Europe, but there weren't many in the United States that I knew of. Certainly not in Blue Island.

I wanted to learn more. So I took the city bus to the mall bookstore and shoplifted a copy of the only book I could find on the topic, appropriately titled *Skinhead*, by a British photographer named Nick Knight. In it, I discovered skinheads, or "skins," first appeared in London sometime in the 1960s among working-class teenagers reacting against hippie culture. Upon further investigation, I learned skinheads were pissed off about the lack of jobs and opportunities to make a decent living, so they rebelled against what they believed were the causes of those problems. They didn't fall for the "flower power" notions of peace and love, and they blamed everyone from politicians to immigrants for their troubles. They shaved their heads, both to distinguish themselves from their hippie counterparts, and to keep their opponents from grabbing their hair during their frequent street fights.

While I learned that not all skinheads were violent—many factions just adopted the music and look, not the nationalist politics or aggressive attitudes towards immigrants—I learned those that *were* prone to violence typically attacked beatniks, gays, upper-class students, and local Pakistanis, who, they claimed, were taking their much-desired jobs. In the early '70s, Scotland Yard cracked down on skinheads in London, and more or less put an end to their riotous activities.

For a while.

Then, thanks to Ian Stuart, whose Skrewdriver lyrics I'd practically ignored as their music beats pulsed through my veins, the more radical offshoot of skinheads made a comeback in the mid-'80s. Stuart formed a political youth action group called White Noise. That, in turn, led to affiliations with the British National Front, a neo-fascist political organization, and the creation of a right-wing music coalition called Rock Against Communism. Skrewdriver shed their initial punk rock aesthetic and soon became the most well-known nationalist skinhead band in Europe.

The ideologies expressed in their music found an instant audience with many punks and skins who had become disenfranchised with the soaring levels of immigration and unemployment in 1980s England. Add to that feelings of alienation and a strong desire to disrupt a system that seemed the source of many of their problems, and many skinheads adopted more radical right-wing politics—and the pro-white nationalist skinhead subculture was born.

To parlay the sudden popularity of the band, Skrewdriver left their independent British record label Chiswick Records—where they were labelmates with more mainstream punk acts such as Motörhead and The Damned—and secured a recording contract with Rock-O-Rama Records, a West German record company specializing in edgier and more extreme Oi! music, a British brand of skinhead-styled punk rock. As a result of that partnership, Skrewdriver's racist skinhead message reached throughout Europe and Canada and their music then became available through Martell's mail-order service in the United States.

Carmine told me Martell had even arranged for Skrewdriver to come to the United States to perform, the plan foiled when several members of the band couldn't acquire travel visas. Martell, with Carmine's help, settled for being the sole conduit to import Skrewdriver and other Rock-O-Rama records into the United States. And so, the Romantic Violence mail-order service became the first in the United States to distribute white power music in America.

It was 1987 and while I'd seen a handful of skinheads—some even non-racist, Black and Asian ones—throwing kids around in the pit at Naked Raygun and other punk rock shows, I'd never actually met one in person. That's because this guy who'd smacked my head, having borrowed and adopted the style in 1984 from his radical British counterparts, was only one of a few dozen existing in America.

"BE GLAD CLARK took an interest in you," Carmine told me. "He knows what's going on. He's sick of watching white people lose ground to all the affirmative action job discrimination bullshit and seeing minorities mess up clean white neighborhoods like Blue Island. He does something about it, too. Doesn't sit back and let shit happen."

"How does he feel about Italians?" I asked clumsily.

"What, you don't think Italians are white?" Carmine laughed. "Who do you think taught all those fucking pasty Krauts and Limeys to be civilized? If it weren't for the Roman Empire and its 1,500-year rule, most of Europe would still be living like savages and have black skin like the invading nigger Moors of Northern Africa. Thanks to us Italians, ethnic Europeans today are still white . . . Italians, Germans, Greeks, English, the fucking Spaniards and the drunk Irish, the Nordics . . . the whole goddamn lot of us." He pulled out a Marlboro cigarette, lit it, and offered me one.

"Thanks," I took a shallow drag, more interested in what he was saying than the smoke in my hand.

"Even those pansy French bastards," he hacked. "Though, on second thought, maybe we should've let them fuckers go. Regardless, if you're a native European, you're white. White power! And don't you forget it."

"So Clark's a . . . white power . . . skinhead?" I asked, still not exactly clear on what exactly that meant.

"Yeah, but he's more than that. He's a neo-Nazi skinhead, here to save white people from everyone who's trying to destroy us, like the Jews and niggers. After he moved to Chicago from Montana, where he's originally from, Clark worked with the American Nazi Party. But he thinks they're a bunch of kooky old white guys who just sit around and complain about how bad things are, so he's using skinhead music to get the message out to younger people. We have a band."

"We?"

"Clark, Shane Krupp, and Chase Sargent . . . you know them from the neighborhood, right? And me. Final Solution. You've gotta hear us. You'll love it. Ain't nobody else doin' it and we've already played a few shows around town. People are starting to listen to what Clark says about whites needing to watch their backs and fight back."

"Like who? I mean, who's hanging out with him?" I wanted Carmine to keep talking.

"Look around, man. Pay attention. Those shaved heads you see hanging out in this alley aren't some bullshit fashion statement like punk rock has become. They're about showing the world what we're about. Our message is spreading. Word is getting around. And it's starting here, in Blue Island, right before your eyes. We're going to take our country back."

I had no reason to doubt him.

Carmine further explained that Martell believed firmly in the supremacy of the white race over other ethnicities. He was sick of "muds"—as he referred to all non-white people—moving into quiet white neighborhoods, bringing crime, and taking jobs. Martell despised drugs, because he saw them as a tool that Blacks and fat-cat Jews with political agendas used to enslave white people, and keep them dumb—docile. Like Adolf Hitler had done for Germany, Martell—and now Carmine, and a small, but expanding group of Chicago skinhead guys and girls—wanted to stop Jews, Blacks, Mexicans, and "queers"—whom Martell considered subhuman—from poisoning white culture in America. He was especially adamant about recruiting and protecting white women, so they could continue to propagate the white race.

"So . . . what . . . he's going around warning people?" I asked, trying to figure out what Martell was really all about.

"For the last two years, he's been putting together the first white power skinhead crew in the country, that's what," Carmine replied. Leaning forward and dropping his cigarette before crushing it with his boot, Carmine said in an uncharacteristically low voice, "And he's doing a shitload more than that."

I kept digging. "Really? Like what?"

He paused, considering how much I should know. "He's catching heat from the cops for some serious stuff that happened this past spring."

Again I pushed for details. But Carmine wouldn't say anything more.

I thought the skinhead look was cool, and their music pumped me up. But, aside from getting roughed up a bit when my bike got stolen, I had no real beef with Blacks, or even Mexicans—let alone Jews or gay people. I'd never even met any. I was just happy to finally be living in the same neighborhood as my friends.

I didn't see much racism in our community, although, because most families had come from the same small village in Italy, there was an overwhelming amount of Italian pride and we tended to stick together.

My High Street friends and I had chased Black kids out of the St. Donatus carnival before, but not as a racist or political act; we simply didn't want outsiders messing with our rituals. Some Mexican families had moved onto our block, and our parents and grandparents weren't too happy about it, so we did hear the random "there goes the neighborhood" remarks. But there was no significant racial tension that I was aware of.

So was I initially drawn to Martell's racist agenda? Not really.

But he was magnetic. Charming. I wanted to be like him, and like Carmine and the other people I saw them hanging around with. Why? Because Martell was the first adult—even though he was only twenty-six years old when I met him—who had ever disciplined me and provided a valid explanation for doing so. He hadn't asserted his authority without good reason. When he scolded me for smoking pot in the alley, it was because he thought it was bad for me and took the time to explain the consequences; it wasn't merely, "Put that joint out, because it's illegal, and I'm an adult, and I said so." This persuaded me that he wanted what was best for my future—so much so that he'd smacked my head. Just like my dad did.

And so, I changed my behavior: I swore off weed, even though I had barely been introduced to it. When Martell and Carmine and their friends were in the alley listening to music or monkeying with their cars, I made sure I was in visible proximity. I followed Martell around and observed his mannerisms. His racial rhetoric sank in, too. Some of my High Street friends had begun moving away to the suburbs. Was that because Blue Island was less safe now, with other races moving in? My new bike had been stolen by Black kids, after all.

I looked at my neighborhood, family, and friends with wary eyes, questioning all of the things I'd once taken for granted. I'd never liked school, which made it easy to accept that teachers lied to us about history—presented it the way that suited them. Maybe Martell knew something about Jews they weren't teaching us in school. Maybe he was right when he claimed the people who wrote the history books were all Jews—and fed us a bunch of altered historical bullshit. Blacks were certainly tied to the increase in crime. I knew that firsthand.

Aside from seeing him with Carmine, Martell kept cropping up more and more in neighborhood discussions. His intensity scared people, cops included. Conversations stopped when he walked into a room. That was something I admired. Intentionally or not, Clark Martell had made me a whole new person. I wanted to carry his weight.

By the end of the summer, when Carmine was busy working his job at a local muffler repair shop, Clark would regularly task me with going to the post office or running off copies of flyers and literature for him. He had begun publishing a newsletter called *Skrewdriver News* that he handed out in front of concert venues when trying to recruit punk rock kids. I'd over-deliver by cheating the copy counts when it came time to pay the cashier. That typically meant we got at least two times what we'd paid for.

Clark would reward me when I did particularly well. He'd give me a pair of his secondhand boots, or a faded Skrewdriver T-shirt, or more music cassettes, which he seemed to have an abundance of. I ate it all up and would squirrel these gifts away so my mom couldn't find them. Then, one day, Clark handed me a tattered red paperback titled *The Turner*

Diaries. Until then, I hadn't read even one of the books my teachers assigned in school, and I'd faked my way through every book report. But I couldn't wait to read the gift from Clark.

I HAD BEEN comfortable as a High Street Boy, but now, I had awoken to the larger world, and wanted more than to just fit into it. I wanted to matter. Ever since I was a lonely little kid, playing make-believe in my grandparents' coat closet, I'd felt called to do something truly big. Now I wanted people to look up to me, the way I looked up to Clark, and for as noble a reason: saving the white race. The more I thought about him and his mission, the more it appealed to me. This was important.

Like most people who are caught up in someone's charisma, I looked for evidence that Clark was right, not wrong. I visited bookstores and sat and read books from the shelves, and took an interest in history and current events. Sure enough, I concluded that giving college scholarships to minorities meant passing over more deserving white kids. I noticed lots of muds, Blacks and Mexicans mostly, working labor jobs and in restaurants—which seemed to prove whites were being shoved aside in favor of lesser-paid illegal immigrants. In place of trustworthy families from Italy, strangers with different ways of living had moved in. I soon began perceiving life through Clark's shrewd lens, and started to believe Blue Island, my beloved home, was in danger.

My family and friends didn't listen to my new ideas. My parents weren't concerned. They shrugged me off and changed the subject. That made it clear they needed to be protected.

A seed began to germinate inside of me. The racist skinhead movement had only just begun in the United States, born right here in my own Blue Island backyard. I could become part of the new movement, spread the word, win Clark's full acceptance and the respect that came from being on the cutting edge of something significant.

Rapidly, living for innocent fun faded, playing Wiffle ball and riding bikes with the High Street Boys didn't seem exciting anymore, and the need to live for a greater purpose came sharply into focus.

I was about to turn fourteen years old and start high school. Sitting in class all day would only slow me down.

I was already learning about things that mattered. Things most people took for granted.

And I didn't need a classroom or some double-talking teacher to try and change my mind.

DILLINGER

JESSIE ANN FOLEY

A couple years ago, after scoring a reservation at one of Chicago's hippest new restaurants, I texted my mom: "Having dinner in your old stomping grounds!"

She called me immediately. "Are you going to Gurney's?" she asked.

"No," I said. "It's called Parachute."

"Yes, I know that," she said impatiently. "I read about it in *Chicago* magazine. You're talking about Gurney's. When I was a kid I used to do Mary Gurney's grocery shopping for her. She was a one-legged bookie who lived on the second floor above the tavern, so it was hard for her to get around."

"But it's not a tavern anymore," I explained. "It's a Michelin-starred Korean American restaurant."

"Huh." She considered this. "Well, that's good. I always wondered what would become of that place after Mary's son got murdered behind the counter. Who would have ever guessed that Gurney's would end up with a Michelin star?"

Sometime around the turn of the twentieth century, my great grandparents left the western coast of Ireland to converge on the southwestern coast of Lake Michigan. They settled in neighborhoods that we now call Albany Park and Avondale but which, back then, were nameless. They married and found work: firemen, school clerks, coffin salesmen. One became the police officer who shot John Dillinger. Most had children, children who traded in the Gaelic lilt of their parents for a nasal bouquet of elongated *a*'s and dropped *g*'s and, in doing so, became not just Americans, but Chicagoans. Whether out of necessity or love, they stayed put for three more generations. Which is how I ended up, one hundred years later, being affectionately ridiculed for wanting to eat award-winning fusion shared plates at the same place where my grandpa used to drink sixty-cent pints of Old Style.

Sometimes when I consider the fact that I have never lived, for any significant period of time, anywhere but the city of Chicago, I feel proud. This city beats inside of me like blood, it is written in my DNA; how could I live anywhere but here? Other times, though, I feel ashamed. Is it really my love for this town, my fierce if unreturned sense of loyalty, that has kept me here all my life? Or is it simply a lack of pluck? What would it be like, I sometimes wonder, to live in a place where you are a stranger? While it's true I've never had to spend Thanksgiving stuck at an airport, or had to troll Craigslist for help moving my furniture, I sometimes crave the delicious anonymity of living in a place where the whisper of memory doesn't trail me everywhere; where I don't care about changing neighborhoods or bandwagon sports fans or someone using the word "soda" with a straight face; where I can even go to the grocery store without running into at least three people I know.

But then, maybe these are the kinds of thoughts that everyone has, transplant or not. We all want the thing that we can't have—like a Chicago parking spot carved out of a blizzard and marked off with lawn chairs and overturned paint buckets. The transient crave roots, and the rooted crave movement. We are all hemmed in by the limitations of our humanness, each of us with our small and precious allotment of one single life.

THE CHICAGO THAT I LOVE WITH THE PROTECTIVENESS OF A LIFE-long resident occupies two separate places in my psyche. First, there's the Chicago of my memory, filled with park district summer camps, block parties, and sidewalks glutted by oversized strollers. It's a city that conjures pleasant and parochial memories: a blizzard blowing furiously outside our bathroom window as we gather to watch Dad punching through the plaster to unfreeze the pipes with a blow-dryer, running up and down the street with celebratory sparklers in those golden Junes of the Jordan-era Bulls.

And then there is my second Chicago: the dreamy, mythologized city occupied by my parents and grandparents. This grainy city glimmers to life in their stories that are so well known to me I can trace the plot lines like grooves in a graffiti-scratched park bench. This is the Chicago where you could accidentally burn down an abandoned theater and never get caught, where you could find a bright green parrot waddling down Montrose Avenue and adopt it as your pet. It is a place where gangsters swiped their hats off when a funeral passed. In this Chicago, every night at 7:30, you might walk down to the tavern to bring your daddy home for dinner.

Once, a few years back, the Chicago of my reality collided with the mythologized Chicago of my ancestors. It began in July 1934, when two East Chicago beat cops staked out a criminal while he was out at the movies with two girls. When he emerged from the theater, immersed in the dream world of the film, they pumped him full of bullets on a crowded street. The criminal was John Dillinger, one of the most famous gangsters of the age. And one of those cops was Tim O'Neil, my great-great uncle.

Family lore paints a picture of Uncle Tim as a simple guy, a lifelong bachelor who was devoted to his mother. He never married or had children, and was especially fond of his niece, Eileen, my grandmother. Uncle Tim didn't have very many material possessions, but when he died, he left my grandmother the few items that he felt were worth something—specifically, the Colt Army Special revolver that discharged the bullets that killed the most famous criminal of the Gangster Age. He also left her yellowed newspaper clippings and his letter of congratulations, signed by J. Edgar Hoover himself, which she held on to faithfully in an old shoebox in the basement of her Troy Street two-flat until her death in 1998.

For many years after my grandma's death, the gun was passed from family basement to family basement. We felt about this object the way a rummaging child feels after discovering an old arrowhead. It had that museum allure, that whispered promise of money, but we couldn't quite figure out just how the hell to sell it. We didn't know the kind of people who buy memorabilia.

Then we heard about the movie.

To mark the seventy-fifth anniversary of Dillinger's death, Johnny Depp was starring in the summer blockbuster *Public Enemies*. My mom and her sisters could practically hear the calls of Grandma and Uncle Tim from Calvary Cemetery. The big-budget Hollywood film about his life was out, and we knew it was time to act. My mom had been a Chicago Public

Schools teacher for thirty years, meticulously poring over the incremental increases in her union handbook as each year went by. She had the sense that we were just plodding along, while all around us, it seemed, people just got rich. She felt that if we could make a pile of money on our family's particular thread of this Chicago story—a story that now seemed much more significant after Hollywood had cast its roving eye on our corner of life and anointed it interesting—that somehow, all that scraping along would have been worth it. Then, at least we could feel like we, too, had gotten away with something in this town.

A River North auction house jumped at the chance to sell the gun, insinuating exclusive access to wealthy collectors and thousands and thousands of dollars. My mom and her sisters put the gun in a small metal lockbox, locked it in the trunk, and drove it over to the auction house. They carried their treasure inside, their eyes cutting from side to side at potential thieves or police who might try to steal it from them. This was Chicago, after all, a city they knew as intimately as Dillinger once did, and they understood that when someone in this city was on the brink of a windfall, the people on the streets could smell it.

The gun was photographed and examined and given a glossy spread on the cover of the bidding catalog. The auction was scheduled for the end of July, nearly seventy-five years to the day after Dillinger's death. As the sultry days rolled along, we all privately dared to hope, our dreams running wild, jackpots whirring behind our eyes and landing in a row on lucky number sevens. In the weeks leading up to the auction, it felt like barely a day went by without some mention of Dillinger on the radio, television, or in the newspaper. The auction house had sent out a deluge of press releases, and buzz about our gun—our gun!—was percolating throughout the city.

The closer the auction got, the wider the arcs of my mother's emotion began to swing. Giddy, rapturous excitement was followed by a cynical low-balling of figures, replaced again with timid hope. We waited.

"I'm going to buy a new mattress, and a washer and dryer," my Aunt Patsy declared, never once doubting that she'd be able to buy all of that and then some. And she wasn't alone. This was no longer about a gun.

It was homage to my ancestors, who never quite seemed to be able to catch a break. The more money we got for the gun, the more all the hard lives of Grandma and Uncle Tim and all the rest of them would begin to make sense.

When the big day arrived and we filed into our seats in the back row of the auction house, our faces were grim. We knew that we were hoping for too much, that the stakes were high, that crushing disappointment was probable. Sitting there, waiting for the sale to begin, my mom and her sisters wrangled down each other's hopes.

"Eight thousand dollars is a lot of money, and that's probably the most we'll get."

"Eight thousand if we're *lucky*."

"And keep in mind, we have to split it between the three of us, and the auction house gets ten percent, and Uncle Sam gets his share. If we walk outta this thing with five hundred bucks apiece, I'll consider it a success."

Of course, we didn't believe any of that. In our heads, we were already poolside, sipping tropical drinks and comparing our tans.

All around the perimeter of the room were velvet-covered tables that displayed artifacts to be auctioned—old-fashioned art deco jewelry, obscure hand-drawn maps, rows and rows of grainy photographs, Tiffany's cuff links and large, jewel-studded earrings. These were all beautiful and interesting, but they weren't the main draw. The Dillinger memorabilia was featured prominently in the front of the room, and you had to walk past it to get to your seat. There was a letter Dillinger wrote to his niece from prison, some black-and-white portraits of his bullet-riddled body laid out on a morgue slab, Uncle Tim's handiwork. There was even a plaster death mask that was taken of Dillinger's face for purposes that were unclear—voyeuristic or medical, or perhaps both. The mask was white and clayish, the mouth gaped open, two open holes where the unseeing eyes had been.

But even these had not generated news coverage. Ours, and ours alone, was the big-ticket item. Because of Chicago's handgun ban, a photograph of the Colt revolver was projected onto the wall. Even though no one there knew who we were, I still felt like we were the most important people in the room. I'd never felt that before—I doubt any of us had—and we fanned ourselves calmly with our bid numbers, pretending that this was just another day at the auction house for regulars like us, trying to project the confident sense of ennui that we imagined rich people exuded.

We eyed and appraised the people around us, trying to gauge by their clothes and their mannerisms just how wealthy they were. I have to admit, we weren't too impressed. There were a few clumps of sharply dressed buyers, but most were dressed so casually it bordered on schlubbish—T-shirts, jeans, scuffed gym shoes. We reassured each other that the ultra-rich are the type of people who don't need to display their wealth. At all times we were aware of the presence of Loreen, the owner of the auction house. She was a blonde woman in her mid-fifties; chic, urban, cosmo-politan and self-assured, wearing a black suit and big, chunky jewelry that jingled when she walked. She had a presence, flitting around from group to group, waving her arms and telling bawdy jokes—she seemed to know everyone.

Right as people began to take their places, she sidled up to my mom and nudged her with a familiar elbow.

"Word is, we got a buyer from Northern California," she hissed.

"Is he here?" My mom looked around, extracting a balled-up tissue from her pocket.

"He's going to be calling in his bid," she advised, "so watch the phones." She pointed at the line of black-clad employees who were filing in behind a table full of telephones, hooking Bluetooths around their ears, and ner-vously clearing their throats. Then she flitted away, the sparse facts she'd pro-vided us about our buyer already working to shape a vision: a winemaker, maybe, or a retired kingpin of Silicon Valley. Our main source of knowledge about Northern California had come from watching *The Parent Trap*.

Our gun was the twelfth item to be auctioned, and as we listened to the gavel bang down on the other items, my heart began to rise into my throat; my palms were purple, clammy, shaking. Each time Loreen banged the gavel I winced, and so did my dad and sister, who were seated, fans trembling in their laps, on either side of me. Behind us, my mom and aunts were utterly still.

Item number 12, I heard Loreen say, *Colt Army revolver used to slay John Dillinger outside the Biograph Theater, Chicago, Illinois, 1934, with related papers by J. Edgar Hoover and other memorabilia.*

Behind me, I felt them stiffen. I prayed—was it wrong to pray for money? But it wasn't for the money alone that I prayed, but for my mom, my aunts, my whole family; but especially my mom, who could let disappointment crush her, and for whom the gun, this dream, meant so much. I looked around and saw that no one in the audience was poised to raise their fans, but the moment Loreen said, *Bidding opens at $5,000,* the phones against the wall began ringing off the hook: jangling, old-fashioned rings that drowned out the excited whispering that was spreading through the room. I turned behind me and looked at my mom, who was wound tight as a spring, eyes round and shining with nerves.

Five thousand do I hear $5,500? One of the Bluetoothed employees, murmuring into her phone, raised a pointer finger in the air and nodded— $5,500. *Do I hear $6,000*—down the table another finger was raised. My heart slammed. Back and forth the two bidders jousted via telephone; I imagined them bent over mahogany desks somewhere in California, phones cradled against their ears, their broad, oak-paneled windows looking out over rolling vineyards, their walls decorated with displays of rare coins. $6,000, $6,500, $7,000. Up and up the bidding went, and the fingers of the employees kept jabbing the air.

I grabbed my sister's hand when the bidding reached $15,000. $16,000. $18,000.

I thought of my grandma, knowing instinctively that she would have supported this sale. She had been a product of the Great Depression— someone whose practical beliefs and habits might be considered by some today as quaint and curious as a phonograph. I never once saw her wear jeans, and when it rained, she wore a plastic kerchief that tied in a bow beneath her chin. She drank highballs and distrusted banks. She certainly never went on nice vacations, and her only nice possession was a ratty-looking fur coat (that she'd bought, unknowingly, at a time when the most gauche item you could buy was real fur). She would have had no problem severing any sentimental attachments to Uncle Tim's gun.

At $20,000, the bidding began to lose momentum. The two employ-ees were slower to raise their fingers—first, they would engage in a hushed, prolonged conversation with the buyer while everyone looked on and we strained to listen. It appeared that the buyers had reached their limit, and each bid increase had to be cajoled, teased out of them.

I pictured Grandma, here at the auction, red hair carefully hot-rolled, wearing her best brooch, and warily clutching her plastic purse to her chest.

At exactly $30,000, when Loreen asked, *Do I have $35,000?* we trained our eyes on the woman on the phone and she looked up at Loreen with regret, and shook her head once. Loreen asked it again: *Do I hear $35,000?* The edge of hope in her voice mirrored our own—after all, there was her commission to think about. The buyer murmured some more into the phone, a last attempt, but finally set her mouth in a tight line and shook her head again.

The gavel came down.

It was a good price, and yet I didn't even have to turn around to know that Mom and aunts were disappointed. We all were. And it was hard to explain why. Maybe it was because the price of my ancestors' memory had been bought by a faceless stranger from California. And it had been he, not us, who had dictated the final value. Maybe it was because of my mom's dreams, or aunt Patsy's reckless hoping. Maybe it was because Dillinger's letter to his niece, which was not expected to sell for more than a few hundred bucks, went for over fifty grand. "I guess people care more about the living Dillinger than the dead one," my sister observed, and for the first time since this whole process began, I thought about the living Uncle Tim. I thought about how, like Dillinger, he must have told his tale of glory to his own beloved niece, perhaps sitting around a table in some North Side two-flat kitchen nook, his elbows resting on the table and my grandmother's pale little Irish feet swinging beneath her chair. I thought about how her blue eyes must have widened, thinking about the girl in the orange dress, and how proud she must have felt for being part of a family like that. And I knew that my sister was right—it's the stories of living that we cling to, not of dying, and that is the way it should be.

When we left the auction, staggering out into the bright sun, it didn't feel like we'd won anything. We went to a fancy Randolph Street restaurant to celebrate, but we picked at our food. My dad complained about how expensive the drinks were. We kept asking my mom how she could be upset about winning thirty grand, but our questions were just as directed at ourselves as they were at her. It seemed ridiculous of us, greedy.

Two weeks later, we got a call from the auction house. Our California buyer had made up some excuse that he no longer believed the gun was authentic. He reneged on his offer. I remember how, when she called her sisters to tell them, my mom sounded almost relieved. It was comforting to be back in the world she knew, where you were free to resent the unearned wealth of others because no one had ever given *you* a break—and you knew, with a strange, fierce pride, that no one ever would.

Loreen scrambled around and found a second-tier buyer who took the gun off our hands for a modest sum.

Aunt Patsy bought a new mattress.

The washer and dryer would have to wait.

MOTHMAN

EMIL FERRIS

I grew up in pre–Urban Renewal Chicago at a time when Chicago was a down-at-the-heels, blue-collar place where the silent picture stars of Essanay Studios still hobbled the streets of Uptown. I get a good portion of whatever strength or inspiration I have from the beauty and tenacity of this amazing city. I love it so much I can be brought to tears while simply riding the El, but enough about that.

The School of the Art Institute of Chicago (SAIC) is my alma mater. The Art Institute of Chicago figures prominently in my life, less as a repository for artifacts than as a restaurant for the eyes. I recall quite a few wonderfully escapist days spent playing hooky from Lane Tech High School during which I perfected my technique for dreaming myself into paintings.

If you've perused the work I have posted here, you've seen monsters. My apologies, but it wasn't possible to grow up in *Mad Men*-era Chicago and not believe in monsters. I mean for goodness sake our mayor at the time of the '68 riots ('hizzoner') Mayor Daley Sr. reassured Chicagoans, "The police are not here to create disorder but to preserve disorder." What true-blue, card-carrying monster wasn't breathing a sigh of relief right about then, I ask you?

Growing up in an ornately grimy Gotham combined seamlessly with my childhood addiction to *Creature Features*, a late-night Saturday airing of famous (and often offbeat) black-and-white B-movies of the monster genre. No doubt these two influences have had a big hairy-clawed hand in making me a lifelong fan of creaturely, revenant, and undead beings everywhere.

EVEN THOUGH DEEZE IS SOMETIMES A TOTAL BUTTHOLE, I AM PRETTY MUCH ALWAYS PROUD HE IS MY BIG BROTHER...

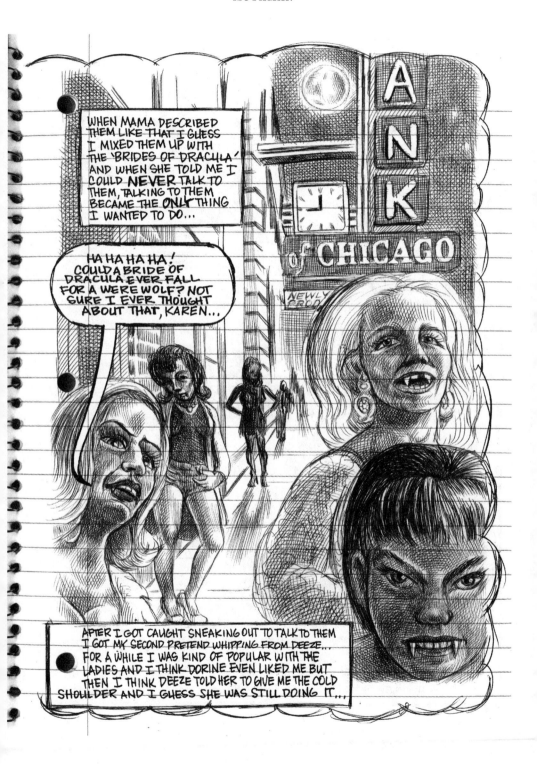

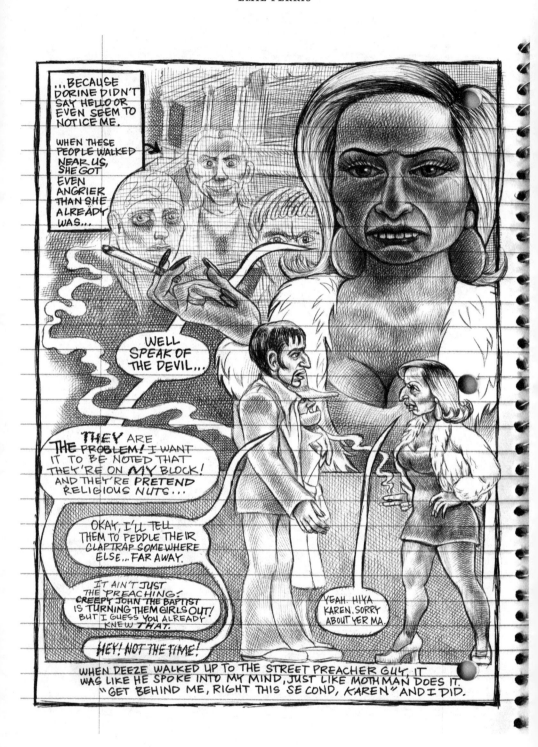

WHILE DEEZE AND DORINE BLABBED ON AND ON, I SPACED OUT AND REMEMBERED WHAT MAMA HAD ONCE CALLED LADIES LIKE DORINE...
BLAH BLAH BLAH BLAH BLAH BLAH BLAH
BLAH BLAH BLAH BLAH BLAH BLAH BLAH BLAH BLAH
THEY'RE LADIES OF THE NIGHT AND YOU ARE FORBIDDEN FROM TALKING TO THEM EVER ABOUT ANYTHING!

MAMA AND DEEZE NEVER AGREED ABOUT RELIGION. MAMA THOUGHT DEEZE "BETTER GET HIMSELF SOME FIRE INSURANCE" (I THINK SHE MEANT SOMETHING ABOUT HELL) AND DEEZE TEASED MAMA BY TELLING ME REAL LOUD THAT "ANNOYED BLONDE SURFER JESUS IS MAMA'S TEENY BOPPER FANTASY DATE."

EVEN THOUGH THE 'PREACHER GUY' **LOOKS** LIKE MAMA'S BLONDE SURFER JESUS, SOMETHING MORE THAN DEEZE'S E.S.P. MESSAGE TELLS ME THAT THE GUY ISN'T WHAT HE PRETENDS HE IS.
MAMA BELIEVED THAT EVEN THOUGH PEOPLE HIDE THINGS BEHIND THEIR FACES (SHE CALLED THEM 'THE MASK PEOPLE') IT'S POSSIBLE TO SEE WHAT'S INSIDE BY LOOKING INTO THEIR EYES.

WHEN I **FORCED** MYSELF TO LOOK INTO THE EYES OF 'THE PREACHER GUY' AND HIS GIRLFRIENDS, I GOT THE FEELING THAT I WAS A SPARROW TRYING TO STARE DOWN A PACK OF HUNGRY ALLEY CATS...

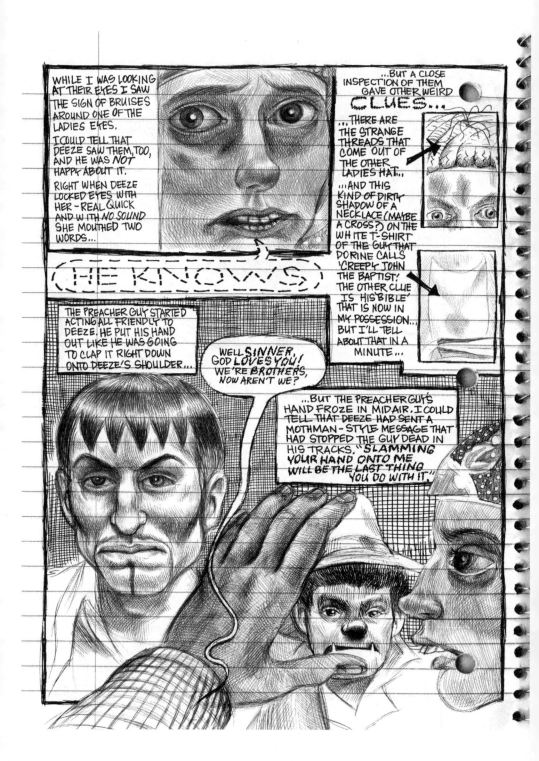

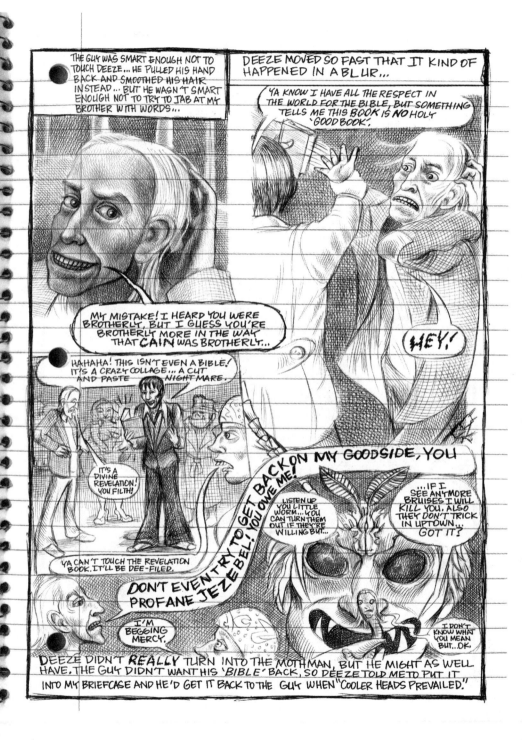

WHEN I PUT THE BOOK INTO MY BRIEFCASE THIS EXTREMELY CREEPY PAGE FELL OUT.

THE SPIEGGEDALIEGA

The many Shadow Travels in in the fragstic of man

I KNOW THAT THE PREACHER GUY IS WEIRD AND MEAN BUT I HAVE TO ADMIT THAT I KIND OF LOVE THE PAGES IN HIS BOOK THAT HE TITLED, "PICTURES OF SINNERS, DRAWN WITH PEN AND PENCIL." I HAVE SOME QUESTIONS ABOUT WHAT HIS BOOK MEANS.

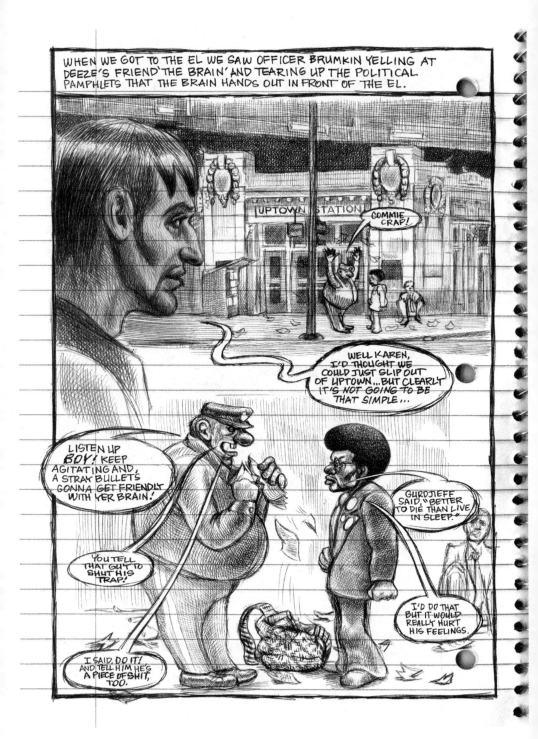

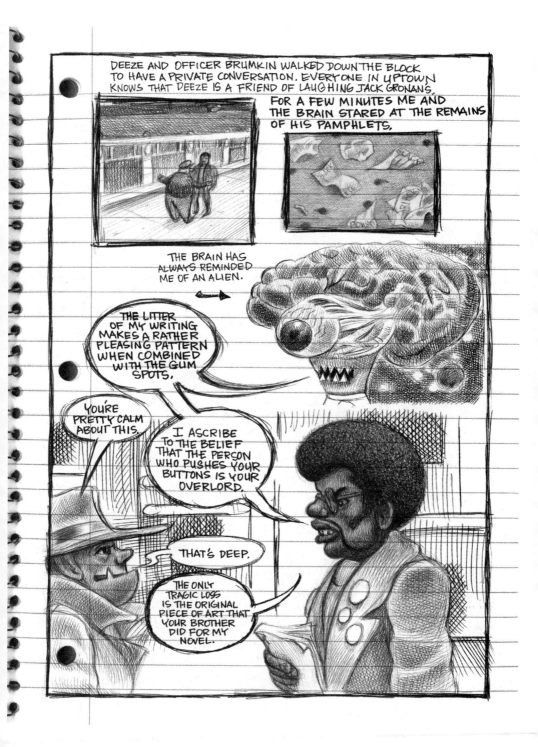

CARLO CRIVELLI 'SAINT PETER MARTYR' 1479

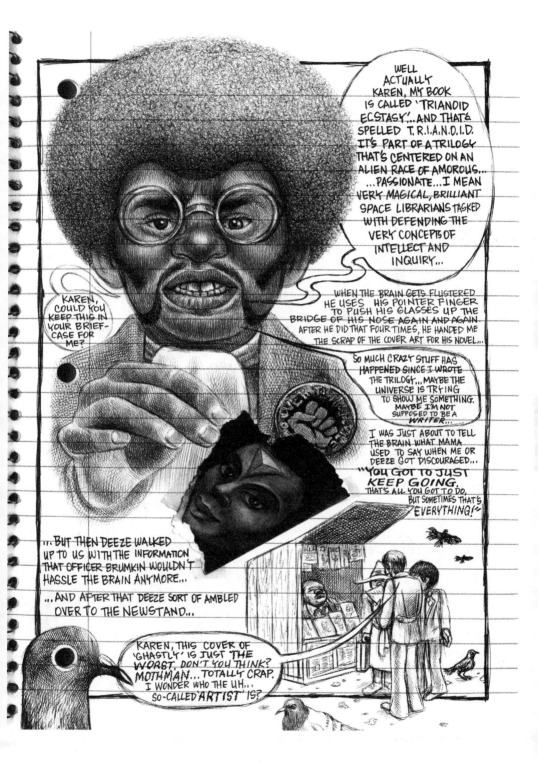

127

WHEN DEEZE WENT OFF TO SHOW SOMEONE ELSE HIS GHASTLY, THE BRAIN DUG INTO HIS BAG AND PULLED THIS OUT AND HANDED IT TO ME...

THE BRAIN SAID THAT IF I COMPARE 'LEFT IN THE LURCH' WITH THE MOTHMAN COVER OF GHASTLY MAGAZINE I WOULD SEE HOW MY BROTHER HID 'THE LURCH' IN PLAIN SIGHT... BUT THE BRAIN WOULDN'T TELL ME WHY DEEZE PLAYED THIS STRANGE TRICK ON THE WHOLE WORLD...

FROM
I AM NOT YOUR PERFECT MEXICAN DAUGHTER

ERIKA L. SÁNCHEZ

My favorite writer, Toni Morrison, said, "If there's a book that you want to read, but it hasn't been written yet, then you must write it." That is what I did with both of my books, *Lessons on Expulsion* and *I Am Not Your Perfect Mexican Daughter*. I loved reading, but I grew up with white stories. Most of the stories at my disposal were about middle-class white kids living in the suburbs. And their problems were so foreign to me. I loved Judy Blume, but I was so confused about the characters' lives. I grew up in a small, roach-infested apartment on the West Side of Chicago, and in the books I read, families had maids and summer homes. I remember one family didn't eat leftovers. I also adored *The Baby-Sitters Club*, and read every single book. There was a time I very naively wanted to start my own club, then quickly realized I lived in the hood.

Needless to say, there was rarely any book that I could relate to. I was lucky enough to find *The House on Mango Street* by Sandra Cisneros in high school, which was beautiful and comforting, but that wasn't enough. It came out the year that I was born, 1984, and there hadn't been anything like it since. I didn't know of other books by Latinx authors. I was desperate for more. I wanted to see myself in literature. Where were all the messed-up brown girls? Poor ones? The ones who sulked in their bedrooms listening to Nine Inch Nails on repeat? I decided that if they didn't exist, I was going to create them.

I DIDN'T KNOW THINGS COULD GET ANY WORSE AT HOME, BUT apparently they can. The apartment feels like the play *The House of Bernarda Alba*, but much less interesting. Just like the crazy and grieving mother, Amá keeps all the blinds and curtains drawn, which makes our cramped apartment even more stuffy and depressing.

Because of my punishment for going into Olga's room, all I can do is read, draw, and write in my journal. Amá also took away my phone. I can't even close my bedroom door because she opens it as soon as I do. When I tell her I need privacy, she laughs and tells me I've become too Americanized. "Privacy! I never had any privacy when I was a girl. You kids here think you can do whatever you want," she says.

I don't even know what she thinks I might do if I'm alone in my room. There's no way I'd try touching myself with her yelling and lurking all the time. I don't bother looking out the window because all I can see is the building next door. And now I can't go into Olga's room, not even at night when they're sleeping, because Amá installed a lock and I can't find the key. I've looked *everywhere*. As soon as I can bust out of here, I'm going to the Continental Hotel to see if I can find anything about Olga. I've tried calling Angie about a million times from a landline, and she still hasn't called me back. She has to know something.

I usually go inside my closet to cry so my parents don't hear me. Other times I just lie on my bed and stare at the ceiling, imagining the kind of life I want to have when I get older. I picture myself at the top of the Eiffel Tower, climbing pyramids in Egypt, dancing in the streets in Spain, riding in a boat in Venice, and walking on the Great Wall of China. In these dreams, I'm a famous writer who wears flamboyant scarves and travels all around the world, meeting fascinating people. No one tells me what to do. I go wherever I want and do whatever I please. Then I realize that I'm still in my tiny bedroom and can't even go outside. It's like a living death. I almost envy Olga, which I know is completely fucked up.

If I tell Amá that I'm bored, she tells me to pick up a mop and start cleaning. She doesn't believe in boredom when there's so much to do around the house, as if cleaning the apartment were as entertaining as a day at the beach. When she says stuff like this, I feel the anger bubble in my guts. Sometimes I love her and sometimes I hate her. Mostly, I feel a combination of both. I know it's wrong to hate your parents, especially when your sister is dead, but I can't help it, so I keep it to myself, and the resentment grows through me like weeds. I thought deaths were supposed to bring people together, but I guess that's just what happens on TV.

I wonder if other people feel this way. I asked Lorena once, but she said, "No, how could I possibly hate my own mother?" What was wrong with me? But that's probably because her mom lets her do whatever the hell she wants.

I DON'T LIKE most of my teachers because they're as interesting as buckets of rocks, but English with Mr. Ingman is always fun. There's something about Mr. Ingman that I liked right away. He looks like a dorky suburban dad, but his eyes are friendly and his weird, jagged laugh is kinda funny. And he treats us like we're adults, like he actually cares about what we think and feel. Most teachers talk down to us, as if we're a bunch of immature dummies who don't know anything about anything. I don't know if anyone's told Mr. Ingman about my dead sister, because he doesn't look at me as if I were some sad cripple.

As soon as we sit down today, Mr. Ingman makes us write down our favorite word and says we'll have to explain it to the rest of the class.

I've loved words since I learned how to read, but I've never thought about my favorite ones. How can you choose just one? I don't know why such a simple task makes me so nervous. It takes me a few minutes to come up with anything, then I can't stop.

Dusk
Serenity
Flesh
Oblivious
Vespers
Serendipitous
Kaleidoscope
Dazzle

Wisteria

Hieroglyphics

Sputter

By the time Mr. Ingman gets to me, I finally decide on *wisteria*.

"So what's yours, Julia?" Mr. Ingman nods toward me. He always says my name exactly how I pronounce it, the Spanish way.

"Yes, well, um . . . I had a lot of words, but in the end I picked *wisteria*."

"What do you like about that word?" Mr. Ingman sits on his desk and leans forward.

"I don't know. It's a flower, and it . . . it just sounds beautiful. Also, it rhymes with *hysteria*, which I think is kinda cool. And maybe this sounds weird, but when I say it, I like the way it feels in my mouth."

I regret that last part because all the guys start laughing. I should have known.

Mr. Ingman shakes his head. "Come on, guys. Let's show Julia some respect. I expect you all to be kind to each other in this class. If you can't do that, I'll ask you to leave. Understand?"

The class quiets down. After we get through everyone, Mr. Ingman asks us why he made us do this exercise. A few people shrug, but no one says anything.

"The words you choose can tell us a lot about yourself," he says. "In this class, I want you to learn to appreciate—wait, no—I want you to *love* language. Not only will I expect you to read difficult texts and learn how to analyze them in smart and surprising ways. I expect you to learn hundreds of new words. See, I'm teaching you standard English, which is the language of power. What does that mean?" Mr. Ingman raises his eyebrows and looks around the room. "Anyone?"

The room is silent. I want to answer, but I'm too embarrassed. I see Leslie smirk next to me. What a jerk. She always looks like she's just sniffed a dirty diaper.

"It means that you will learn to speak and write in a way that will give you authority. Does that mean that the way you speak in your neighborhood is wrong? That slang is bad? That you can't say *on fleek* or whatever you kids are saying these days? Absolutely not. That form of speaking is often fun, inventive, and creative, but would it be helpful to speak that way in a job interview? Unfortunately not. I want you to think about these things. I want you to think about words in a way you've never done before. I want you to leave this class with the tools to compete with kids in the suburbs, because you're just as capable, just as smart."

After Mr. Ingman gives us a short lesson on the importance of American literature, the bell rings. This is definitely my favorite class.

ON SATURDAY MORNING, Amá is making flour tortillas. I can smell the dough and hear the rolling pin from my bedroom when I wake up. Sometimes Amá lies in bed all day, and other times she's in a cooking-and-cleaning frenzy. It's impossible to predict. I know she's going to make me help her, so I stay in bed reading until she forces me to get up.

"Get up, huevona!" I hear her yelling from the other room. Amá calls me huevona all the time. She says I don't have the right to be tired, because I don't work cleaning houses all day like she does. I guess she has a point, but it's a weird thing to call a girl if you really think about it. Huevos means "eggs," so it means that your eggs (balls) are so big that they drag you down and make you lazy. Telling a girl her balls are too heavy is bizarre, but I never point this out because I know it will piss her off.

After I brush my teeth and wash my face, I go to the kitchen. Amá has already covered the table and counters with rolled-out tortillas. She's bent over the table, stretching a little ball of dough into a perfect circle.

"Put on an apron, and start heating these up," Amá says, pointing to the tortillas scattered throughout the kitchen.

"How do I know when they're done?"

"You just know."

"I don't know what that means."

"What kind of girl doesn't know when a tortilla is done?" She looks irritated already.

"Me. I don't. Please just tell me."

"You'll figure it out. It's common sense."

I study the tortillas as they heat on the comal and try to flip them before they burn. When I turn the first one, I see that I've left it too long. That side is almost burned. Amá tells me that the second one is too pale, that I have to leave it on longer, but when I do, it gets too crisp. When I burn the third one completely, Amá sighs and tells me to roll them out instead, while she heats them. I take her rolling pin and try my best to shape the little balls into circles. Most of them end up in weird shapes, no matter how much I try to fix them.

"That one looks like a chancla," Amá says, looking at my worst one.

"It's not perfect, but it doesn't look like a slipper. Jesus." I feel myself grow more and more frustrated. I take a deep breath. I don't want to fight with her because I heard her crying in their bedroom last night.

"They have to be perfect."

"Why? We're just going to eat them. Why does it matter if they're not in perfect shape?"

"If you're going to do something, you have to do it right, or else you shouldn't do it at all," Amá says, turning back to the stove. "Olga's were always so nice and round."

"I don't care about Olga's tortillas," I say, throwing off my apron. I've had enough. "I don't care about any of this crap. I don't see the point of going through all this trouble when we can buy them at the store."

"Get back here," Amá yells after me. "What kind of woman are you going to be if you can't even make a tortilla?"

AFTER TWO WEEKS of no TV, no phone, and no going out whatsoever, Amá says maybe she'll end my punishment today. Little does she know that I'm going to the Continental after school. I'm tired of waiting for permission to go anywhere, and something about Olga is driving me crazy. Maybe I can convince Lorena to go with me.

I put on bright red lipstick, my favorite black dress, red fishnets, and black Chuck Taylors. I flat-iron my hair until it falls straight down my back. I don't even care that I look kinda fat or have a giant pimple throbbing on my chin. I'm going to try my best to have a good day. Well, as good as it can be when your sister is dead and you feel like you might lose your mind at any moment.

When Amá sees me come out of my room, she makes the sign of the cross and doesn't say anything—that's what she does when she hates what I'm wearing or I say something weird, which is always.

I put the leather journal Olga gave me for Christmas in my backpack. It was one of the most thoughtful gifts I've ever received. I guess even when it didn't seem like it, Olga was always paying attention.

When Amá drops me off at school, she kisses me on the cheek and reminds me that we have to start looking for a dress, that I can't show up to my party looking like I worship Satan.

Lorena meets me at my locker and gives me a hug before class. Sometimes I don't know how Lorena and I are still best friends. We're so different and look like complete opposites. People even look at us funny when they see us together. She likes spandex, and bright and crazy patterns and colors. She wears leggings as pants. I prefer band T-shirts, jeans, and dark dresses. Most of the clothes in my closet are black, gray, or red. When I started listening to New Wave and indie, Lorena got into hip-hop and R & B. We always argue about music—and everything else, for that matter—but I've known her forever and we understand each other in a weird way I can't describe. She can tell what I'm thinking just by looking at me. Lorena is ghetto, loud, and acts ignorant as hell sometimes, but I love her. She'll fight anyone who even looks at me funny. (One time, Faviola, a girl we've known since grade school, made fun of my pants, and Lorena knocked her desk over and told her she looked like a scared Chihuahua.) The bell rings before I can ask Lorena to go downtown with me after school. I run to algebra before I'm late. Not only do I hate math with every fiber of my being, I suspect my teacher Mr. Simmons is a racist Republican. He has a handlebar mustache, and his desk is covered with American flags. He even has a tiny Confederate one he probably thinks we don't notice. What kind of person would have something like that? He also has a dumb Ronald Reagan quote about jelly beans taped to the wall, which is another obvious clue: *You can tell a lot about a fellow's character by the way he eats jelly beans.* What does that even mean? How exactly do people eat jelly beans differently? Is that supposed to be deep or something? No one else seems to notice or care about these kinds of things, though. I tried to explain it to Lorena, but she just shrugged and said, "White people."

While Mr. Simmons goes on and on about integers, I work on a poem in my journal. I only have a couple of pages left.

> *Red ribbons unraveling*
> *with the noise of my chaos.*
> *A light beating like a drum.*
> *I opened my wings and took*
> *a swim in a warm, euphoric dream*
> *of hands pressed to faces,*
> *opened to the mad dancing*
> *and combusted into a new constellation.*
> *The dream too warm*
> *for the flesh, too rough for the soft*
> *touch of fingertips, holding my universe*
> *in a single grasp. Everything sank, falling*
> *to the ground, became blue.*
> *The sunsets raining behind me*
> *like a monsoon.*

As I'm daydreaming about more images for my poem, Mr. Simmons calls on me, of course. He probably noticed my hatred for him pulsing around me.

"Julia, what is the answer to problem four?" He takes his glasses off and squints at me. He says my name the wrong way (*Jewlia*), even though I already told him how to pronounce it. Amá has never let me say it the English way. She says she's the one who named me and that people can't go around changing it for their own convenience. We agree on that, at least. It's not like it's hard to pronounce.

"I'm sorry. I don't know," I tell Mr. Simmons.

"Were you paying attention?"

"No, I wasn't. Sorry."

"And why not?"

My face feels hot. Everyone is watching me, waiting for my humilia-tion like vultures. Why can't he just back off? "Look, I said I was sorry. I don't know what else to tell you."

Mr. Simmons is really pissed now. "I want you to come to the board and solve the problem," he says, pointing at me. I guess he was never taught that it's impolite to point at people.

I want to get all Bartleby about it, tell him I don't fucking feel like it, but I know I shouldn't. I've gotten in enough trouble lately. But why does he have to pick on me? Doesn't he know my sister is dead? My heart is racing, and I can feel a thick pulse in my left cheek. I wonder if my face is twitching.

"No."

"What did you say to me?"

"I said no."

Now Mr. Simmons is pink as ham. His hands are on his hips, and he looks as though he wants to bash my skull. Before he says anything else, I shove my stuff into my backpack and run out the door. I can't deal with this today.

"Get back here right now, young lady," he yells after me, but I keep going. I can hear everyone screaming, laughing, and clapping as I walk out the door.

"Damn, son!" I hear Marcos yell.

"Oh hell no, she told *you!*" I think that's Jorge, which makes me almost forgive him for having a rattail.

The sky is clear—a blue so bright and beautiful that it hurts to look at it. Maybe I should've waited until the end of the day to see if I could con-vince Lorena to go with me, but there's no way I'm going back inside now. The birds are carrying on, and the streets smell like frying chorizo. Cars are honking. Men and women are selling fruit and corn from carts. Mexi-can music is blaring from every direction. Most of the time I hate walking through my neighborhood because of the gangbangers and guys whistling from their cars, but today nobody even looks at me.

I know I shouldn't have left school, but Amá is always talking about how it's a sin to waste this and that and it feels like a sin to waste a day like this. Besides, now I don't have to wait all day to go to the Continental.

As I walk to the bus, I watch a helicopter fly toward downtown until it disappears into a tiny black speck. I can see the hazy skyline in the distance. As long as I can find the Sears Tower, I know I can't get lost.

A green balloon floats past a power line, then gets tangled in a tree. I remember a movie I watched in first grade about a red balloon that chased a French boy throughout the streets of Paris. I imagine this balloon coming loose and chasing a little Mexican girl throughout the streets of Chicago.

I walk into the most unappetizing diner in the whole entire city. The counters are avocado green, and most of the stools are torn. Even the windows look greasy. It makes me feel like I went into a time machine. It reminds me of the painting *Nighthawks*, but even more depressing. I'm not sure where I am exactly—I think I'm near the South Loop.

I sit down at the counter, and the waitress asks me what I'll have in a thick European accent. Maybe she's Polish or from one of those other countries in Eastern Europe. I can't tell exactly. She looks tired but pretty in a way that doesn't call too much attention to itself, in a way that doesn't say, "Hey, hey, look at me!"

I only have $8.58 in my pocket, and I still have to get back on the bus or train, so I have to choose carefully. What I really want is this meal called "The Hobo," which is made of eggs, hash browns, cheese, and bacon— practically everything I love—but it's $7.99. I won't have enough left to get back home. I order a cheese Danish and a cup of coffee, even though the smell of bacon makes my mouth drip.

I read the newspaper on the counter while I drink my coffee, which is so awful I can barely stomach it. It tastes as if they boiled old socks and dumped the liquid into a coffeepot, but I gulp it down anyway because I'm not about to waste my two dollars. And the Danish is stale, of course. I should have seen that coming. I scoop out the cheese and eat it with my finger.

"Shouldn't you be in school?" the waitress asks as she refills my mug.

"Yeah, I should be, but one of my teachers was being a total jerk."

"Hmmm." She raises an eyebrow; she seems suspicious.

"He was, I swear."

"What did he do?"

"He called on me to solve a problem on the board. I didn't know the answer, but he kept insisting. It was so embarrassing." I realize how stupid this sounds when I say it out loud.

"That doesn't sound too bad," she says.

"Yeah, I guess it doesn't, huh?" We both laugh.

"Well, I think you should probably go back before you get in trouble." She smiles.

"My sister is dead," I blurt out.

"What?" she asks, as if she's misheard.

"She died last month. I can't concentrate. I guess that's the real reason I left."

"Oh, no," she says, her pretty face now sad and severe. Why did I tell her this? It's not her problem. "You poor girl. I'm so sorry."

"Thank you," I say, still not knowing why I just told her about Olga. She squeezes my hand, then walks to a table behind me.

I write in my journal for a little while and try to figure out what to do next. Might as well make a day of it since I'm already going downtown. Whatever I do has to be free or close to it, or else I'll have to walk home. After some brainstorming and doodling, I decide on the Art Institute, which is one of my favorite places in the whole world. Well, in Chicago. I haven't seen much of the world yet. They have a suggested donation, but I never pay it. Key word: *suggested*.

When I ask the waitress for my bill, she tells me someone's already paid for me.

"What? Who? Wait, I don't understand."

"The man who was sitting over there." She points to an empty stool at the end of the counter. "He heard you were having a bad day."

I can't believe it. Why would someone do something like that without asking for anything in return? He didn't even hit on me or stare at my boobs or wait around for me to thank him. I run out to the street to find him, but it's too late. He's gone.

I take out my notebook and stare at the address for the Continental. I'm not very good with directions, but I think I can probably figure it out without a map. I walk northwest. It's not that hard when you know where the lake is. The buildings are blocking the sun, so it's starting to feel cold. I wish I would have brought a jacket.

A homeless man with no legs screams in front of a Starbucks. I think he's drunk because I can't understand what he's saying. Something about a llama? A mother and daughter brush past me with two giant American Girl bags. I've heard those dolls cost hundreds and hundreds of dollars. I can't wait until I have enough money to buy whatever the hell I want without worrying about every single penny. I, however, would never spend it on something as stupid as a doll.

The Continental is small but lavish, lots of blue and off-white. It's called a "boutique hotel," whatever the hell that means. The woman at the front desk hangs up the phone when I approach her. "Can I help you, miss?" Her hair is drawn into a slick, tight ponytail that looks like it hurts, and her perfume smells like a dusty flower in summer twilight.

"Did you ever see this girl come in here? She was my sister." I give her a picture of Olga at tía Cuca's barbecue a month before she died. She's holding a plate of food and smiling with her eyes closed. I figured it was best to use the most recent one I could find.

"I'm sorry, but we're not allowed to give any information about our guests." She smiles apologetically. I see a tiny smear of pink lipstick on her teeth.

"But she's dead."

She winces and shakes her head. "I'm so sorry."

"Can you at least tell me if you've seen her?"

"Again, I'm so, so sorry for your loss, but I can't. It's against our policy, sweetheart."

"Why would a policy matter if she's dead? Can you just look up her name? Olga Reyes. Please."

"The only people we're allowed to give information to is the police."

"Fuck," I mutter under my breath. I know it's not her fault, but I'm so frustrated. "OK, well, can you at least tell me if this hotel is connected to the Skyline? Are they owned by the same company?"

"Yes, they're a part of the same conglomerate. Why do you ask?"

"Thanks." I walk out the door, without bothering to explain.

BEFORE ENTERING THE museum, I take a walk around the gardens outside. Everyone is desperately trying to hang on to the sunshine, enjoying the unexpected warmth before winter takes a cold gray crap on the city and makes us all miserable again.

Though the trees are changing colors, flowers are still in bloom, and there are bees everywhere. Everything is so perfect I wish I could keep it in a jar. A young woman in a flowered dress is breastfeeding her baby. A man with long gray hair is lying on a bench, with his head on his wife's lap. A couple is making out against a tree. For a split second, my mind tricks me into believing the girl is Olga, because they have the same long ponytail, skinny body, and flat butt, but when she turns around, she looks nothing like my sister.

When I tell the woman at the counter that I will pay zero dollars instead of the suggested donation, she eyeballs me as if I were some sort of criminal.

"Don't we all have a right to art? Are you trying to keep me from an education? That seems very bourgeoisie, if you ask me." I learned that word in history class last year and try to use it whenever it's appropriate, because Mr. Ingman always tells us that language is power.

The woman just sighs, rolls her eyes, and hands me the ticket. She probably hates her job. I know I would.

I walk over to my favorite painting, *Judith Slaying Holofernes*. We learned about the artist, Artemisia Gentileschi, in art class last year. My teacher Ms. Schwartz told us something bad happened to her, but wouldn't tell us what, so I looked it up after class. It turns out that her painting teacher raped her when she was seventeen. What a scumbag.

Almost all the Renaissance and Baroque paintings we studied in class were of baby Jesus, which is not very interesting, so when I saw Artemisia Gentileschi's paintings of biblical women killing all those horrible men, my heart trembled. She was such a badass. Every time I see *Judith Slaying Holofernes*, I notice something new. That's what's so great about art and poetry—right when you think you "get it," you see something else. You can find a million hidden meanings. What I love most about the painting is that Judith and her maid are slicing off the man's head, but they don't even look scared. They're totally casual, as if they're just washing dishes or something. I wonder if that's how it really happened.

When Ms. Schwartz said that one of her paintings was at our museum, I decided I needed to see it right away. This is my fourth time this year. I love art almost as much as I love books. It's hard to explain the way I feel when I see a beautiful painting. It's a combination of scared, happy, excited, and sad all at once, like a soft light that glows in my chest and stomach for a few seconds. Sometimes it takes my breath away, which I didn't know was a real thing until I stood in front of this painting. I used to think it was just some saying in pop songs about stupid people in love. I had a similar feeling when I read an Emily Dickinson poem. I was too excited and threw my book across the room. It was so good that it made me angry. People would think I'm nuts if I try to explain it to them, so I don't.

I crouch down to get a better look at the bottom part, which I never paid much attention to before. The blood is dripping on the white sheet, and the fibers of the silk are so delicately painted that it's hard to believe they aren't real.

I can't get enough of this place. I can be here forever and ever, studying all the art and walking up and down the dramatic marble staircases. I love the Thorne Miniature Rooms, too. I can spend hours imagining a tiny version of myself living in those fancy little houses. I always have to come to the museum alone, though, because no one will ever join me. I tried dragging Lorena once, but she just laughed and called me a nerd. I suppose I can't argue with that. I asked Olga one time, but she was going shopping with Angie that day.

As I wander around, I find a painting I've never noticed before—*Anna Maria Dashwood, later Marchioness of Ely* by Sir Thomas Lawrence. I gasp when I see the woman's face, because my sister's eyes are staring back at me. I never paid attention to that expression before—neither joyous nor somber, but as if she were trying to tell me something.

I walk around and around, and lose track of time. I look at my favorite paintings again—*The Old Guitarist* by Pablo Picasso, the *Cybernetic Lobster Telephone* by Salvador Dalí, and the one made of dots by Georges Seurat. Every time I see it, I promise myself I'll go to Paris some day. I'll roam through the city by myself, eating cheese until I burst.

IT'S RUSH HOUR when I finally get on the train to go back home. The bus is too unreliable at this time. All the men and women in suits are all sweaty and tired. If I end up being an office lady who wears slacks and changes into white sneakers to walk home from the train, I'll just jump off a skyscraper.

The train is crammed with people, but I find a window seat facing backward, next to a man in a filthy coat, who smiles and says, "Good evening," when I sit down. He smells like pee, but at least he has good manners. I take out my journal to make some notes. I love to watch the city from above—the graffiti on factories, the honking cars, the old buildings with shattered windows, everyone in a hurry. It's exciting to see all the movement and energy. Even though I want to move far away from here, moments like these make me love Chicago.

A couple of Black kids near the doors start beatboxing, which makes a man frown and shake his head. I think it sounds amazing, though. I wonder how they can make that kind of music with their mouths. How can they sound exactly like machines?

I go back to the poem I started in Mr. Simmons's class, when a woman with a burned face makes her way through the crowded aisle, asking everyone to spare some change. When she gets closer, I see that her green T-shirt says *God Has Been So Good to Me!* The letters are so bright and shiny, they feel like they're yelling. She puts her hand in front of me, and I reach into my backpack to pull out the rest of the money I have left. The mystery guy at the diner paid for my food today, so why not?

"Have a blessed day," she says, and smiles. "Jesus loves you."

He doesn't, but I smile back anyway.

I look out the window and watch the skyline lit up by the evening sun. The buildings reflect a dazzling orange-red, and if you glance, it almost looks like the buildings are on fire.

I bet the school has already called my parents and I'm in some deep shit again. It was worth it, though. I open my journal to a blank page and write, *God Has Been So Good to Me!* before I forget.

DETENTION

JAMES McMANUS

I was born in the Bronx, but I spent the years from fourth grade through high school in Chicago and its suburbs. Most particularly in St. Joan of Arc Parish in Lisle, where I was a twelve-year-old seventh-grader in the fall of 1963. Nearly all the events in "Detention" actually occurred, though not in the order in which they appear in the story.

FOR SEVENTH WE'VE GOT OUR FIRST NOT-A-NUN TEACHER, MISS Moore. She's smart so she's hard, though she almost never gives weekend homework. And unlike most nuns, she's strict but not mean. She's not allowed to cane you either. Only Sr. Regina, the principal, can. Miss Moore can still write detentions and rap your knuckles with a three-sided ruler, which John Krawczyk said smarts a hundred and fifty times worse. He said it could rupture a blood vessel or fracture a knuckle, so you'd be in a cast for two months; canings through pants-shirttail-underpants only throb for like forty-five minutes. But Krawczyk—make that Kraw*dick*—is full of it. The pain obviously depends on the caner, the cane, how hard they swing it, how many swings, where they land, corduroys or khakis, etc. Only priests can do it with shirt up and underpants down. Only nuns can cane girls, and never with panties down. "Uh, that'd be my job," John Vogel said when we first heard that rule. "Panties-pull-downer, eighteen hours a day, double shifts." Miss Moore says she won't enjoy hitting anyone's anything, but we won't enjoy it either, so we shouldn't make her do it.

On the first day of school she passed around a sheet of class rules and read them in a soft, soothing voice. Behave as if St. Joan or God the Father is watching, no talking unless called upon, no passing notes, proper uniform attire at all times, three tardies equal one absence, always sit at your assigned desk. Mine's in the first row, far left. Reid Schaefer, our quarterback, sits next to me. Vogel's behind me, and Krawdick sits behind Reid. Vogel, with his shoulders and enormous round head, is our center. I'm a wide end. Krawdick loves football but his parents forbid him to play it because he's only got one kidney.

The girls are on the other side. Only ten boys v. thirteen of them, so they also take up most of the middle.

Miss Moore wears sweaters or blouses and fairly short skirts. You can only get a decent look at her legs when she's up at the board. Her outfits show as much as the girls' uniforms do, though she still writes detentions for too-short skirts or blouses not buttoned up all the way. (Except for the top one. In Religion, Sr. Francona said girls' throats aren't wanton or concupiscent "in and of themselves," unlike breasts, which are a sin of delectation to look at unless it's by accident and only for a couple three seconds.)

Boys mostly get them—detentions—for swearing or horseplay. The closest I've come was when Miss Moore caught me jumping to touch the "207" above our door. "Second time I've told you, Mr. Killeen. Next time I bring out my pad." I almost told her receivers are *supposed* to practice jumping, but my dad would nail me if I got even one, let alone a second for backtalk. My mom would say I'd disgraced our whole family before Jesus and Mary and Joseph.

About once every other week Miss Moore makes Angie Barotka or Misty Bender or someone else kneel with her arms out. Her hem doesn't touch, or she talks back: detention. The pleated plaid skirts are usually long enough, unless the girl's having a growth spurt, but fast girls like to roll them when they think no teacher will notice. You also get the feeling Miss Moore isn't dying to write them for venial infractions, but Regina forces her to—like she'd fire Miss Moore if she didn't write a certain minimum, like a cop's monthly quota of tickets.

Just this morning, she stopped in the middle of a polynomial and stalked back past the globe. "On those knees, Miss Barotka." Angie must've been shooting a beaver—but just to Miss Moore, not a boy. "Oh, maaaan," Angie said, taking her sweet sulky time, while the goody-goods whispered, "What, not *again!*" I swung around, craning my neck. The shoulders of Angie's blazer bunched against her spoiled-brat face. Fat Frankie Boyle sits next to her, so he had the best seat in the house—or would've if he dared to turn sideways. Miss Moore's hip was an inch from his ear, in her stretchy gray wool Friday skirt. She crossed her arms, shifted her weight. If a buttock or cantaloupe could poke out an eye . . .

"This is how you steward your talents, young lady?" Exactly how Regina would put it.

"I steward?" said Angie.

"How you choose to maintain or present yourself? Keep those arms out and straight."

As the blazer bunched higher, Angie's forehead got redder. I pictured her blurting, "Jeez, look at *your* skirt!" What she said was, "So like, I'm a stewardess?"

As we silently howled, Vogel whispered, "Cane 'er already!"

"Only if you're lucky someday," said Miss Moore. Out came the pink pad. "For now, just a slatternly hussy." Again, what Regina would say. "You'd need to develop some poise."

When Angie mouthed, "Hey, *you're* the hussy," we hooted with respect, disbelief. "Thank you, ma'am," muttered Reid. "May I please have another?"

"Panties down," I said, under my breath. "Right on her talents."

Miss Moore could probably hear us, though not exact words. Otherwise it'd be one of us getting detained, even rulered. "Unroll it this instant," she said.

As Angie adjusted the waist, I stood up to see better. She made sure the plaid hem rode higher, of course. A lot higher.

"Remain kneeling while I write this all up," said Miss Moore. "No one needs to be talking or ogling now. Keep working on problems nine through twelve . . ."

IT'S HER FIRST semester of teaching, not just at St. Joan, and sometimes
you can tell she's still nervous. She only got her degree from St. Mary's
in June. She's better at History and Math than Religion, which is why for
Religion we've got Francona again. Sr. Mary Francupiscence, O.S.B.

English is between Math and lunch. While Miss Moore's diagramming *The young women devoutly pray for peace with the Soviet Union*, she puts
devoutly on the predicate line, God knows why. She sees me raise my hand
out of the corner of her eye, but she doesn't call on or even look at me. She
clears her throat and says, "Wait." Not to me, to herself. The mistake's only
there for eight seconds before she erases it, draws the diagonal underneath,
starts writing *devoutly*. But she made the line too short and her cursive too
round, so the last few letters are scrunched like a haywire Slinky.

Vogel whispers, "Devilishly prayed?"

Krawdick says, "Deviantly."

When she turns around, her cheeks and throat are pink, but it just
makes her look even prettier. "Sorry 'bout that. Any questions?"

Not even Ruth Ann asks her one. While we copy down the sentence,
Miss Moore slide-steps to the left, flexing and relaxing her calves, then
starts diagramming the next one.

Reid slides me a corner of loose-leaf. *The stewardess gave a piece
to the Soviet deviant.* I knew it'd be something like that, so I made sure
not to laugh. It seems kind of embarrassing, I guess, but for us, not for
her. The next time she turns around I look at her face, in her eyes. Don't
stoop, buddy, my dad always says, meaning, don't stoop to their level—
even though when he and my mom got back from parent-teacher confer-
ences last month, he said, "Miss Moore isn't long for our school." When
my mom said they'd just agreed she seemed devoted as any nun, he said,
"She does, but she's gonna land a husband real soon." "Kev!" my mom said.
Ellen, who's a Sacred Heart freshman, gave her usual smirk. "Yeah, we
heard about her. Hubba-hubba." "I'm not saying," he said. "I'm just saying."

What I'm just saying is, despite my resolution thirty seconds ago to
look at my teacher more virtuously, as soon as she swivels to point out
a predicate nominative, I can't help noticing the lacy pattern of her bra
showing through the side of her blouse, though she probably passes the

pencil test. She's explaining how verbs change to agree with plural subjects when she suddenly catches her breath, makes this weird squeak, and backs up.

"Mr. Killeen, please come up here."

What'd *I* do? Did I say "bra" out loud or just think it? Because it's like she was reading my mind, like that kid on *The Twilight Zone* who zapped you for thinking bad thoughts about him. *Stop scrutinizing my lingerie!*

"Chop chop," she says, as I scrape back my chair. "Hustle up."

"Get your ass over there, Duh," whispers Reid. "Hold out them knuckles."

When I get up to her desk, even though she's wearing her black low high-heels, I'm probably tall enough to be with her if she wasn't my teacher, or even if she is. She can probably read these thoughts too, maybe easier because I'm so close. The thing is, I can't stop them!

The ruler sticks up from her mugful of pens. I wince when she reaches for it, but it's only to pluck out two Kleenex. "Please kill that spider." She points. "Right—*there.*" Laurie shrieks like it's a tarantula or something, but it's just a daddy longlegs. Not spinning a web or anything, just crouching in the chalk tray, camouflaging itself in the shadow of an eraser. "Use these."

Our fingers touch, and I catch a whiff of soap or shampoo before she backs farther away. When I kill spiders and centipedes for my mom or my sisters, I use two or three, but of course I don't ask for an extra. I zero in, push down, and pinch.

"Got him?"

I nod. People holler and clap, the goody-goods all going, "*Shhhhhh-hhh!*" Miss Moore says, "Quiet! Be quiet. But thank you, da Vinci." She smiles.

"You're welcome." I almost say, "Now you don't have to worry anymore, Miss Moore," but that'd be pitiful overkill.

"Uh, Miss Moooore," Krawdick says, "it's *Duh* Vinci. *Duh,*" which cracks people up even harder. If it weren't for the spider situation, he'd've never had the nerve to say it out loud, plus without even raising his hand.

Instead of reprimanding him, though, she asks, "Isn't that what I said?"

"Just wanna make sure you spell it right. Not d-a, d-u-h."

149

She nods and says, "Ahhh," pretending to write *Duh* on her palm. I shake my head. *Thanks!* I crushed the spider's body, but two of its legs are sticking out, feeling around like they're trying to inject me with poison. As I go to drop it in her garbage pail, she says, "Uh, no. No-no-no-no. Take it to the boys' room, please, flush it down, then march straight back in here. No need for a hall pass. Just go."

I don't run but I walk pretty fast, so it takes like exactly a minute. I'm almost back when the bell rings, echoing three times as shrill down the long, empty hall. Every locker is closed, with daylight gleaming off the beige-and-blue tiles, all the scuffs. I've still got two fifths of a boner from touching her finger when the door blasts open and people start rushing out past me.

Not Angie and Misty, however. They squeeze slowly past either side of me, doo-wopping like the Shirelles, "D3 an' Duh Vinci, sittin' in a tree," each letting one cup—Misty's left, Angie's right—brush my biceps. I flex, but too late. "K-I-S-S-I-N-G . . ." Misty smooches the air near my eyebrow, lets me inhale her perfume. They do this about once a month, which I hate but look forward to. I've got less of a chance with either of them than I do with Miss Moore or Miss Universe. A minute from now they'll be sharing short Cokes with their eighth-grade hood boyfriends, who shave and sneak flasks into school. But I do wish I'd worn looser whities.

"First comes love, then comes marriage, then comes Duh Vinci with a ba—"

"Then comes Duh *Vinci*, you mean." I didn't know Reid was behind me.

"You wish," Angie gloats without turning around. "Ya both do," taunts Misty.

"Duh does, at least," says Reid. "He's also got the hots for D3."

"No shit, Sherlock."

"That hussy!"

"The Singing Nun's just scared of spiders," I call after them, making my voice crack, so I feel even more like a pity.

MISS MOORE DOESN'T sing or play guitar, at least not at school, but her first name's Dominique so some of us call her the Singing Nun. The real Singing Nun's a Dominican sister from Belgium. Her song "Dominique" is Number 1 on the WLS Silver Dollar Survey, even though it's in French. It's not about a girl either. Vogel said that in Belgium and France and their colonies they use the same names for boys as for girls, and vice versa. The song's about St. Dominic, the abbot who founded her order. Her Dominican name is Luc-Gabrielle, but her nickname's *Soeur Sourire*, which is French for Sr. Smile. I've only seen her once on TV, and I guess she smiled more than the average person or nun. She definitely had a big nose. Her wimple covered her hair and the tops of her glasses covered her eyebrows. She didn't look at all like Miss Moore.

The way her eyebrows and lashes swerve outward, Miss Moore looks like Juliet Prowse, Frank Sinatra's fiancée. Both have reddish-brown hair and green eyes, though Miss Moore's more curvaceous. But even when we talk about her figure at practice or lunch, I try to remember that ogling her curves is a sin of concupiscence. She's a devoted teacher and a good Catholic woman. If she was *that* kind of woman, Regina wouldn't've hired her.

At our lunch table, Krawdick says he doesn't see Juliet Prowse but agrees that D3 is curvaceous. "You fuckin' A she is."

"From the Latin for stacked," Vogel says. "*Curvus, curvare, curvaceus.*" He's the one who started calling her D3, for Dominique Double-Deckers. "If laying your teacher's a sin," he says, "then send me to Hell in a hand basket," loud enough for the monitors to hear him. On Fridays it's Feeney, Bonita, Miss Moore.

"Fine li'l teach-ah, waitin' fo' may," Vogel sings, "she just the girl from a-cross the way . . ." Reid sings along while pretending to play the organ. His mom packed him egg-salad sandwiches, and you can see chunks of yolk while he sings. I sing too. But we can't even get through the opening verse because nobody's sure what the words are.

"Louie Louie" is Number 13. The only reason stations can play it is Jack Ely recorded the vocals so Pope Paul and the FBI couldn't understand them, but he *still* got kicked out of the Kingsmen and the Pope still bans Catholics from listening. The governor of Indiana banned it too, so no Chicago station whose signal reaches over the border can play it. Yet even though Lisle is farther from downtown than Whiting or Gary, some spooky electromagnetic weirdness lets us hear it every time Bob Hale or Dick Biondi announces he'll be spinning it.

Krawdick always says he can top that. His brother Stan drove into Old Town to buy the 45, so John can listen to it on his hi-fi *any time he wants,* as long as Stan ain't around. That's how he was supposed to be able to decipher each word. "This'll settle all arguments," he tells us, handing Reid a sheet of legal paper. For weeks he's been promising to write down the lyrics and show us, and I guess now's the time. "Ladies and quarterbacks first."

Vogel and Rendeck and I swing around to read it over his shoulder.

Louie Louie

Louie Lou-eye, oh no, sayin' me gotta go,
yeah-yeah-yeah-yeah-yeah-yeah,
I said Lou-ay Lou-eye, oh ba-bee,
I said we gotta go.

A fine little girl, she's waitin' for me.
She's just a girl from across the way.
She say I take her out, all alone.
She's never the gal I-uh lay at home.

Lou-ay Lou-eye, oh no, I said me gotta go,
aye-yi-yi-yi-yi-yi, baby

CHORUS:
I said, Louie Lou-eye, oh, no
I said we gotta go.

GUITAR SOLO
Me see . . . Me see: got makeup, remove her clothes.
It won't be long till she slip it off.
I take her in my arms again.
I tell 'er I just gotta lay 'er again.

CHORUS
I said we gotta go now.
I said what's goin' on round here?
Let's go!

But before we can even finish reading, Krawdick starts explaining what everything means. "The singer's married . . . his mistress's name's Mary Lou, nickname's Louie. 'Take her by' means take her by the place where he lays her."

Reid chuckles heartily. "Dickfor, you're *so* fulla shit . . ."

Krawdick looks horrified, even though Vogel's let go and the sheet hasn't torn even slightly. Something stings my left earlobe.

"What's this awfulness I'm hearing?" The voice—her shampoo! "What's *this*?" says Miss Moore, snatching the sheet from my hand.

I try to turn around, but she yanks my ear in the other direction. "What's what?" I say, doing my best not to whimper.

"Is this yours?"

"We found it by the eighth-graders' table."

"Oh my goodness." She's reading it under her breath. "Oh my dear Lord!" She twists my ear harder. "Rest of you weirdos, straight back upstairs!" I've never heard her sound half this pissed off. "Wait by your desks!"

Leaving their desserts on the table, they trudge down the aisle toward the stairs. Sr. Feeney starts herding them. Oh Jeez, how I wish I was with them!

"You, mister, are coming with me. Up, right now. *Up!*" She lets go of my ear and starts guiding me—shoving me, actually—toward the stairwell. Just about everyone's hissing or clapping or hooting. As Sr. Bonita shooshes the eighth-graders, Angie stands up and yells, "*Way da go, Vinci!*" I pull away from Miss Moore and take the stairs two at a time. She yells at me to stop; I keep going. I only stop at the second landing because I can't think of where else to go. Not that I'd leave the building, but I'm scared I might knock her down the stairs in self-defense. And now here she comes, charging up the last flight.

"You *run*," she gasps, "from a *teacher*?"

"I just thought, we're coming here anyway." I lower my head.

"We most certainly *are*. To the *principal*." She grabs my left arm with both hands and swings me across the hall, pushing me into the glassed-in area outside Regina's office. The secretary, Mrs. Unferth, isn't at her desk, and Regina's door's closed. Miss Moore knocks, tries catching her breath, tells me, "Sit!" Two chairs are piled up with dittos and mail, so I have to take the one by the door. My lungs burn and heave.

It sounds like Regina's in there with a man, though how could Fr. Jude get here so fast from the rectory? When neither of them answers the door, Miss Moore licks her thumb and pulls back the top carbon, which must be Angie's detention. She checks her little watch and starts jotting: time, date, name, reason(s), number of character points deducted. All hundred?

I can't rat out Krawdick, of course. Once she calms down, she'll see that the lyrics aren't in my handwriting, and maybe recognize his. Not that I'd point out the difference. All it would do is get us both into trouble, not get me out of it. Plus that's how they nail extra culprits. *Tell us your accomplices and we'll go easy on you.* Then they nail you anyway and your friends want to kill you.

When the door opens, Regina looks out, and the man keeps on talking. "Oh, Monique, I'm on the phone, sorry. It's so good you're here. Please come in." The man is just a guy on the radio.

Miss Moore glares down at me. "*Glued* to that chair, mister. Hear me?"

"Yes, ma'am."

In she goes past Regina, who looks past me into the hallway. I don't think she recognizes me, even though I've held the paten under her chin fifty times, seen her tongue sticking out past the gold in her molars. She's taller, more bug-eyed than when taking Communion. She doesn't seem to see me at all.

She closes her door. PRINCIPAL, it says. Not principle. I've always used *Not my pal* to remind me which one means "boss of school." Below the black letters is a faded-green palm frond neatly folded into a crucifix.

My left ear is all pins and needles, so I offer it up for my sins. I could hear better if I cupped my good one against the door, but what if they suddenly open it? Leaning sideways, with less than half a butt cheek still touching the chair, I hear murmurs but not any words. Mixed with the radio, it's all humming buzz.

And then someone says, "Oh my *God!*"

I get down on one knee, not just to hear better but to aim a prayer up at where Jesus's feet would be. I picture the single nail driven through both of them, the blood running down from the wound, which oozes more as He shifts His weight from heel to heel, trying to make it less excruciating. *Dear Lord, who suffered and died for my sins, I beg Your forgiveness for reading banned lyrics, for listening forty-eight or -nine times to a song proscribed by His Holiness, for having concupiscent thoughts about my teacher, impurely touching oneself while picturing her in lingerie I do not know how many times but roughly two hundred, for embarrassing myself and my family, especially my father and grandmother, who as You know heads the fundraising drive and works in the rectory, respectively. I pray for a miracle, that this detention be somehow vouchsafed from me, that I still be allowed to serve on Your altar. Please fill me with Your Holy Spirit and grant me this miracle, one of the first I've ever asked for, Amen.*

I get back on the chair. For the worst detentions, they call your parents and Regina tells Jude or Ted. I'll be out as an altar boy. Definitely suspended, maybe expelled. My dad will completely blow his top, use the belt, make me quit football, ground me till Christmas or longer—like, Easter. Jude might give me a hard pants-down caning, on top of the one Regina's about to administer.

The door creaks partway open. Miss Moore slips out, pulls it closed. The pad and lyrics are still in her hand. No Regina, no cane, no detention—not yet. Miss Moore looks jumpy, though not the way she looked with the spider. "OK, come with me." I get up and follow her, but she swings back around, gets behind me. People rushing back upstairs from lunch turn and gawk. Except for them and for her being behind me, this is how I usually picture us at night: just walking along, looking for a place to make out. I smell her sweat and shampoo as she reaches around me to open our door. "Take your seat." I try to let her go first, but she puts her hand in the small of my back, gentler than I expected. "Go on and sit down."

Everyone's back now and mostly in their seats. Krawdick shakes his head to show how disgusted he is. "I'm dead, right?" I glare: No, jagoff, even though this is mostly your fault. I yank back my chair and sit down.

Miss Moore stands behind her desk, blinking. Knuckles pink and white on the back of her chair. Everyone shuts up and stares. She's the most beautiful woman I've ever seen in real life, and maybe even up on the screen.

"Sr. Regina is about to make an announcement," she says.

What the—?

Reid leans over, reeking of rotten-egg salad. "What the *hell'd* you tell her?"

"Nothing!" I hiss. "Vergina called her Monique and they both disappeared."

The beige speaker above the board crackles. "Boys and girls, this is Sr. Regina. I have some very sad news to report. Our president has been shot. John Fitzgerald Kennedy has been rushed to a hospital in Dallas, Texas." Then just static for a while. A couple of chairs creak, but nobody says anything. "In the meantime we pray for his speedy recovery. Thank you."

Miss Moore asks us to stand, pushing back her own chair, standing up straight, pressing her fingers together. All of our chairs scrape and creak. "Everyone pray with me now. Pray your very hardest for President Kennedy. 'Our Father, who art in Heaven, hallowed be Thy Name . . .'"

One by one, we catch up, though some people talk and don't pray. Even the fast girls are sobbing. Miss Moore's eyes water as I recite along with her, and she looks back at me for maybe two thirds of a second. Reid belches quietly into his fist, to be as respectful as possible.

We're not even done with the prayer when Regina's voice crackles again.

IT'S WAY WARMER out than this morning—about sixty-five. Sunny, then cloudy, then sunny every couple of minutes. Probably even warmer in Texas. A beautiful day on which one of the worst things ever has happened. Plus why was he even *in* Texas?

The teachers made the seventh- and eighth-graders walk home with younger siblings, so instead of Laurie or Vogel and Reid, I'm poking along with two pests. Sheila's in fourth, Kevin's in second—both way too young to understand anything. They keep asking what happened, what happened?

"Why'd the man hafta *shoot* him?" asks Sheila, who will not stop crying.

"We don't know yet. Let's try to walk faster, to try and find out."

"But who was it that *did* it?"

"Some guy in Texas. The FBI'll find out by the time—" "FBI?"

"He *shot* him," says Kevin, aiming his trigger finger. "*Ptchew-ptchewww!*"

Before we got dismissed, Rendeck said we'll get hit now by Soviet missiles, though no sirens have sounded. Castro's coordinating with Khrushchev, he said. I keep scanning the sky when the kids aren't looking. They'd never shut up if they knew what might be coming.

Our game with St. Edward's been canceled. Special Masses will be offered tonight and tomorrow. I wasn't scheduled to serve this weekend, and now I can't call the rectory to volunteer. I think Gramma's still there, but I obviously couldn't stop to find out. Regina's there too, I assume, finding out how to handle things. If she tells Ted about my detention, he might not tell Gramma because it would be too embarrassing. Her grandson the altar boy caught with *those* lyrics? That'd go over like a Budweiser fart in the sacristy.

Gramma calls days like this Indian Summer, but it's like God is an Indian *giver*, giving us the first Catholic president and taking him back for no reason. I still don't know if He answered my prayer, but if *this* is the answer, it's the most vicious miracle ever, damning me to the scaldingest cranny of Hell, where traitors to religion and country go. I'll be down there getting perpetually blistered and stabbed in the penis with Benedict Arnold, Judas Iscariot, Geoffroy Thérage, and Thomas and Oliver Cromwell. I'd rather take my punishment up here and get caned by Miss Moore.

Kevin's kicking a pebble, and Sheila keeps dragging her feet through the leaves. Most of them blew off a month ago, but half the front lawns still need raking. It's not till we pass the Armbrusters', whose gutters overflow with oak leaves and twigs, that it dawns on me: theologically, that *can't* be how it works. The miracle, assuming it's been granted, is only that Miss Moore lets the detention slide because of the news on the radio, not the assassination itself. In all the commotion after the second announcement, the crying and questions and even the idiots celebrating as we lined up for early dismissal, Miss Moore never gave me the copy for my parents to sign. She might not've even turned in the top sheet to Regina. *The president's been shot? Oh, my God! Oh, and here's this detention . . .*

No good Catholic would pray for *any* president to get shot, and God knows I didn't. (Plus what about all the millions of prayers for him to recover from his wounds? A lot of good *they* did. So why would He answer just mine?) But: if a teacher happened to write a detention as an infinitely worse thing was happening a thousand miles away, when she heard about that thing, she might decide of her own volition, with the help of His grace, to grant amnesty or a dispensation or something. It'd just be miraculously good timing, His way of balancing out the hideous timing of her walking up behind five of us just when *I* happened to be holding the lyrics.

OUR MOM DOESN'T get up from the couch because she's feeding Brian, watching the news. She gives us big but sad hi's, swallows like she's going to cry. Her due date's December something, but she looks twelve months pregnant. Colleen's on her other side, sipping red Fizzies water out of one of her bottles.

"What's the latest?" I ask.

"He said he had a rendezvous with death in Dallas." She gulps. "He took off his glasses."

"His glasses?"

"Walter Cronkite. He got teared-up when he had to announce he was dead."

If Mrs. Unferth had called about the detention, my mom would've mentioned it by now. "They think it was the Soviets?"

"The priests in the operating room said he died of his bullet wounds."

I shook my head, nodded. "The doctor couldn't sew them back closed?"

"Fr. Huber gave extreme unction to remit all his sins. Not that he'd've had many . . ."

"Of his bullet wounds, OK, but who shot them? Whose gun? A Russian's?"

"Oh my gawden of roses—I hope not."

Colleen burps and says, "Ahhhh!" She's giving her Barbie a drink from her bottle, letting the sticky red juice dribble into their laps. I glance out the window but can't see the sky from this angle.

At the station identification, my mom says, "We'll find out when your father gets home."

GRAMMA WENT STRAIGHT from work to pick up Ellen at Sacred Heart. When they finally get home, Teen Angel heads up to her room—so what else is new?

My mom's making pot roast, waddle-scooting back and forth to the living room to follow the news. She says someone named Lee H. Oswald's been captured by the Dallas police. We'll know more after they do good cop/bad cop, but why didn't they just stop him from shooting the president to begin with?

Walter Cronkite says his body is being flown back to Washington. Vice President Johnson has been sworn into office.

"This monster, this . . . *Oswald*," says Gramma. If she's heard about the lyrics, I'd be able to tell from her voice. She sniffles and smokes for a minute. "Now this *Texan* takes over?"

OUR DAD DOESN'T get home until 6:45, with the bad-week look on his face even as the kids and our mom hug and kiss him. He hardly even laughs when Kevin tries to sack him for being a Giants fan. He says one of his buyers didn't seem too broken up by the shooting, plus he got a flat outside of Danville. After he goes to the bathroom, he comes down to the kitchen to shake up a triple martini, though lately he calls them martunis.

It's against family rules, but Gramma lets him eat on the couch while watching TV. My mom scooches over with Brian.

They're now saying Oswald's a member of the Fair Play for Cuba Committee, though he sure doesn't look like he ever sat on any committee. He's twenty-four, wears T-shirts, and lives in the Soviet Union. C'mon! I want to ask my dad if this proves he was part of a sneak attack by Khrushchev, but he likes to finish eating and pour out Martuni No. 2 before talking serious business.

When a snippet about the Kennedy kids comes on, he puts down his fork. Without looking away from the screen, he lights Gramma's Kent. Except for when he gave me Grampa Vince's mitt and talked about how much he and Gramma missed him and how sad she was that my dad never had a chance to play catch with him, it's the first time I've seen my dad with wet eyes.

But of course that's the signal for everyone else to cry too. Gramma finally says, "Jackie made sure *sniff-sniff* two priests have *gulp* stayed with the body."

"That's good, Mutha," my dad says, lighting a Chesterfield.

"Msgr. Robert Mohan and Fr. Gilbert Hartke. Every second since they took his casket off the plane."

"Jebbies? Benedictines?"

"Fr. Mohan's a Sulpician." She lowers her chin to say, *Look how disappointed I am.*

"Hartke's Dominican."

"Hey, just like the Singing Nun," Ellen chirps, while our mom says, "Such a comfort to Jackie."

"The souls of the just are in the hands of a Merciful God," Gramma says.

"I just don't see why," Ellen says, "how He'd let—" She glares at the TV, shakes her head, and sashays upstairs. Let it happen, she was going to say.

To which Gramma would've said, *Ours is not to know the reason why.*

But here's the kicker: Grampa Vince died when my dad was two and Uncle Don was five. John John and Caroline are now in the same situation.

SATURDAY MORNING, INSTEAD of going to confession as usual, I detour to Reid's house. Whether I'd got Jude or Ted behind the screen, I couldn't've confessed to reading the lyrics without tipping them off about the detention. Not confessing a sin *half* that size would itself be a sin of omission, and maybe a mortal. But if the detention goes through, I can always confess it next week. What scares me right now is that Reid's back from church already, and he might've confessed to reading them with his friends. *And which friends might they be, my son?*

He has on his Notre Dame sweats, though their game today with Iowa's been canceled. He tells me his dad says the Bears are still playing the Steelers in Pittsburgh, but it won't be on TV. We agree that's b.s. They always show NFL road games, but tomorrow's won't be on because of the shooting. His dad says we'll need a distraction by then after missing the college games. "Three lousy hours," he says. "How much news can you *watch*?" His dad's a Double Domer, so he knows what he's talking about.

Reid gets his ball and we run patterns for each other in the outfield across the street. His flags and posts have to be shorter than mine because I don't have his arm. My zags and hitches are crisper, but usually he tells me, "Go long." Without any pass rush or DB to hound me, he hits me in stride with a spiral just about every time. I'm walking back, out of breath from a thirty-yard bomb, when he says, "You didn't rat Krawdick out, huh?"

"Aw, man, what, you think I'm a dickfor? *He's* got the dick in his craw for accusing me—"

"What'd your old man say about the detention?"

"He actually hasn't heard yet, with all the commotion. So what about the song? You confess it?"

He nods. "But only to listening. This time, buttonhook at the hash. HUT-hut-hut-HUT!" A dozen more passes and questions and it turns out he had Jude, who made him say five Our Fathers, make ten ejaculations, and promise not to listen again—almost exactly the same penance Ted gave me last week. Ejaculations are short little prayers, like "Holy Mary, Mother of God, I place my faith in Thee" or "Sacred Heart of Jesus, I place my trust in Thee," but Reid says he switched some of his to "Here comes Ruth Ann Patton, she lays in puberty." She's sort of Krawdick's girlfriend, but Reid digs her too, not that he'd ever admit it.

"I changed some of mine to 'Thou shalt not admit adultery.' He ask you who else saw the sheet?"

"Ah-ah. I almost said, 'Only ten, Liverlips? No problem. Just lend me a few of your *Playboys.*'"

"But only for the articles, Father."

"Thass right." He flips me the ball. "Got your ten ejaculations right here for ya, Jude," says Reid, pumping his fist like he's pounding a three-foot-long doozer.

JOGGING HOME, I realize Miss Moore probably asked me to kill the spider because I was the closest boy—end of the front row, get there the quickest, etc. But I still think I'm her favorite, or was, except for Ruth Ann and maybe Marybeth Marino. Definitely favorite boy. She's given me A's on all three papers so far, A+ on the "Young Goodman Brown" one. She puts little checks next to sentences she approves of, and writes things like *You've made this point wonderfully, Vince.*

Though I've never shown my friends passed-back tests or papers, when Vogel saw the one with A+ at the top, he said, "Singing Nun's polishing Pope Vince's *ferula*, I guess. Are you speaking *ex cathedra* when you tell her what grade you should get?" In the locker room last week, Reid held open his butt crack and made his voice sound like hers: "Now, Vincent, you *must* desist brown-nosing me." At least he didn't fart in my face. But Krawdick said, "Yeah, ya got shit schmeared all over your schnoz," poking me in the eye as he tried to wipe off the shit with his towel. We both landed a couple of solid shots before Vogel and Reid helped Brother Frank break it up.

So at least they won't be hassling me about sucking up to D3 anymore.

"LEE H. OSWALD *has been detained by Dallas police until prosecutors can charge him with the felony murder of President Kennedy. He will be transferred tomorrow morning at . . ."*

"Godless bastid," hisses Gramma. She must be the one who hung the black sash across the president's picture. Hearing her swear is bizarro enough, but I'm watching TV on the couch while eating a PB&J and nobody says anything? Plus my dad's at the A&P, shopping! What's the world coming to?

The casket, wrapped in a flag, lies in state, right where Abraham Lincoln's was ninety-eight years ago. Long lines of mourners outside, in the rain. Inside the rotunda, priests with rosaries; sailors in spats, with fixed bayonets; oldster presidents Truman and Eisenhower; altar boys with extra long candles. How'd they land *that* assignment? I also can't tell if this is happening right now in Washington or they're splicing in snippets filmed earlier. I dash to the kitchen for milk.

"Bobby would rather be dead than have him be president," my mom says.

"Disciple of Christ, whatever he is," Gramma says. She's too mad to cry anymore. Eyes glaring, smoke blasting from her nostrils, she looks like a dragon with a freckly bosom.

"It must be God's will," says my mom, "though I still don't see how . . ."

"All I can say is, no other leader would be blessed with *half* this much clergy."

On my way upstairs, my mom says, "Oh, Mrs. Unferth called," and I stop. Before I can even get nervous, she tells me school's been canceled till Tuesday because the funeral got moved up to Monday. Ellen's door opens immediately. "Sacred Heart too?" she shouts down.

"Haven't heard yet!" my mom yells. "Banks will be closed, so I'd think so!"

BACK UP IN my room, I keep 'LS on 3 while going over the reasons to think it won't go or hasn't gone through yet. If Regina got her hands on the lyrics, I'm done for; Miss Moore still has them and I might have a chance. She knows I didn't write them, which has to help calm her furies. Five guys passing it around, Vince loses at musical chairs—at musical pass-the-banned-lyrics.

If possession's nine tenths of the law, what's . . . detention?

Vengeance is mine, saith the Lord, not Dominique's. She's also more likely to forgive and forget over a three-day weekend than if we went back on Monday, I think.

New teachers don't know every rule yet. Mrs. Unferth's in charge of procedure but wasn't in the office when we were. Regina was way too distracted. No one's called my parents about it.

Being an altar boy could help me or hurt me. We're supposed to set an example, meet a higher standard, etc., so me getting caught with them could be considered worse by Regina or Jude than if one of the hoods did. They might want to *make* an example . . .

That Gramma works at the rectory and her son leads the fundraising drive might stand me in good stead, as he'd say. But if they cut his son or her grandson any slack, it'd be unfair to all other students.

I think I can handle getting caned by Regina, even by Jude with my pants down. When Phil Dixon got caned by him for punching out Mike Waligora two days before they graduated, it just made Phil seem even cooler. Everyone said he didn't cower or complain but just took it; he *smiled*. (Though how could they know this if it happened in Jude's private office?) But if I get expelled, or suspended from serving, for being stupid enough to get caught with banned lyrics, no one would think it was cool— the lyrics maybe, but definitely not getting caught.

Miss Moore gets the caning assignment and it makes it a whole different ballgame. I'm afraid that I might get a doozer.

WHEN IT COMES on at 10:45, I'm in bed, even though it isn't a school night. I dial down my Zenith to 1½ and hold it against my good ear. I can't remember exactly what Krawdick wrote down, but his only mistake seems to be in the chorus, where Jack doesn't sing "I said" every time. Pretty close, though.

I turn off the Zenith and try to fall asleep, but I've still got it stuck in my head. I've also got to disagree with myself that Monique is too old to ask out. It won't be that long, three years and four months, till I can take her by Tops Burgers in, say, a T-Bird convertible. Save up for it by caddying, playing poker, maybe inheriting the rest from Uncle Barry, who suddenly dies of no-pain cancer out in Montauk. Or buy it now and let *her* drive to Tops.

She lets us hold hands, maybe kisses me goodnight when I walk her to her door. Lips closed at first, then slightly open. Or we stay in the T-Bird but move to the little backseat after putting the top up. Sometimes she likes to rassle like Elly May Clampett, grow her hair longer like that, wear tight dungarees. If I try anything, though, she scolds me for my "dirty mind" and "forward comportment."

THOUGH IT'S BACK in the forties, my dad and I wear our blue Dacron suits to nine o'clock Mass. His idea, but why argue? I'll need him on my side any day now. With our maroon ties (for St. Joan and his old Fordham Rams) we're practically red, white, and blue. We're taking his Olds, to get there in time to save a pew for the ladies and kids, who were taking too long to get ready.

He's far from over it, but at least he doesn't have bloodshot eyes anymore. He talks about how he and Uncle Don, the Kennedy brothers, and I have all served on God's altar. "You're up for next week, right?" The schedule's not out, but I nod. "Keep it going, buddy," he says. "Kevvie's next." When I tell him I've already taught him the *Introibo*, he tugs my lapel.

He parks and heads off with the ushers while I rush to get dibs on a pew. Most of the early birds look pretty solemn, anxious to hear what our pastor has to say because everything's been so confusing.

Five minutes later the rest of our family crowds in, the ladies dolled up like it's Easter: my mom in her navy wool pregnant coat; Ellen in mascara and lipstick, like she's going on a date in the city; Gramma in her beaded black dress and net veil, and of course her fox stole.

By the time Ted emerges from the sacristy, people are lining the walls. Flynn and Donohoe, eighth's biggest Holy Rollers, are serving. *Introibo ad altare Dei*, etc. The Barotkas have squeezed in across the aisle, three pews ahead of us, Angie at the end in a blue skirt four inches above the backs of her knees. So it won't seem like I'm ogling, I pretend to adore Station X, a carving of Jesus being stripped of His garments, on the pillar above her dad's head.

Ted barrels along, saying some lines before the servers can finish their response to the last one. *Agnus Dei, Filius Patris* . . . If I squint I can see Station XII. Not that I can make out the carving from here, but I know it shows

His death on the cross. As Francona likes to say, *Don't despair, one thief was saved; don't be presumptuous, the other was damned.* I see Angie kneeling before the congregation, her back to the altar, arms held straight out; crucified in only a loincloth, with no crown of thorns and ropes instead of nails, like the thieves, being scolded and scourged by Miss Moore: *this* for your backtalk, *this* for that skirt, *this* for your wayward comportment. My doozer's so hard that it hurts.

When Ted finally gets to the rostrum he already looks tired, more salt than pepper, though after the sermon he still has to give Communion to like two hundred people. Gramma loves him so dearly, she sighs.

"We are stricken this morning by the assassination of our beloved fellow Catholic, John Fitzgerald Ken-nedy. Many millions the world over join us in lamenting his untimely death." He mentions twelve Catholic countries, even some Protestant ones. "Some will ask, 'Why does God countenance such tragedy?'" He pauses to watch all the head-shaking. "Then we remember His only begotten son suffered a miserable death to cleanse mankind of its sins. This teaches two important lessons. First, that suffering is never wasted. And second, to always trust that God the Father knows best." Gramma fingers her Sacred Heart scapular, nodding and shaking and weeping.

"John's devotion to country and Church were equivalent, one and the same. He served both by valiantly fighting for freedom of religion in the Pacific, in Cuba, behind the Iron Curtain. But now a godless coward, a Communist cur, has cut down our John, and we seek the Lord's justice. There's an appointed time for everything: a time to weep and a time to mourn; a time to be born, a time to die; a time of war, a time of peace; a time to love, a time to hate; a time to heal, a time to execute.

"We also pay tribute to John as a husband and father, a good Catholic family man. The demands of the presidency often took him abroad, as when he visited his Holiness this past July. Yet he always made sure to share with his little son and sweet daughter whatever time was his own, mindful as well of three other souls in the Nursery of the Kingdom of Heaven, each delivered from Limbo through the sacrament of baptism. They are fatherless now, though not spiritually." The parents in front of us, especially dads, nod and murmur. Moms weep. My mom and Gramma act like they're in a heaving and sniffling contest.

". . . always at his side, gracious Jacqueline. Always true to the obligations of wife- and motherhood, she gave new dimension to the role of First Lady. Her pink outfit now stained forever with the blood of her husband, Divine Providence blessed her by allowing her hero the comfort of dying in her arms." Which reminds me of when Marilyn Monroe sang "Happy Birthday" to the president just before she died, and Gramma said, "Jackie'll be positively green-eyed."

Donohoe's yawning, trying to hide it by making his eyes extra pious. Flynn thumbs the zits on his neck. Fr. Ted's sermon must be a homily, I guess, because diocesan law forbids eulogies during funeral Masses. Plus I still can't decide whether to take Communion with unconfessed sins, a couple of which might be mortals. If I don't, though, I'll have to explain why I didn't.

"This morning, even though his body is yet to be interred, John speaks to us in the words of St. Paul: 'As for me, my blood has already flown in sacrifice. I have fought the good fight. The reward of heaven will be granted unto me, as to all those who welcome His coming.'" Fr. Ted pauses, gazing at the nave, just like always. Gramma knows what's coming too, and she whispers along with her boss: "Eternal peace grant unto John, O Lord, and let perpetual light shine upon him, in the name of the Father and of the Son and of the Holy Ghost, Amen."

WHILE MY DAD turns in the collection money, I wait at the bottom of the steps, two yards over from the famous blood stain. You can still make it out—grayish maroon, shaped like Italy—after dozens of scrubbings, from the most humid Sunday of July, when Ruth Ann's grandmother fainted while standing at the top of the steps, knocking her dentures and most of her teeth out. Five days later, she died of a hemorrhage. Our family had always waited right there, ever since my dad became an usher. Now we wait here, a couple three yards to the right.

My mom had to pee, so our other car's already gone. So's Angie and everyone else from my grade. The day's just too dismal, I guess, for after-Mass chitchat. Cars keep arriving at the curb to pick up the oldsters. Everyone left is talking about the Bears or Lee Oswald. "Sauté his Red balls," one dad says. "Chair's way too good for this twerp."

The sun's like a flashlight behind the low blanket of clouds, though it could also be God watching over me, still trying to decide whether to grant me my miracle. If an ICBM is headed this way, you couldn't see it because of the clouds, plus the shear of light comes too fast to shield your eyes anyway. With mortals on my soul, unless we shoot it down before the warhead detonates, my skin'll melt here and/or in Hell when I die. The same difference, I guess, except that the melting in Hell lasts a trillion times longer. But my ear hardly hurts anymore.

I finally spot my dad coming down the steps—with *oh Jesus* Miss Moore! She must've been way in the back and, like me, skipped Communion. She lives out in Naperville, so her parish is Peter & Paul, but so why's she at *this* Mass? She and my dad are shaking their heads, solemn as all get out, though they seem to relax as they reach the last step.

"I believe you know this young scoundrel," he says. He's dying to ask, *No Communion?*, but he'll wait till we get to the car.

"I do," she says, friendly but sad. Her left shoe is right on the stain.

"He tells us so many good things about you."

"I'll just bet he does," she says, pulling up the collar of her trench coat. Her eyebrows go up too. "Like father like son, eh?" she says, complimenting or mocking our suits. "Did he say he killed a spider for me?"

"He *did*, huh?" Like killing a spider has a double meaning, or like he's flirting with her—or *I'd* been, by killing it for her. "When was this?"

"On Friday." Her sad voice again. "Just before, you know, we heard."

Well, not *just* before, I think. She squints like she's reading my mind again.

"Must've been something," he says. "Having to announce or explain that."

"I couldn't *begin* to explain it—except to say what a terrific role model he was for our boys." But she never said anything like that! When she looks back at me, holding my eye, I hear a low rumble. I also hear "Drip Drop" by Dion.

A man in a black Corvette is looking over at us from the curb. Thick brown pompadour, green pilot sunglasses, younger than my dad. Almost like a greaser version of the president, with sideburns, had arisen, after only two days, from the dead. He's got the top down, so the heater must be cranked up on high.

My dad turns and looks as another dad whistles. "Triple-black," says a high school guy behind us. "Sixty-one duck tail."

"OK, here's my ride," says Miss Moore. "Kevin, you have a good day, if that even makes sense anymore."

"It does," says my dad, cupping her elbow. "You too."

"And say hello to Mrs. Killeen. Vincent, I'll see you on Tuesday." All pretty friendly, unless they both deserve Oscars. All three of us might, come to think of it.

She walks toward the Vette in slow motion: mysterious bombshell in trench coat, in one of those dirty French movies. As she reaches for the handle, the man leans across to push the door open. They both have brown hair, so it could be her brother; I'll have to find out if she has one. She dips and slides in, and I make myself look up away from her stocking, the kind with the seam down the back. She's never worn that kind to school.

"You," says my dad, "are one lucky guy."

She settles into the seat, which I'm glad is a bucket. Dion keeps singing, "Heh," so that's what I say to my dad. What else am I going to tell him?

"Drip Drop" ends as the Vette rumbles off from the curb. She waves; we wave back. I won't be surprised if the next song's the one that caused all the trouble, though it might get me out of it now. I hear the organ's 3-2-3 rhythm, the drums, the first words. They keep it on 'LS all the way to wherever they're going and it's bound to come on any minute.

THE UNTOUCHABLES

MAXINE CHERNOFF

Set in the early 1960s, "The Untouchables" is a coming-of-age story in which a preteen becomes aware of sexual orientation, social boundaries, and the fragile nature of truth.

The protagonist, Jane, lives in a time and a climate that is both innocent and charged. She loves, for instance, childhood rituals such as visiting the parakeets at Woolworth's, an American institution, but she is perplexed and intrigued by more "adult" issues she witnesses around her and seeks explanations from her parents, who are themselves uncomfortable with certain truths and not eager for their daughter to grasp them. When it comes to kissing or a failed pregnancy or the sexual orientation of the female gas-station attendant Ike, who intrigues Jane, this family is strictly "party line" about preserving innocence despite their daughter's naturally developing curiosity.

Chicago in the 1950s and mid '60s—anywhere during that era—was steeped in tradition, and families were mostly not forums for information or lively discussion. Like a detective, Jane seeks to obtain her own answers and follows her instincts to learn how lives unfold and what the "real" story is. Whether at the art museum with her friend's more upscale mother, observing her old babysitter locked in a passionate kiss, or exploring how Ike at the gas station became the manly woman she is, Jane has a passionate need to know and will risk causing discomfort to any adults impeding her quest.

This story is set on the Southeast Side, a postwar neighborhood of similar, six-room homes, where often a child's freedom was limited to endlessly riding a Schwinn bike around the block. The actual gas station and a person who inspired Ike existed on the corner of Eighty-Seventh and Jeffrey Boulevard. The neighborhood was a mix of Eastern European and German Jews, and Catholics: Poles, Serbians, Croatians, and Mexicans. About four blocks south was "Pill Hill," where wealthier families lived, Jewish doctors and lawyers and some African American sports figures, including the Cubs' Ernie Banks and Billy Williams. The postcard Jane gives Ike is a Hopper painting from the Art Institute, a great presence in the lives of many Chicagoans aspiring to enrichment. A world containing greater possibility for expansion seems almost within reach of Jane, who already sees the limits of her parents' fears and secrets. She is an explorer and freer spirit, trying to find the "hidden" Chicago that will unleash truths she needs to grow and mature into the more modern and tolerant woman she will become.

JANE KNEW THAT HER FATHER, A LEATHER-GOODS SALESMAN, was of the merchant class. She had been studying the caste system in school and worried that his job might put him in jeopardy, since Untouchables dealt with animal skins. As long as her father only sold the stuff, he'd be safe. Salespeople were never Untouchables. She would have liked her father to have been a Brahmin, but after all, her family lived next to a gas station and showed no particular interest in learning or religion. Usually this pleased her. While her Catholic friends were tortured in Sunday clothes, Jane could ride around the block on her old Schwinn bike singing, "Some Enchanted Evening," her favorite song from *South Pacific*. Every time she passed the Shell station, she'd ride over the hose that made the bell ring. Sometimes it punctuated the song mid-chorus. Other times it accompanied her as she reached for a high note. When she got bored, she'd park her bike, walk back to the gas station, put her quarter in for a Coke, and swig the bottle down, leaning against the red metal housing of the machine. No one noticed her. She could stare at anyone she pleased. Mostly she looked at the m'woman, which was what her father called the person who pumped gas on weekends.

Jane had concluded that she was definitely a woman because the badge on her shirt didn't lie flat over her breast pocket. It puckered, as her own pockets had begun to. But no woman in her right mind would have her hair way above the ear or that short on the neck or let grease accumulate all over her face and hands without trying to clean herself up. Once Jane asked her mother about the m'woman but was told to be quiet. If she asked why, her parents' silence would become an impermeable barrier. Victoria Pranz's mother had told Jane that the m'woman was probably a lesbian. Victoria's mother was definitely a Brahmin, an art professor at the University of Chicago, though her status was questionable, considering her recent divorce.

Dr. Pranz would be a Brahmin too, Jane calculated, by virtue of his classical music training. Even though he'd given up the flute to practice dentistry, he might have played in a symphony. Once Victoria had told Jane that dentists have the highest suicide rates. From then on Jane had stared at Dr. Pranz, trying to detect a sudden sadness behind his jocular manner and jaunty little Vandyke. When he left Mrs. Pranz, Jane wondered if he'd take to wandering aimlessly along Lake Michigan until a surge of emotions vaulted him into the water. But when he came to pick up Victoria on Saturdays, he never looked anything but animated. Sometimes he'd include Jane in a special outing. En route he'd hum to the classical music on the car radio. One morning they'd gone to Calumet Harbor to tour a merchant-marine ship from Denmark. Someone depressed couldn't have thought of such pastimes. Jane's own father, absorbed in the Cubs' problems with left-handed hitting, or bills or edging the lawn, looked far sadder than Dr. Pranz. Perhaps Brahmins were naturally more content than the merchant class.

On Sundays Victoria and Jane rode their bikes together. On the particular Sunday it happened, Jane was in the lead, Victoria well behind. That was a difference between them. Victoria dallied, taking in details, reserving judgment. Maybe she'd inherited her mother's preoccupation with seeing. Jane remembered a horrible Columbus Day spent at the Art Institute with Victoria and her mother, who paused for one, sometimes two minutes, at every painting before moving on. Even worse, Mrs. Pranz asked Jane what she thought of several Cézannes, as if Jane could tell her something she didn't already know. "You're the artist," Jane had finally said when Mrs. Pranz seemed dissatisfied with her replying, "I think they're OK."

When Jane went over the gas hose this time, her tire skidded in some grease and she went flying over the handlebars, landing on both palms and knees. Before Victoria caught up with her, the m'woman had rushed out of the gas station and was helping Jane up. She made a greasy fist around Jane's forearm. Pulling Jane to her feet, she surveyed the damage.

"Guess you'll be all right," she said and offered Jane a clean flannel cloth.

Jane stared at her palms, which were red and smarting under the grease, and at her poor knees, which had taken the brunt of the fall. One was bloodier than the other. Jane dabbed at them with the rag. Before Victoria arrived on the scene, the m'woman had walked back into the garage.

"She talked to me!" Jane told Victoria as they walked their bikes home.

"Who?" Victoria asked, cocking her head like her mother while waiting for the reply.

"The m'woman came out when I fell. She has a lady's voice. She gave me this cloth." Jane held it out.

"Yuck," Victoria said.

By then they'd reached Jane's house. As Jane expected, her mother asked Victoria to go home. Whenever Jane got hurt, her mother used the occasion to lecture not only about safety but whatever had been on her mind since the last injury.

"Let's go to Woolworth's," her mother said, wiping the last grease off Jane's legs. "I need some yarn, and I'll buy you a vanilla Coke."

Bandages on both palms and knees, Jane limped to the Fairlane. She made a half-hearted effort to comb her hair and wet her lips shiny as her mother started the car and headed off.

"Jane, I was wondering, honey, whether I've told you enough."

"About what?" Jane asked, alert to a very different line of questioning.

"About growing up," her mother said.

"I guess it's just happening anyway," Jane said, looking down at her hands, which, with the extra bandages and the stiffness they caused, appeared huge.

"I mean something else," her mother mumbled. Why wasn't Mrs. Pranz her mother? She had brought home a gynecological test and taken

Victoria to a health seminar on her eleventh birthday. Whenever Jane's mother wanted to talk about sex, she got all self-conscious and stuttery and even drove funny.

"Mom, you're going twelve miles an hour. I think the speed's at least twenty-five."

"Do you know about babies?" Jane's mother blurted out as she parallel-parked the car in front of Woolworth's. Parking had taken three tries.

"They're those little things with diapers, right, Mom?"

Before her mother could reply, their attention was caught by the couple standing in front of Woolworth's. The thin young man had his arms around the girl, who was younger still, perhaps sixteen. Her hands were tucked demurely in her pockets. What fascinated Jane was how their bodies connected at the tongue, and how they twisted against each other for what seemed like forever.

"They're Frenching," Jane explained to her mother, who looked either confused or stricken. "Hey, that's Nina Treesom!" she added. Nina lived across the alley and had been dating a college boy.

"Hi, Nina," Jane said, as her mother whisked her past them into the store.

"Yarn?" her mother asked, a tired monosyllable. The woman pointed them toward the back of the store, Jane's favorite area, where she could watch the parakeets crowding together, chirping on their perches.

Her mother bought pink and blue and yellow mohair, promising Jane she'd make her a sweater. Every so often she took on such projects, but most ended in failure. There was a whole box of half-made sweaters and scarves in the bottom of the linen closet. Jane said that would be nice but spent her time over the vanilla Coke thinking about the m'woman. After the flannel cloth was clean, Jane would return it to her. Maybe the m'woman would explain to her why she dressed that way. Maybe she was from another country, but Jane hadn't detected an accent.

"The couple you saw outside Woolworth's," her mother began once she was back behind the wheel, "had better be careful." She was shaking a manicured index finger toward Jane's nose.

"Mom, that was Nina. Remember, she used to walk me to school when I was in kindergarten?"

"Nina or not, one thing leads to another." Squinting to look serious, she added, "Remember Tammy Swartz?"

"Yes," Jane said, recalling Mrs. Swartz's hefty daughter who'd gone away one summer to work at a resort in the Wisconsin Dells.

"She didn't go to college after that summer, Jane, like Mrs. Swartz told everyone. She had a baby."

"But she wasn't married."

"I'm telling you, Jane, it's dangerous to be a woman." She was looking crazed again. They took a sharp left. The tires squealed around their corner, engraving the afternoon on Jane's eardrums, and they were home.

Jane lay on her bed and wondered whether the m'woman worried about such matters. It would be nice to worry about nothing at all or just dumb things like her father did. Jane wondered what the m'woman's status would be in India. Then she remembered that unmarried women were always a disgrace to their families.

WHEN JANE WALKED into the gas-station garage, the m'woman was reading the Sunday paper and smoking a cigarette. She had stretched out her legs so that her work boots rested against the edge of the counter.

"Excuse me," Jane said.

The m'woman looked up and smiled at her.

"I have your cloth." Jane held it toward her.

"Thanks," the m'woman said. "Are you all healed?"

"I'm fine," Jane said. She noticed that the insignia over the m'woman's pocket read "Ike." She smiled to think that the m'woman and the President shared the same name.

"I'm Jane."

"I'm Sheila."

"Your pocket says 'Ike.'"

"I'm Sheila Ikenberry. People call me Ike."

"I'm twelve."

"I'm thirty-two."

Then the gas-bell rang, and a blue Chevy was waiting at a pump.

"Right back," Ike said.

Jane picked up the paper Ike had been reading. It was folded at the classified car ads.

"I'm looking for a car," Ike continued upon her return.

"My dad buys Fords."

"Right now I have a Studebaker." She pointed outside to a two-toned sedan colored like toast with jelly. "It's getting kind of old, and I live way out in the sticks. I need a more dependable car for winter."

"My mom drives my dad's car. Someday I'll probably have my own car. I wouldn't mind a Thunderbird."

"Right now your bike is fine, I'd guess."

"Sure it is. I'm talking about the future."

"What do you want to be in the future?" Ike asked.

This is leading somewhere, Jane thought. If she just said the right thing, Ike would explain herself. "Maybe a truck driver," Jane said, hoping to prod her along.

"When I was little, I wanted to be a nurse."

A Plymouth pulled up. The man got out of the car and walked into the gas station.

"Got some change for the Coke machine?" he asked. Ike gave him quarters, nickels, and dimes.

"Your hair's pretty short," Jane said while the man was opening his Coke.

"Yeah, it's convenient for me that way." Ike picked up her paper and started looking down the column again. "I used to wear it longer when I was your age." She drew circles around two car ads in a row.

"Do you have any pictures?" Jane asked.

"Of what?"

"Your family, or how you looked before you cut your hair."

"Not on me," Ike said. "Why don't you come by next Sunday? I'll bring a photo of me when I was your age."

"I'll try," said Jane. "Mostly I'm free on Sundays."

"Want a Coke?"

"I don't have any money."

"I'll treat you to one," Ike said, "and then I have to close up for the day."

All the time Jane drank the Coke, she watched Ike reading the ads. Ike never looked up or seemed to notice that Jane was staring. If she did notice, she ignored it, just as she did Jane's riding over the gas-station hose again and again.

THAT TUESDAY Mrs. Pranz took Jane and Victoria back to the Art Institute. In one gallery right near *American Gothic*, which Jane remembered from her previous visit, she saw a painting she hadn't noticed before. It was a gas station painted at night by someone named Edward Hopper. The station itself was lit up, and the majestic red pumps were topped off with white globes. There was a lone attendant standing at one edge of the painting and a road that went off into darkness. Jen liked how the painting admitted that gas stations mattered. She hoped Mrs. Pranz would ask her about it. For once she'd have had something to say.

On the way out Mrs. Pranz asked the girls what they'd like in the gift shop. Victoria picked out some stationery with Degas dancers. Jane chose a few postcards. Between a Renoir mother and child and Van Gogh's bedroom, Jane slipped the Hopper painting.

BECAUSE IT WAS raining that Sunday, it was harder for Jane to get out of the house. She knew she couldn't just say she was going to the gas station or mention Ike's name, even as Sheila Ikenberry. She was glad for one thing. Her mother had gotten all involved in the sweater and forgotten about Jane's education in being a woman.

"I'm taking a bike ride," Jane said. Her father, who was reading *National Geographic*, didn't look up.

"In the rain?" her mother asked, peering over her glasses.

"I need a few things at Woolworth's," Jane said, "and I want to look at the parakeets."

"Don't look too long," her father said, "or they'll charge you."

IKE WAS SITTING exactly where she'd been last week. She was wearing a rubber raincoat over her slacks and shirt.

"Lousy weather to pump gas," she said when Jane walked in. "On days like this I wish I *had* been a nurse."

"I guess you still could be," Jane said but regretted it immediately. It was the kind of thing her mother would have said to cheer someone up.

Ike smiled and opened the drawer under the cash register. "Voilà!" She produced a picture of herself as a little girl. "That's me at six. I couldn't find me at twelve. Pretty cute, huh?"

She was sitting on a stuffed bear at a zoo. Her hair was short and the little skirt she wore revealed thick, sturdy legs. Because she was smiling into the sun, her face was wrinkled up.

"Where was it taken?" Jane asked.

"The Bronx Zoo. That's where I grew up. Not in the zoo. In the Bronx," she laughed.

"Why did you come to Chicago?"

"Just to follow a friend. The friend was going to move here, so I did too."

"Where's your friend now?"

"That's a long story." Ike looked out the window.

"I brought you something," Jane said, reaching under her rain slicker and pulling out the postcard. She placed it on the counter next to the cash register.

"A postcard of a gas station," Ike said. "Now when I'm at home, I'll be able to remember where I work on the weekends." She laughed. "It's really very nice, especially those old-fashioned pumps."

"It's of a painting at the Art Institute."

"Right. A pretty nice painting."

"I go there all the time with Victoria and her mom. Her mom's an art professor."

"I saw you yesterday with your mom. Pardon me for saying this, but your mom's driving leaves something to be desired."

"She just learned two years ago. Believe me, she's gotten better. Did your mom drive?"

"My mom didn't drive and neither did my dad. My older brother drove, though. He taught me one summer."

"Why didn't they drive?" Jane asked.

"You ask a lot of questions," Ike said. "How about a little break? Can I buy you another Coke?"

They were at the machine when Jane saw her father approaching. He was wearing a rubber raincoat identical to Ike's.

"Jane, I saw your bike. You're wanted at home," he said.

"Dad, this is Sheila Ikenberry."

"Pleased to meet you," he said, turning to hold the door for Jane.

"Do you spend a lot of time there?" he asked when they were out of the rain under the overhanging porch of their house.

"Not really," Jane said. "Ike saw when I fell off the bike. She came out and asked if I was all right. I guess that got us talking."

"You know, Jane, there's something strange about that woman."

"Daddy, you call her 'the m'woman.' Anyone can see there's something strange about her."

"You probably shouldn't hang around there. Let's not tell Mom for now. She's off in all directions with worries."

"Yeah, what's her problem?"

"Well, we didn't tell you, but for a while we thought that she might be having another baby. Then we found out that she wasn't."

"Is that why she needed yarn?" Jane asked.

"No, she needed yarn later. After she found out she wasn't going to have another baby."

"Why would you want another baby," Jane asked, "when you have me?" For a reason she didn't understand, she felt tears forming in her eyes. She knew her eyes turned greener when she cried. She didn't know if she was crying because she wanted her parents all to herself or didn't want them at all.

They were standing in the foyer when her mother asked where Jane had been. Her father held his finger up to his lips, looked Jane in the eye, and said, "Oh just around the neighborhood. I treated her to a Coke at the Shell."

THE NEXT SUNDAY Jane looked up Martinegro's Shell Station in the phone book. When Sheila Ikenberry answered, Jane said she thought she'd just say hello. Then she told Ike that her mother had been pregnant but that things hadn't worked out.

"I mailed that postcard to my friend," Ike said. "You know, the one of the gas station? I thought she'd get a kick out of seeing what I've made of myself."

DISCOVERING MY FEMININITY IN MENSWEAR

M SHELLY CONNER

In 2017 Lena Waithe became the first Black woman to win an Emmy for comedy writing for her Thanksgiving episode of Aziz Ansari's series *Master of None*. The episode, based on her experience coming out as a Black queer woman to her mother on Chicago's South Side, is emblematic of our mirrored experiences. In short, Waithe and I are both Black/queer/female writers from the South Side of Chicago. We are masculine of center and, until recently, we both had locs. On cutting her locs, Waithe notes, "I felt like I was holding onto a piece of femininity that would make the world feel comfortable with who I am."

Black women's hair occupies a contentious space, especially for non-Black women. Much has been written on how Black women navigate hair care even as our hair has been banned, regulated, and appropriated by others. The investment in defining the feminine is one in a cluster of social and cultural issues. In 2016, when I first wrote "Discovering My Femininity in Menswear," my long locs served as a feminine counterweight to the bow ties and wingtips in my closet. Even before the shift in my clothing aesthetic, my long hair—from childhood pigtails to adulthood locs—worked to balance my androgynous figure and athletic inclinations. I hid beneath them until it seemed that, even in my bow ties, I found people were consumed with the hair that was becoming increasingly complicated in my life. I wanted to learn to swim. I wanted to be in charge of my own hair care and not employ a loctician. I wanted to choose to comb or not comb it and to no longer be perpetually startled by its touch against my neck. In 2016, I shaved the lower half of my hair and the following year I cut the rest.

Since writing "Discovering . . ." I have discovered as many feminine attributes of myself in masculine-leaning aspects as I've discovered masculine attributes in more feminine-leaning aspects and activities. This means: I ride my motorcycle; I cook and BBQ; I teach; I read; I write essays, such as "Dapper: Fashioning a Queer Aesthetic of Black Womanhood"; I fish; I garden: I build things; and I swim. I do all of these things and more, no longer restricted by social constructs of my gender.

MY MOTHER WANTED A BALLERINA, BUT I'VE ALWAYS BEEN MORE of a cowboy. Mayfair Academy of Fine Arts has been serving Chicago's predominantly Black South Side since 1957. Lured into classes by tap dance, I was entrapped into years of ballet. Tears always accompanied those Saturday morning classes, where I was taunted by cliques of pre-pubescent prima donnas. I sought refuge in my room, skinny legs wrapped protectively in durable jeans, hidden from the jeers of my peers.

I always equate dresses with two things: unsolicited commentary on my size, and impracticality. I was a cowboi, not the woman forced to sit side-saddle—restricted to following or falling; never fighting or leading the cavalry. Dresses signified damsels in dis-dress (see what I did there?). Even when women characters were badass, a frequent mark of their capture was being forced into a dress. Think Selena (Naomie Harris) in the zombie-apocalypse thriller *28 Days Later* upon her capture by the all-male military faction desperate for ~~female companionship~~ rape. Selena spent most of the film as a leather trench coat–wearing, machete-wielding badass. Once captured, the militia's first action is to force Selena and her teenaged charge into dresses. Dresses were for tripping up women characters for the quintessential fall. They were tools of inequality, leaving women easily accessible.

Dresses did not make me feel feminine; they made me feel vulnerable. I realize that vulnerability is a key element to the social construct of the feminine; and make no mistake, my critique of dresses is purely about their function for the social construct perpetuated in media and culture.

Of course I find them aesthetically pleasing. I just don't enjoy how I feel wearing them.

The first steel horse that I owned was a bicycle that epitomized the feminine: banana-seat, sunshine-yellow paint, tassels, and a mesh basket. It did not match the stallion or Harley Davidson of my imaginary. I pedaled twice as hard to keep up with the boys on the block; I yearned for the rugged rubber of their BMX tires. More important, I began to realize that their masculinity (nascent as it was) afforded them a freedom of adventure and beingness from which I was excluded. My mother wouldn't allow me a dirt bike, and the 1980s did not produce a female version, splattered in pastel pinks and yellows with a slanted frame bar. My only recourse was to ditch the basket, rip off the tassels, and switch out the tires. Before gender-neutral bikes, there was my transgender one.

I take issue with gender binaries—that there is *either* masculine or feminine. The way the words function is problematic and was evident the first time I wore a bow tie. It did not imbue me with masculinity. I did not become butch, stud, or any other masculine-male identity. Wearing a bow tie did, however, provide a buffer for me to experience some of the liberties attributed to the masculine. My mannerisms and behaviors were no longer regulated by my style of dress. Regardless of how I was perceived— femme-bodied, masculine of center/androgynous—the shift was in how I felt. I felt free to be me—at times feminine, masculine, androgynous, or combinations of these: classifying bow ties, neckties, suits, and wingtips as menswear becomes extremely oppressive. The clothing allows me to embrace myself fully. For one who felt dresses to be too difficult a performance, masculine attire provided the outlet for my range of gender identity—particularly for my repressed feminine energy.

From Sojourner Truth's assertions in "Ain't I a Woman?" to the misogynoirist insults hurled at Serena Williams's body, women of color have continually battled social constructs of "womanhood" that exclude them. Masculine of center, queer women of color are even more affected by these definitions and their associated violations. To be a queer woman of color in "menswear" is an act of resistance on multiple levels. It is the embodiment of intersectionality. It asserts womanhood on its own terms while embracing historically problematic associations. It's the equivalent of eating a fried-chicken and watermelon dinner in public (because fried chicken and watermelon are delicious) and daring anyone to attribute racial stereotypes to the meal. Menswear-inspired clothing intervenes into traditional constructs of womanhood.

I sometimes wonder what life would be like without such strict gender categories. My love affair with "menswear" is a direct result of fleeing the limitations of women's wear and its significance of inequality.

As an adult, I asked my mother why she tortured me with ballet. She replied, "To get rid of that country gait of a walk you have."

"Did it work?" I asked.

"Nope."

Always a cowboi.

DEATH OF THE RIGHT FIELDER

STUART DYBEK

"Death of the Right Fielder" began as a prose poem. Well, actually it began with the single sentence that opens the piece. I had no idea where it was going, but by the time I hit "He always played deep" I had the tone of the piece, a tone I realized was black humor, and that realization told me what liberties I could take—what directions were open—in utilizing all that was real about the material: my recollection of growing up playing the pastoral game of base-ball in parks surrounded by the sometimes violent inner city.

AFTER TOO MANY BALLS WENT OUT AND NEVER CAME BACK WE went out to check. It was a long walk—he always played deep. Finally we saw him, from the distance resembling the towel we sometimes threw down for second base.

It's hard to tell how long he'd been lying there, sprawled on his face. Had he been playing infield, his presence, or lack of it, would, of course, have been noticed immediately. The infield demands communication—the constant, reassuring chatter of team play. But he was remote, clearly an outfielder (the temptation is to say out*sider*). The infield is for wisecrackers, pepper-pots, gum-poppers; the outfield is for loners, onlookers, brooders who would rather study clover and swat gnats than holler. People could pretty much be divided between infielders and outfielders. Not that one always has a choice. He didn't necessarily choose right field so much as accept it.

There are several theories as to what killed him. From the start the most popular was that he'd been shot. Perhaps from a passing car, possibly from that gang calling themselves the Jokers, who played sixteen-inch softball on the concrete diamond with painted bases in the center of the housing project, or by the Latin Lords, who didn't play sports, period. Or maybe some pervert with a telescopic sight from a bedroom window, or a mad sniper from a water tower, or a terrorist with a silencer from the expressway overpass, or maybe it was an accident, a stray slug from a rob-bery, or a shoot-out, or assassination attempt miles away.

No matter who pulled the trigger it seemed more plausible to ascribe his death to a bullet than to natural causes like, say, a heart attack. Young deaths are never natural; they're all violent. Not that kids don't die of heart attacks. But he never seemed the type. Sure, he was quiet, but not the quiet of someone always listening for a heart murmur his family repeat-edly warned him about since he was old enough to play. Nor could it have been leukemia. He wasn't a talented enough athlete to die of that. He'd have been playing center, not right, if leukemia was going to get him.

The shooting theory was better, even though there wasn't a mark on him. Couldn't it have been, as some argued, a high-powered bullet trav-eling with such velocity that its hole fuses behind it? Still, not everyone was satisfied. Other theories were formulated, rumors became legends over the years: he'd had an allergic reaction to a bee sting, been struck by a single bolt of lightning from a freak, instantaneous electrical storm, ingested too strong a dose of insecticide from the grass blades he chewed on, sonic waves, radiation, pollution, etc. And a few of us liked to think it was simply that chasing a sinking liner, diving to make a shoestring catch, he broke his neck.

There *was* a ball in the webbing of his mitt when we turned him over. His mitt had been pinned under his body and was coated with an almost luminescent gray film. There was the same gray on his black, high-top gym shoes, as if he'd been running through lime, and along the bill of his base-ball cap—the blue felt one with the red *C* which he always denied stood for the Chicago Cubs. He may have been a loner, but he didn't want to be identified with a loser. He lacked the sense of humor for that, lacked the perverse pride that sticking with losers season after season breeds, and the love. He was just an ordinary guy, .250 at the plate, and we stood above him not knowing what to do next. By then the guys from the other outfield positions had trotted over. Someone, the shortstop probably, suggested team prayer. Then no one could think of a team prayer. So we all just stood there silently bowing our heads, pretending to pray while the shadows moved darkly across the outfield grass. After a while the entire diamond was swallowed and the field lights came on.

In the bluish squint of those lights he didn't look like someone we'd once known—nothing looked quite right—and we hurriedly scratched a shallow grave, covered him over, and stamped it down as much as possible so that the next right fielder, whoever he'd be, wouldn't trip. It could be such a juvenile, seemingly trivial stumble that would ruin a great career before it had begun, or hamper it years later the way Mantle's was hampered by bum knees. One can never be sure the kid beside him isn't another Roberto Clemente; and who could ever know how many potential Great Ones have gone down in the obscurity of their neighborhoods? And so, in the catcher's phrase, we "buried the grave" rather than contribute to any further tragedy. In all likelihood the next right fielder, whoever he'd be, would be clumsy too, and if there was a mound to trip over he'd find it and break *his* neck, and soon right field would get the reputation as haunted, a kind of sandlot Bermuda Triangle, inhabited by phantoms calling for ghostly fly balls, where no one but the most desperate outcasts, already on the verge of suicide, would be willing to play.

Still, despite our efforts, we couldn't totally disguise it. A fresh grave is stubborn. Its outline remained visible—a scuffed bald spot that might have been confused for an aberrant pitcher's mound except for the bat jammed into the earth with the mitt and blue cap fit over it. Perhaps we didn't want to eradicate it completely—a part of us was resting there. Perhaps we wanted the new right fielder, whoever he'd be, to notice and wonder about who played there before him, realizing he was now the only link between past and future that mattered. A monument, epitaph, flowers, wouldn't be necessary.

As for us, we walked back, but by then it was too late—getting on to supper, getting on to the end of summer vacation, time for other things, college, careers, settling down and raising a family. Past thirty-five the talk starts about being over the hill, about graying Hoyt Wilhelm in his forties still fanning them with the knuckler as if it's some kind of miracle, about Pete Rose still going in head-first at forty, beating the odds. And maybe the talk is right. One remembers Willie Mays, forty-two years old and a Met, dropping that can-of-corn fly in the '73 Series, all that grace stripped away and with it the conviction, leaving a man confused and apologetic about the boy in him. It's sad to admit it ends so soon, but everyone knows those were the lucky ones. Most guys are washed up by seventeen.

MY MOTHER'S MÉXICO

ANA CASTILLO

Now that I am nearly the age my mother was at the time of her sudden death from cardiac arrest, it feels that at seventy she died relatively young. She suffered from diabetes and the debilitating disease had steadily withered her away. In the physical sense she stopped being the imposing stern figure in my life but a diminutive, frail version of herself. Toward the end, she was completely dependent on me to tend to her smallest needs. And yet, she never stopped being an intimidating presence.

The day of her death, she was on her way to dialysis and her last words to me were in Spanish, "Hasta pronto, mi amor." My mother was not an immigrant. She was born in the United States and was part of the nearly one million Mexicans and their American-born children who were repatriated in 1929–30 after the stock market crash. She consequently grew up speaking Spanish. While she lived for most of her adult life in Chicago, she never gave up her language and the customs she was raised with in Mexico.

By the time my mamá became too ill to fend for herself at home, among her last lessons was teaching my preadolescent son how to make the tortillas he so appreciated from her kitchen. Centuries pass, generations go by, and migrations continue, and yet the lessons of a Mexic-Amerindian woman to her children in some ways vary little. The teachings of the huetlatolli (the elders) include respect for your elders, accountability and contribution to the well-being of your community, and self-respect. How this gets accomplished in the twenty-first century in a new nation, in some ways more hostile to our people than ever, was left to my son and me. While I searched within, as a single, young mother while my own mother was alive and well, I collected these basic tenets. Mamá did more than pass them on to me—by accepting her legacy, in many respects, I have become her.

M Y MOTHER'S MÉXICO WAS THE BRUTAL URBAN REALITY OF LUIS Buñuel's *Los Olvidados*. Children scamming and hustling, fire-eaters, hubcap stealers, Chiclet sellers, miniature accordion players with small, dirty hands stretched out before passersby for a coin, a piece of bread: "Please, señor, for my mother who is very sick." This was the Mexico City of my family. This was the México from which my mother spared me.

In that Mexico City in the 1930s, Mamá was a street urchin with one ragged dress—but not an orphan, not yet. Because of an unnamed skin disease that covered her whole tiny body with scabs, her head was shaved. At seven years old, or maybe eight, she scurried, quick and invisible as a Mayan messenger, through the throngs of that ancient metropolis in the area known as "La Villita," where the goddess Guadalupe Tonantzin had made her four divine appearances and ordered el indio Juan Diego four times to tell the Catholic officials to build her a church. "Yes!" and off he went, sure-footed and trembling. Mamá, who was not Mamá but little then, bustled on her own mission toward the corner where her stepfather sold used paperbacks on the curb. At midday he ordered his main meal from a nearby restaurant and ate it out of stainless-steel carryout containers without leaving his place of business. The little girl would take the leftovers and dash them off to her mother, who was lying on a petate—in the one room the whole family shared in a vecindad overflowing with families like their own with all manner of maladies that accompany destitution. Her mother was dying.

María de Jesús Rocha de Castro spent her days and nights in the dark, windowless room reading novels, used paperbacks provided by her new husband from Veracruz, seconds like the food he shared with her. She copied favorite passages and verses into a notebook, which I have inherited, not through the pages of a will but by my mother's will: she carried the notebook, preserved in its faded newsprint cover, over decades of migration until, one day, it was handed over to me, the daughter who also liked to read, to write, to save things.

María de Jesús named her second daughter after a fictional character, Florinda, but my mother was the eldest daughter. She was not named for romance like my tía Flora—aromatic and evocative—but from the

Old Testament, Raquel, a name as impenetrable as the rock in her parents' shared Guanajuatan family name, Rocha: Raquel Rocha Rocha. And quite a rock my mother was all the days of her life, Moses and Mount Sinai and God striking lightning all over the place, Raquel the Rock.

One day, María de Jesús—the maternal grandmother whom I never knew but was told I am so much like—asked her eldest daughter to purchase a harmonica for her. Of course, it would be a cheap one that could be obtained from a street vendor not unlike her bookselling husband. This the child did, and brought it to her mother's deathbed, a straw mat on a stone floor. And when the mother felt well enough, she produced music out of the little instrument, in the dark of that one room in Mexico City, the city where she had gone with her parents and two eldest children with the hope of getting good medical care that could rarely be found in those days outside the capital.

Instead, María stood in line outside a dispensary. Dispensaries were medical clinic substitutes, equipped to offer little more than drugs, certain common injections, and lightweight medical advice. In a rosary chain of women like herself—black rebozos, babies at the breast—she waited for hours in the sun or rain, on the ground. So many lives and that woman at the end, there, yes, that one, my mother's young mother waited, dying.

In the 1970s while I was living alone in Mexico City, I had a medical student friend who took me to such a dispensary where he worked most evenings. The place, located in a poor colonia, consisted of two dark rooms—one for the receptionist and the other for consultation. The dispensary was crammed to the ceiling with boxes of drugs, mostly from the United States, administered freely to patients. I knew almost nothing about medication, but I knew that in the United States we did not have a once-a-month birth control pill, and that belladonna could not be taken without a doctor's prescription. And yet, drugs such as these were abundant in the dispensary, and my young friend was not a doctor but, in fact, was a failing medical school student, permitted to prescribe at his own discretion.

María de Jesús was newly widowed during her dispensary days, and why she married again so soon (the bookseller) I cannot say, except that she was so sick—and with two children—that shelter and leftovers may have been reason enough. She bore two children quickly from this second marriage, unlike the first, in which, among other differences, it took seven years before the couple had their first child, a son born in Kansas, and two years later a daughter, my mother, born in Nebraska.

My mother often told me my grandfather worked on the railroads as a signalman. This is what brought the Guanajuatan couple to the United States. From this period—the 1920s—I can construct a biography of the couple myself because María de Jesús was very fond of being photographed. She wore fine silks and chiffons and wide-brimmed hats. Her mustached husband with the heavy-lidded eyes telling of his Indian ancestry sported a gold pocket watch. They drove a Studebaker.

After the Stock Market Crash of 1929, Mexican workers in the United States, suddenly jobless, were quickly returned to the other side of the border. My grandparents returned not with severance pay, not with silk dresses nor wool suits, not with the Studebaker—but with tuberculosis. My grandfather died soon after.

When María de Jesús died (not surprisingly, she was not saved by the rudimentary medical treatment she received at dispensaries), her children—two sons, two daughters—were sent out to work to earn their own keep. Where the sons went, I don't know as much. But I know about the daughters—Raquel and her younger sister, Flora—because when they grew up and became women, they told me in kitchens, over meals, and into late evenings, that by the time they were ten years old, they worked as live-in domestics.

My mother was a little servant. Perhaps that is why later, when she became a wife and mother, she kept a neat home. My tía Flora was sent to the kitchen of an Arab family. And in adulthood, her tiny flat was always crowded, filled with crazy chaos, as she became the best Mexican cook on both sides of the border. It was a veritable Tenochtitlán feast at Flora's table in her humble casita at the outpost of Mesoamerica—that is to say, the mero corazón of the Mexican barrio of Chicago: spices and sauces of cumin and sesame seeds, chocolate, ground peanuts, and all varieties of chiles; cuisines far from shy or hesitant, but bold and audacious, of fish, fowl, and meats. Feasts fit for a queen.

When my mother was about seventeen, her guardian grandparents decided to take their US-born grandchildren closer to the border. The strategy of the migrating abuelos was that the US-born grandchildren could get better work or, at least, perhaps better pay on the US side. They settled in Nuevo Laredo. One year later, my mother was raped—or at a minimum clearly taken advantage of—by the owner of the restaurant on the US side of the border where she had found work as a waitress. (She never said which it was, or at least, she never told me.) He was married with a family and considerably older than the teenager who bore his son. The best my great-grandfather could do at that point on behalf of my mother's honor was to get the man to provide for her. He paid the rent on a little one-room wooden house, which, of course, gave him further claims on my mother. Two years later, a daughter was born.

Three years more and Mamá's México ended as a daily construct of her reality when, with machete in hand, she went out to make her own path. She left her five-year-old son with her sister Flora, who was newly-wed (and soon to be widowed), and, with her three-year-old girl, followed some cousins who had gone up north. A year later, she would move to Chicago alone with both children. Mamá remembers this as the longest year of her life.

In Chicago, my mother went to work in factories. Doña Jovita, the curandera who took care of Mamá's two children while she worked, convinced the young mother to marry her teenage son. The next summer, I was born. Mamá stayed in factories until the last one closed up and packed off to Southeast Asia, leaving its union workers without work and some without pensions, and sending my mother into early retirement.

Mamá, a dark mestiza, inherited the complexes and fears of the colonized and the strange sense of national pride that permeates the new society of the conquered. Although she lived in Chicago for over forty years, she spoke only Spanish. She threw out English words—*zas, zas, zas*—like stray bullets leveled at gringos, at grandchildren, at her African American Avon manager.

When I was twelve, I saw Mamá's Mexico City for the first time. My mother and I traveled from Chicago to Nuevo Laredo by car. It was possibly the hottest place on earth in the month of July. Mamá didn't have much choice about when to travel, since the first two weeks of July were when the factory where she worked closed down and workers were given vacation time. Mamá paid a young Mexican who was looking for riders to take us to the border. The car broke down, we slept in it at night, we were refused service at gas stations and in restaurants in the South. Finally, we got to my great-grandmother's two-room wooden house with an outhouse and a shower outside.

I had made friends with the little girl next door, Rosita, on a previous visit to Nuevo Laredo. At that time, we climbed trees and fed the chickens and took sides with each other against her older brother. That's how and why I learned to write Spanish, to write to my friend. My mother said it was also to exchange letters with Mamá Grande, my mother's grandmother, but I wanted to keep up with Rosita. My mother, after long days at the factory, would come home to make dinner, and after the dishes and just before bed, she, with her sixth-grade education and admirable penmanship, would sit me down at the kitchen table and teach me how to write in Spanish, phonetically, with soft vowels, with humor, with a pencil, and with no book.

On the next visit, Rosita was fourteen. She had crossed over to that place of no return—breasts and boys. Her dark cheeks were flushed all the time, and in place of the two thick plaits with red ribbons she once wore, she now left her hair loose down her back. She didn't want to climb trees anymore. I remember a quiet, tentative conversation in the bedroom she shared with her grandmother who had raised her. Not long after that, Rosita ran off—with whom, where, or what became of her life, I was never to know.

In Nuevo Laredo we were met by my tía Flora—who had also traveled from Chicago—with her five children, ranging from ages fourteen to four. The husbands of these two sisters did not come along on this pilgrimage because they were men who, despite having families, were not family men. They passed up their traditional right to accompany their wives and children on the temporary repatriation.

There were too many children to sleep in the house, so we were sent up to the flat roof to sleep under the stars. My mother had not known that she needed permission from my father to take me into México, so with my cousin's birth certificate to pass me off as Mexican-born, we all got on a train one day, and I illegally entered Mexico City.

Our life in Chicago was not suburban backyards with swings and grassy lawns. It was not what I saw on TV. And yet it was not the degree of poverty in which we all found ourselves immersed overnight, through inheritance, birth, bad luck, or destiny. It was the destiny that my mother and her sister had dodged by doing as their mother, María de Jesús, had done decades before (for a period of her life at least) by getting the hell out of México, however they could. It was destiny in México that my mother's little brother refused to reject because of his hatred for capitalism, which he felt was embodied by the United States. Leonel came out of the México of Diego and Frida and was a proud communist. Dark and handsome in his youth, with thin lips that curled up, giving him the permanent expression of a cynic, the brother left behind came to get us at the little hotel in México City where my mother's stepfather, who was still selling books on a street corner, had installed us the night before. He'd met us at the train station, feeding us all bowls of atole for our late meal at the restaurant where his credit was good.

My cousin Sandra and I opened the door for Tío Leonel. We didn't know who he was. We told him our mothers had gone on an errand, taking the younger children with them. My tío Leonel did not step all the way into the room. We were young females alone, and for him to do so would have been improper. He looked me up and down with black eyes as black as my mother's, as black as mine, and knitted eyebrows as serious as Mamá's and as serious as mine were to become.

"You are Raquel's daughter?' he asked. I nodded. And then he left.

He returned for us later, Mamá and me and my tiá Flora and her five children, eight of us all together, plus big suitcases, and took us to his home. Home for Tío Leonel was a dark room in a vecindad. Vecinndades are communal living quarters. Families stay in single rooms. They share toilet and water facilities. The women have a tiny closet for a kitchen just outside their family's room, and they cook on a griddle on the floor. I don't remember my uncle's common-law wife's name. I am almost certain that it was María, but that would be a lucky guess. I remember my cousins were all younger than me and their cuh-razy chilango accents. But I don't remember their names or how many there were then. There were nearly ten—but not ten yet—because that would be the total number my uncle and his woman would eventually have. Still, it felt like ten. So now there were four adults and at least thirteen children, age fourteen and under, staying in one room.

We didn't have to worry about crowding the bathroom because the toilets were already shared by the entire vecindad. There were no lights and no plumbing. At night sometimes my uncle cleverly brought in an electrical line from outside and connected a bulb. This was not always possible or safe. The sinks used for every kind of washing were unsanitary. Sandra and I went to wash our hands and faces one morning and both stepped back at the sight of a very ugly black fish that had burst out of the drainpipe and was swimming around in the large plugged-up basin.

For entertainment, we played balero with our cousins, who were experts. Balero was a handheld toy where the object of the game was to flip a wooden ball on a string onto a peg. My little cousins could not afford a real balero, even the cheap kind you find in abundance in colorful mercados, and made their own using cans, found string, and stones or cork.

A neighbor in the vecindad who owned the local candy stand had a black-and-white portable TV. At a certain hour every evening, she charged the children who could afford it to sit in the store to watch their favorite cartoon show.

I was twelve years old, Sandra was thirteen, and her older brother was fourteen. We were beyond cartoon shows and taking balero contests seriously, and we were talking our early teen talk to each other in English. It was 1965 and the Rolling Stones were singing "(I Can't Get No) Satisfaction" in English over Spanish radio on my cousin's made-in-Japan transistor, and we insolent US-born adolescents wanted no part of México. Not the México of the amusement park, La Montaña Rusa, where we went one day and had great fun on the roller coaster. Not the México of sleeping under the stars on the roof of my tío Aurelio's home in Nuevo Laredo. Not the México of the splendid gardens of Chapultepec Park, of the cadet heroes, Los Niños Héroes, who valiantly but fatally fought off the invasion of US troops. We wanted no part of *this* México, where we all slept on the mattress our mothers had purchased for us on the first night in my tío Leonel's home. It was laid out in the middle of the room, and six children and two grown women slept on it crossways, lined up neatly like Chinese soldiers on the front line at night in the trenches, head-to-toe, head-to-toe. My tío and his wife and children all slept around us on piles of rags.

We had, with one train ride, stepped right into our mothers' México, unchanged in the nearly two decades since their departure.

YEARS LATER, WHEN I was living on my own in California, I met my family at the appointed meeting place—my tío Aurelio's in Nuevo Laredo—and traveled south by van with everybody to Mexico City. My tía Flora, this time without any of her children, came along, too. It was 1976, the birthday of the United States, but in México, my elders were all dying. The great-grandmother, Apolinar, had died earlier that same year and we had only recently received word of it. The great-uncle and border official, Tío Aurelio, had a heart condition and also died before this visit. My tía Flora's veracruzano bookselling father had died that year, too. We had only the little brother Leonel to visit. The young anticapitalista—once so proud of his sole possession (a new bicycle, which eventually was stolen), devoted to his family in his own way (although the older children had gone off on their own, while the youngest sold Chiclets on the streets)—was on his deathbed at forty.

Leonel was suffering from a corroded liver, cirrhosis ridden. By then, his lot had improved so that he had two rooms, a real bed, and electricity, but not much more. We stood around his bed and visited awhile so he could meet his brother-in-law and some other members of my mother's family whom he had never known before.

We went to visit his oldest daughter, around my age, at the house where she worked as a live-in domestic. She could not receive company, of course, but was allowed to visit with us outside for a bit. We dropped in on her older brother, too. He had an honest-to-goodness apartment—three whole rooms and its own kitchen. All grown, he worked in a factory and had a young family of his own.

One evening, my tía Flora and I ran into Leonel on the street, not far from where the cousin with the apartment lived. He was now a yellowish wire of a man and appeared quite drunk, his pants held up by a rope. He glanced at me, and then asked my tía Flora, "Is this Raquel's daughter?" My tía, in her usual happy-sounding way, said, "Yes, yes, of course she is the hija of Raquel." And then Tía, who is more veracruzana than chilanga—that is, more palm than granite—laughed a summer-rainstorm laugh.

Of course I was and am the daughter of Raquel. But I was the one born so far north that not only my tío but all my relatives in México found it hard to think me real. The United States was Atlantis—and there was no Atlantis—and therefore having been born there, I could not exist. He nodded at my aunt, who was real, but not at me, who was a hologram, and went on his way.

"My poor brother," my tía said, "he looks like Cantinflas," comparing him to the renowned comedic actor, famous for his derelict appearance and street ways. That was the last time we saw him, and by the end of summer, he was dead.

If the double "rock" in Mamá's name (and the "castle" at the end through marriage) had dubbed her the stoic sister, the flower in Flora's name perfumed her urban life and warded off the sadness of trying times. And those had been many in my tía's life, multiplied with the years as her children grew up far from México in Chicago's poverty.

So it was that night that my tía and I, riding a city bus, jumped off suddenly in a plaza where trios and duos of musicians gathered for hire, and we brought a late-night serenade to Mamá and family at our hotel. That was when my tía Flora and I bonded as big-time dreamers. After the serenade and after Dad (who came on this trip) had brought out a bottle of mescal and we had all shared a drink with the musicians, Mamá told me some of the stories I share here now.

By migrating, Mamá saved me from the life of a live-in domestic and perhaps from inescapable poverty in Mexico City. But it was the perseverance of Raquel the Rock and the irrepressible sensuality of Flora the thick-stemmed calla lily that saved me, too. "Ana del Aire," my mother called me (after the popular telenovela of the 1970s). Woman of the air, not earthbound, not rooted to one place—not to México where Mamá's mother died, not to Chicago where I was born and where my mother passed away on a dialysis machine, not to New Mexico where I made a home for my son and later, alone for myself—but to everywhere at once.

And when the world so big becomes a small windowless room for me, I draw from the vision of María de Jesús. I read and write poems. I listen to music. I sing—with the voice of my ancestors from Guanajuato who had birds in their throats. I paint with my heart, with acrylics and oils on linen and cotton. On the phone, I talk to my son, to a lover, and with my comadres. I tell a story. I make a sound and leave a mark—as palatable as a prickly pear, more solid than stone.

MY FATHER'S PILLOW TALK

CHARLES JOHNSON

My father would not have approved of me writing this essay about him. He was a private man, one not at all interested in my sharing intimate details of his life, or having other people talking about him, "putting his business in the street," as the old saying goes.

But I've been a father myself, raised a boy and girl, now have a four-year-old grandson, and I think it's important at this moment in our cultural history—especially given the centuries devoted to the demonization of Black men which continues to this very day—that we reflect deeply on the crucial role that strong fathers play in shoring up a family and, by virtue of that, providing a solid foundation for our communities. So in this essay I dare to talk about my dad, even though he'd feel uncomfortable with my doing so if he was alive. He wasn't perfect, but through his daily example I learned how challenging it is to be a full-grown man—providing for one's wife and children, treating all others with respect, negotiating successfully the world of work and how to move through a racist society with grace, dignity, and confidence. The example my father set for me in regard to these matters made him the only man on earth that I ever felt I had to answer to or please. To fail him or my mother in any way—well, that was a thought I dreaded more than any other.

Of all the roles we play during our lives, I believe that parenting is the most important. The moment one has children—who are so vulnerable, so dependent upon us from their first breaths—is the moment one stops being a child oneself. (And, if the truth be told, parenting is actually a lifetime sentence.)

And so, against what would have been my father's objections, I composed "My Father's Pillow Talk" as a way to honor him as well as all those Black men from Reconstruction forward who knew how to "make a way out of no way."

N MY FATHER'S HOUSE, THERE WERE GENTLE RULES THAT HAD TO be honored. One was about bedtime. All the lights had to be out by 11 P.M. Everything had to be finished by that time: my homework, any drawings I was working on, and my chores, which included washing and putting away the dishes, and making sure the kitchen was clean and orderly for our family's use the next morning when my parents and I were up promptly by 7 A.M. I always felt at ages fourteen and fifteen that doing the dishes every night *ought* to be annoying to me—or to any teenager. But even though I would have preferred to be drawing, it was a chore I discovered that I enjoyed because, unknown to my quietly pious parents, I'd secretly begun the practice of meditation, which I'd read about in one of the books on yoga that came to our house from the three book clubs my mother belonged to. Fifty years ago, I'd stand there at the sink for thirty minutes, my hands immersed in warm, sudzy water, my thoughts absorbed by this one simple activity, and for a brief time I forgot everything, including myself, as I carefully cleaned then dried each plate, spoon, fork, pot, cup, and glass we'd used, as a family, during the day.

I was aware of the water's temperature as it slowly cooled, the fragility and ephemeral quality of the iridescent bubbles as they burst on the water's surface, how the water itself wrinkled the skin on my hands, and the way porcelain, glass, tin, and stainless steel felt against my fingers. I made sure that not a speck of food or grime remained on anything—the same way I'd clean away eraser crumbs and the residue of pencil lines from a drawing I'd finished inking. For thirty minutes every night I knew the kind of tranquility that only comes from being mindful of every minute detail in what one is doing. Once I was finished, something my father often said when he concluded a chore echoed through my mind. Whenever he lifted that last heavy box, or hammered home that last nail, he would remove the cigar from his mouth, smile, happily cast his gaze at the last remaining item that brought a period of work successfully to an end, and he would say, *That's the one I was looking for.*

After straightening up the kitchen, I made my way to my tiny bedroom. All the space was taken up by my desk, dresser, bed, the stacks of novels that I read (I made myself finish one book a week starting my freshman year in high school, then it became two and sometimes three) and my twenty-five-dollar drawing table before which I sat dreaming of one day becoming a professional artist. Sometimes its broad, rectangular surface seemed to me to be like a movie screen onto which I could project images that hitherto existed only in my head where no one could see them, and at other times it felt like a magic carpet I could ride into unexplored realms of the imagination. Although my father bought me that drawing table as a Christmas present, it would symbolize that fourteenth year of my life, the first real crisis I experienced as a young man, the one time my father's world and mine collided.

The trek to my bedroom took me past my parents' bedroom. If their door was open, I would see my father in his pajamas and on his knees beside the bed where my mother was already sleeping. His head was bowed, both his callused hands were pressed together in prayer, and whatever he was saying was spoken so low, so softly that I couldn't make out the words. It looked to me as if he was talking to his pillow. I knew at that time in our lives, as a family, he probably had a lot of difficult words to bounce off that pillow. Some, no doubt, were about me.

For a few seconds I quietly studied him as he prayed. He was a proud, frugal man. He had only simple, inexpensive pleasures. For example, playing billiards on a table he set up in our garage, where I spent many summer nights doing my best to beat him at eight-ball. If you have seen the character called Hoke, played by Morgan Freeman in the film *Driving Miss Daisy*, then you have seen my father. In my hometown, he and my mother were respected by everyone who knew them. He was a South Carolina boy born into a big family in 1922. Six boys. Six girls. A family of farmers where even toddlers were taught to work early, carrying tools and water to their older siblings laboring in the fields. Not once in my life did I hear him utter an oath stronger than the word "Shoot!" He was content to own but one carefully preserved suit, which he wore to Ebenezer A.M.E. Church, where he loved to hear the minister preach and the choir (which included a couple of my cousins) sing. Despite his workaholic habits, he told his employers that he would do overtime and time-and-a-half on holidays, but he would never, never work on a Sunday because, as he put it,

"Sunday was for church." Around our house, my dad was never idle, nor did he let me do much woolgathering. If he wasn't painting, he was repairing something; if he wasn't repairing something, he was planning some improvement he intended to make (and thirty years later, whenever he came to visit my home in Seattle, he was forever tinkering with things I'd been too busy to attend to). He was the one man I saw day and night, the closest example I had for measuring my strengths and weaknesses. He was my first meditation on manhood. My challenge. My Rosetta Stone.

So I studied him the way I would a book, working to decipher his words, his life, which seemed to unfold so far away from the liberal arts and humanities I was exposed to in school. Every day I wondered what the meaning of his life might possibly mean for my own. My generation, the notoriously rebellious baby boomers, was the first in American history to be taught that we should be creative—that creative expression was essential to being fully human. *His* generation, however, was just taught that it had to work. And, I swear, I think he enjoyed finding the most humbling labor he could for his only child—like a Zen master testing one of his disciples, putting him to work in the monastery kitchen precisely because he didn't enjoy doing the dishes, helping him see that even in the most repetitive, dirty, and boring task you might discover insight and inspiration.

Looking back, I remember coming home after my freshman year in college with no job lined up for the summer of 1967. On my first night back, my father announced to me that I'd better set my clock early—around 5 A.M.—because he had already secured a job for me: as one of the student garbagemen employed by the City of Evanston. I, being a good Confucian son, did that job for two summers, tramping down hot alleyways with older Black men, hauling the filth of the affluent on my back in a big, plastic tub, sweeping away dead rats and maggots. After work, after sharing a beer with men who did this all year round for a living, I'd come home filthy, smelling from head to toe of sewage-tainted water from garbage cans. It was the kind of honest, blue-collar work—and the men who did such work—that my father felt I needed to know, because—well, because *he* was one of them. And, briefly, so was I.

Because of the differences between us, I waited patiently when I was fourteen to see if he would slip or make a mistake, which I thought would give *me* permission to slip or make a mistake, too. But except for one time (which I'll talk about in a minute), he never did, not even when a Black criminal stole every penny he saved to buy this very house we were in, where every night I washed the dishes and watched him as he talked to his pillow. I know that theft must have hurt him, because he was the kind of man who on paydays when his coworkers went off to drink up their wages, dutifully brought his paychecks home for my mother to take to the bank. There's no need to elaborate on this anecdote, except to say that when the police came to the apartment we lived in to get a description of the perpetrator, I watched him lean against the doorway, smoking his ubiquitous cigar, silent as a tree, and staring—just staring—off into space, reviewing his options after this disaster, figuring out how to make his next move—how to make a way out of no way. He managed to do just that, getting us into our first home on the schedule he had planned, and this was not strange because whenever he set his mind to doing something it was like a dog chewing single-mindedly on a bone until whatever he desired or thought right was done.

All in all, we were happy as a family. And that included me until the day when I finally told my father what I planned to do with my future.

I'm sure I chose the wrong moment to spring my decision on him. In the early 1960s, he was working three jobs to support my mother and me, without complaint—a day job doing construction, an evening job as a night watchman for the City of Evanston, Illinois, and on the weekends he helped an elderly white couple do repairs on their home. Late one afternoon, I approached him in our living room as he let his weight sink into the soft cushions of a chair, tired after working construction all day and with just an hour or so before he had to head out the door for his evening job.

"Dad," I said, "I've figured out what I want to do with my life."

Without looking up, he mumbled, "That's good."

I took a step closer to him. "Really, I'm serious. You know I always get good grades in my art classes. That's what I really care about. And that's what I want to be. An artist."

When I said that, he looked at me with the gravest concern. He'd never known any successful Black American artists, because in 1962 there were very few one could point to. He said, "Chuck, they don't let Black people do that. You should think about something else."

I told him I didn't *want* to think about anything else.

But having said what he believed, he said no more. And, true to his nature, he did not budge. But those eight words felt as if he'd delivered a death blow to me. Art was the only passion I had. Yet his was the irrefutable voice of 244 years of slavery, then the decades of segregation, discrimination, and disenfranchisement that had shaped his childhood and consciousness. How could I argue with *that*?

For days after this brief conversation I was gloomy, crushed, and directed many an evil thought his way. I started talking to *my* pillow night after night, because a future without creating was inconceivable to me.

Finally, I dashed off a letter to a perfect stranger in New York, a liberal, Jewish man I'd read about in *Writer's Digest*. I never expected him to answer me, but in 1962 he was what I was burning to be: an illustrator, editor, prolific writer, and he offered a two-year correspondence course in cartooning. His name was Lawrence Lariar. He was cartoon editor of *Parade* magazine, a former Disney studio "story man," as they were called, and for twenty years he served as editor for *Best Cartoons of the Year*. In the 1960s, he boasted that he'd published one hundred books. Among those books were several works of mystery fiction. These were bad imitations of Mickey Spillane (who was pretty bad himself), which he wrote under pseudonyms like Adam Knight, Michael Lawrence, and Michael Stark. These pulpy crime novels have long been forgotten and rightly so. They had titles such as *Stone Cold Blonde*, published in 1951, with this blurb on the back, "When private detective Steve Conacher sets out to investigate the murder of one of his best friends (who also happens to run a plush house of ill-repute) he tangles with some of the loosest women and rottenest men in New York." And here's an example of the kind of prose one found in *Stone Cold Blonde*: "Mary Ray was the queen of New York's call girls. But Mary had an enemy who dealt in murder and Steve Conacher vowed to track down the killer before others died. But he had to slug his way through plenty of slime— and illicit temptation—before he nailed the murderer."

Lariar was a true hack writer, and there is much to be said in support of pulp fiction, at least for its short-lived entertainment value. To do him justice, I have to add that when I finally read *Stone Cold Blonde* in my twenties, I recorded in my writer's workbook that Lariar did an admirable job of creating his diminutive detective Steve Conacher, how the pacing of the story never slowed, that one party scene is hilarious, and that he managed to evoke the nightclubs and characters in his version of New York City quite well. In the early '60s, I had not read any of his novels, though—I was more interested in drawing stories than writing them.

But I wrote him a desperate teenager's letter. I told him what my father had told me. To my surprise, I received a bristling letter back from Lariar within a week. "Your father is *wrong*," he said. "You can do whatever you want with your life. All you need is a good drawing teacher." I wrote him back, asking if he'd be my teacher. His reply was all right, but I'd have to pay for his two-year course. There were no free lunches with Lawrence Lariar.

It was only later when I became his student and traveled to New York to visit Lariar during my sophomore and junior years in high school that he told me how much pleasure he found in the anger of his neighbors when he invited groups of Black artists to his Long Island home for lessons.

I showed his first letter to my father. I read it aloud to him, emphasizing the words, *Your father is wrong.* My dad listened deeply. A kind of quietness came into his eyes. I was talking again about something—the arts—alien to him. Nevertheless, he gave me a shake of his head that said, "OK, you win." He admitted that he was wrong. That he had slipped. And he agreed to make the monthly payments for my two years of study with Lariar. Long before anyone knew me as a writer, when I was seventeen, I began publishing illustrations for the brochure of a Chicago entertainment company (and also stories in my high school newspaper). I still have that first professional dollar I made in 1965, which I happily waved in my father's face when I earned it, framed in my study. For seven really wonderful years, before I became a creative writer, I published hundreds of drawings in Black magazines like *Negro Digest, Ebony,* then the *Chicago Tribune,* a Black imitation of *Playboy* called *Players,* my college newspaper, regular editorial drawings for a newspaper in Southern Illinois, two collections of political satire and, toward the end of this period, I created, hosted and co-produced in 1970 an early how-to-draw PBS series called "Charlie's Pad" that was entirely based on my lessons with Lariar, who remained a dear and supportive friend until his death in 1981. Furthermore, my dad even acquiesced to my attending an art school that accepted me in Illinois (though I decided at the last minute not to go).

He was not a man who expressed any interest in "culture," or the suite of disciplines we loosely identify as the humanities. But when he died nine years ago, he had five—I counted them—*five* preachers at his funeral in rural South Carolina. *That* was culture. His culture. I realized one of these ministers knew my father extremely well when he said from the pulpit, "Mr. Johnson was never in the choir. He didn't serve on any committees or as a deacon. He didn't say much, but he was there *every* Sunday, and he apologized to me if he had to be out of town." Lariar taught me how to draw professionally, but my dad taught me how to work, how to regard everything I did, seen by others or never seen, as being a portrait of myself, and even a kind of sacrifice. The oneness of the work and the worker. He taught me that loyalty, reliability, resilience, truth and the willingness to accept the fact that we can be wrong, unselfishness, resourcefulness, faith, morality, and humility were ideals to strive for every day. He taught me how to talk to my pillow during good times and bad, which prepared me, as a Buddhist, to chant Sanskrit verses on my zafu, another kind of pillow. These things for him were always unstated dimensions of what it means to be cultured and human and civilized—things I learned from watching *him*, not in a fourteen-week college course. And he taught me something even more important. When he financially backed me up on something he barely understood, I realized that he had shown me the true definition of love: helping others because you believe in them, regardless of whether their dreams outstrip your own understanding.

And so, as I wrote this . . . I heard his voice urging me to complete this true, autobiographical story. When I reached the end, *this* page, my father's words were there again, saying:

That's the one I was looking for.

THE POWER AND LIMITATIONS OF VICTIM-IMPACT STATEMENTS

REBECCA MAKKAI

I was spending the week in Denver teaching at a writers' workshop when the Brock Turner verdict came in. I felt helpless and infuriated, and that night, over drinks, a friend and I discussed it. I came back to my hotel room and couldn't sleep, and so I wrote this essay. I'm not normally one for a quick, reactive piece—I don't write all that quickly, and I know it's not healthy for me to hang on every change in the news cycle—but this felt cathartic. One of the reasons it came so fast is that this is stuff I've been chewing on, thinking about, talking about, for years. I never thought I'd write about it, though. After a few awkward attempts in high school and college to fictionalize things, I'd decided I didn't want my writing hijacked by this subject. That changed for me with this essay, perhaps because the times have also changed. And I think the change has stuck; my next novel (like a lot of novels being written right now) deals with female rage.

L AST WEEK, THE SANTA CLARA COUNTY DISTRICT ATTORNEY'S office released a victim-impact statement written by a twenty-three-year-old woman raped on the Stanford campus. The statement, which has gone viral, is sharp, clear, stunningly open, occasionally funny. Its author is a very good writer in the purest way: she makes us feel some sliver of what she felt.

I was startled to learn that she'd read this statement out loud in court to her assailant—that she hadn't just been able to slip it under the judge's door in the middle of the night and leave it at that. I wrote my own victim-impact statement at sixteen, and, on Monday, as I read about the Stanford case, I tried to remember what the procedure had been; I thought I had handed mine in like a term paper, or sent it through the mail. And then, on Monday night, it came back to me, twenty-two years after the fact: I did read my own statement out loud, in court, to my abuser. I'd had a choice, and I chose to do it. I might have been braver then than I am now.

That I didn't remember this before has less to do with my blocking it out than with the fact that the memory is overshadowed by bigger plot points. Because, as soon as I delivered the statement, I was accused of plagiarism.

It was the summer of 1994, and I'd been listening to "Janie's Got a Gun" on repeat since May. That summer, I read James Joyce for the first time; I also still had an American Girl doll in my closet. I was ten years past learning to ride a two-wheeler; I was ten years from publishing my first short story. From the age of seven to thirteen I had been sexually molested by a family friend who occasionally lived in our house; in the summer of 1994, I was a few months from losing my virginity to someone I liked. I was closer to a healthy sense of sexuality, both chronologically and emotionally, than I was to the abuse.

At our local Children's Advocacy Center, in suburban Illinois, a place filled with cheap stuffed animals, they asked me to point to the violated parts of a paper doll, as if I were a preverbal toddler. A lawyer named Sean (I was old enough, apparently, to call him that) asked me to write a victim-impact statement.

It strikes me now that there's a remarkable volume of literature sealed in case files across the country. People writing the most honest things—in many cases, the only personal essays—they'll ever write. I was an aspiring writer who took herself terribly seriously, and so I tackled that thing as a writing assignment. I used metaphor. I used vivid examples. There were *scenes*. I went through at least ten drafts. I was torn between the desire to show how well I was dealing with things and the imperative to show that I was not OK, that this man's actions had derailed my life in a thousand ways. Because how could both be true? I wound up editing any mention of

209

recovery out of the letter. Weren't my actions a show of strength already? When Sean saw the letter, he was so pleased that he asked if I'd give permission for it to be shown, anonymously, to other victims as a model. I was thrilled.

I read it on the witness stand, in the baggy dress I'd been advised to wear because I had a large chest and we didn't want the judge to get the wrong impression of me. He was supposed to see me as the child I'd been, and a chest wouldn't help. I was counseled not to wear makeup.

The defense lawyer was either inept or trying, actively, to throw the case. He disclosed in court, although he didn't need to and the statute of limitations had passed, that the defendant had admitted to raping two women. The lawyer mispronounced words. He sweated through his shirt. And then, in his closing statement, he accused me of not writing my own victim-impact statement. He knew teenagers, he said. He had a teenage daughter, he had a teenage nephew. And his teenage acquaintances could not write that well.

The implication broadened from there. If I had fudged this statement, what else might I have fabricated? Even though the guy had already pleaded guilty, even though this was a statement of emotional impact, not my actual testimony, the victim was not to be trusted.

What unnerves me now about this resurfaced memory is that, for the past twenty years or so—from college on—public readings have been sacred to me. They are places where, regardless of the size of the crowd, I feel in control, where people are there to listen. Some of the best moments of my life have been readings in bookstores on the days my novels were released and I was surrounded by friends. To remember, suddenly, that I once performed a public reading of such a different kind makes me look forward to my next reading less.

How can you know six months or a year after a rape what the impact on your life will really be? A victim-impact statement is necessarily limited by when it was written. At sixteen, I had the benefit of three years of distance, some therapy, and a small sense of how the events of my childhood might affect the rest of my adolescence, at least. But a victim-impact statement is not a living document. I cannot call the courthouse to update it every time I notice something new—that, for instance, whenever I pass a certain car dealership I've driven by almost every day of my adult life I'm washed over with the exact queasy feeling I get when I pass roadkill. Or that, at the age of thirty-eight, I still avoid using the common noun that is homophonous with my abuser's name.

The judge in my case wasn't having any of the defense lawyer's games. I'd like to say I was lucky, but can you call it luck when it's what everyone deserves and few get? In his sentencing statement, the judge said—and these are words I remember precisely, because they went straight to my sixteen-year-old ego—"While her written statement bordered on the eloquent, so did her testimony." It was perhaps the best literary review I'll ever receive. He then handed down what was, at the time, a fairly harsh sentence in Illinois for aggravated third-degree child sexual abuse: ten months of work release.

I don't imagine that victim-impact statements sway judges. I don't imagine they reform criminals. I knew better, even at sixteen, than to expect my letter to sway anyone. If I wanted to prove something with my statement, it was that I was a good writer. That's not as shallow as it sounds. I wanted, specifically, to prove to my abuser that I was now a grown-up who could talk circles around him. That I owned the narrative in a way he never could. That I was smarter than him. That he'd picked the wrong kid.

I wrote a few terrible stories in college about sexual abuse but, until now, haven't touched the subject again. Someone asked me once if I was scared to write about it. That's not it at all. I don't feel compelled to write about it anymore, because it's already out of my system. I had the chance to speak, and—because in this case I had a judge who listened, because I felt heard—I moved on.

It's a mercy that impact statements don't need updating, even if some of us would love for rapists to receive weekly reports for the rest of their lives on the damage they've caused. If I could revise mine, twenty-two years on, it would say that I am over it, and that it is no part of who I am. It would also say the opposite.

GRAVE NEWS

SAJA ELSHAREIF

Based on a true story, this piece takes place in Mokena, a southwest suburb of Chicago. It tells about a family that comes together when Baba, the father in the story, is deeply affected by events in Gaza. While the four children do not really know their relatives back home, they are affected by their father's reactions, the idea of losing everything, and the possibility of never again seeing their extended family.

Through actual news clips and family moments, this piece explores what it means for family members to be there for one another, the differences between generations of immigrants, and the reality of a war that has long been unknown and misunderstood by most Americans.

Finally, this story explores what it is like to grow up in Chicago, one of the most diverse cities in the United States, where first-generation immigrants from a variety of countries likely face a similar divide between generations, a noticeable difference in lifestyle choices, and the ever-growing distance between themselves and their parents' homes.

The piece is part of a larger collection in progress, which is a compilation of short stories based on my father's childhood in Gaza, Palestine. I have found inspiration in the most minute details of my father's recollections and how they relate to my own life. I hope that retelling these stories will help to inform others about events that have affected my family personally and also to bridge a common ground with immigrant and non-immigrant readers of all generations.

NEW YORK TIMES: **JERUSALEM, JULY 24, 1995**—*As Israel and the Palestine Liberation Organization raced against a deadline for new agreements, the West Bank and Gaza Strip were jolted today by their most severe violence in recent months.*

BBC: GAZA, UPDATED ON BBC SEPTEMBER 1, 2014, AND ORIGINALLY PUBLISHED IN B'TSELEM'S RECORDS IN 2009—*Around 1,391 Palestinians were killed, including an estimated 759 civilians . . . Reports say this included 344 children and 110 women.*

BBC: GAZA, SEPTEMBER 1, 2014—*The UN says at least 2,104 Palestinians died, including 1,462 civilians, of whom 495 were children and 253 women.*

THE NEWS HAS been an additional member of my family for as long as I can remember. Images of charred bodies, amputated limbs, and bleeding children continue to be daily visitors in our household.

Baba usually has his laptop, the television, and the newspaper all within reach, constantly streaming the most recent events. It's almost like he is divided between us and them: his family here and his family there.

The news acts as his portal, his connection to "back home." He isn't merely reading, nor is he listening for information. He is searching for familiarity: a familiar place, name, or face.

Most days, the four of us children hadn't even paid much attention to the scrolling headlines or flashing images. It wasn't that we didn't care, it just wasn't personal. It wasn't a Mokena police blotter report about the rare break-in in a neighboring subdivision, or a suburban news article reporting about the closing of a mom-and-pop store. The news my father tuned into seemed so far away. And yet, it was on in the next room, buzzing in the background, as we transitioned from dinnertime to our usual evening activities.

While my friends at school hardly ate dinner with their families, at our house Mama always made dinnertime a priority. Every night, we waited for Baba to get home from work, then my sister and I set the table, someone lowered the TV volume, and we each took our seats. If anyone had fallen asleep, Mama would keep calling their names until they joined the rest of us. No matter the annoyed looks and protests she would get, she reminded us of how lucky we were. She would say, "People wish they could have dinner with their families once a week, let alone every night." Perhaps Mama was right, but when the usual teasing began, I wondered.

"Hey Moe, are you going to eat all that?" Ahmed would sneer. This was a daily occurrence. At dinnertime, my two brothers, Ahmed and Mohammed, would often exchange comments under their breath. They either made fun of each other or ganged up on my sister, Asmaa. I was the oldest, so they were a bit softer in their insults to me, but still irritating.

"Don't call me Moe!" Mohammed would answer. Asmaa and I would stifle our laughter, shaking our heads at Ahmed's annoyingness and Mohammed's vulnerability.

At dinner, we would take turns talking about our days, which typically meant hearing about Baba's patients in the radiology department, discussing Mohammed's career choice (last he wanted to be a lawyer), or laughing at Mama's strange encounters with baggers and cashiers in grocery stores. Tata, my maternal grandmother, said almost nothing at all, because the rest of us spoke mostly in English.

By the time empty plates piled high, Mama would race Tata to the sink, and my sister and I would clear the rest of the table. Someone would make a full pot of coffee, and my brothers would somehow disappear, only to reappear again once the cleaning was over.

Today Baba was the last one sitting at the table. When he finally got up, a boyish grin formed across his face. The six-foot tall, broad-shouldered man with salt-and-pepper hair brought his plate to the sink, where a much more petite Mama in polka-dot pajamas was washing dishes.

"Here, I cleaned my plate really well, so there's one less to wash," he said, smiling as he squeezed her shoulder.

"Sahetein," she said proudly. "Since you loved the mlokhia so much, come help wash the pots."

"Fiiiine, honey. I guess that's what husbands are for." He playfully sprayed her with the dish hose.

When all was done, my sister, grandmother, and I went to the family room, where we usually spent the rest of the evening. Asmaa and I ignored the coffeepot's beeps and waited for our parents to tell one of us to pour for everyone else. Ahmed had gone up to his room to study for a chemistry exam, and Tata was sitting next to Mama on the couch, her head swaying as she fought sleep. The TV had been turned up just enough that it was audible.

"Go take a shower, so you can finish your homework. You have school tomorrow," Mama told Mohammed for the tenth time that evening.

"I will, Mama, I will," he said, eyes glued to his cell phone.

"Moe, you're such a baby," Asmaa said, rolling her eyes.

Baba had just joined us in the family room, folded prayer mat in hand, when he suddenly stopped in his tracks.

"Shhh, listen!" he said sharply, as he dove for the remote and turned up the TV volume near maximum. Quickly coming around, he sat next to me. Balancing on the edge of the couch, he leaned forward, elbow resting on his knee, balled fist holding up his chin.

Just when I started to wonder whether anyone else had noticed how deeply my father's brows had furrowed, Mohammed began to make his usual escape from seemingly sensitive situations. Squeezing past the rest of us, who were waiting to see what the commotion was about, he had suddenly decided that taking a shower seemed like a good idea.

BBC: GAZA, JAN. 6, 2009—*United Nations investigators found that Israeli missiles killed thirty to forty Palestinians in the immediate vicinity of the Jabalia school in Gaza Strip, where hundreds of others had taken refuge during the Israel-Hamas conflict, Tuesday. The attack against the Jabalia school, also known as the al-Fakhoura school, which was run by the UN Refugee Agency in the Middle East, was among the six attacks against UN compounds cited in the report by a three-member investigative board.*

"Mama, what's going on? What's he saying?" Asmaa whispered, struggling to keep up with the newscaster's formal Arabic.

"That was my school," Baba said, pointing in disbelief to a building that was only half standing. Sometime during the news report, he had stood up, but not to his full height. He leaned forward a bit, with his head tilted slightly to the right, and his eyes almost squinting. It was almost as if he was doubtful of the information being presented in front of us. He continued this way, until the half-standing building reappeared on the screen. This time, the videographer showed a clearer shot of the destruction, and with this new view came a whole new sense of meaning. Perhaps my father had recalled memories that he had forgotten, or perhaps he had just realized that it really was his elementary school being televised. Either way, it seemed that something had broken inside of him, as he came crashing down on the couch, and held his face in his hands.

It was strange to see something that belonged to my father on TV. The only time my school appeared on TV, it was a name in a scrolling marquee, indicating a weather-related closing. The newscaster in a bulletproof vest showed Baba's school, now mostly a heap of rubble. Some people stood in awe, surrounded by children crying and struggling with their backpacks. As chaos took over the screen, people ran left and right.

The newscaster continued to talk about the situation surrounding the school and then switched to another reporter, who was in the residential part of the village

"That's my street," Baba said slowly. Winces began to steal into the places that usually wrinkled softly into smiles.

Mama squeezed between me and Baba. Holding his hand, she solemnly watched the report beside him.

Back and forth, our eyes shifting between the screen and my father, we watched as he watched the television. The death count escalated every few minutes on the bottom of the screen, and the live coverage showed the violence approaching my father's childhood home. The outbreaks continued.

My sister and I briefly exchanged glances and looked at Tata. Her trembling hand held the edge of her hijab.

"Ya haram . . . Ya haram," she whispered.

No one else spoke. No one asked for a translation or said anything at all. I don't even remember whether the newscaster continued to report the story.

If Baba hadn't told us that the street on TV was his, *we* wouldn't have recognized it at all. How would we? Our street was a concrete, paved street that led to a cul-de-sac with large brick houses. The homes in our subdivision featured vaulted ceilings, in-ground pools, and three-car garages. Neighbors usually waved in passing, but to me it seemed they were too busy leading corporate jobs to really get to know one another. The street on TV, however, was brick and lined with cement buildings that were nestled closely together. There were more pedestrians, fewer cars, and people embracing one another as they emerged from their homes. Graffiti and red stains covered the unfinished, gray exteriors of the homes. We knew better than to ask what the red stains were.

It was strange to watch people discover their losses for the first time. It wasn't something any of us had experience with. While my father took in the news from thousands of miles away, the live coverage showed people seeing destruction within their hometown for the first time. Emotion was fresh and real. Some had visible tears streaming down their faces, others shrieked and screamed, and some remained completely silent. It was difficult for me to watch. No one said it, but I knew we were all afraid of seeing one of my father's family members, or even worse—hearing their names as one of the deceased.

My brothers finally joined the rest of us. Their faces remained serious, meaning they had been keeping up with what was happening from the top of the stairs. Ahmed didn't crack any jokes and Mohammed looked slightly embarrassed for leaving.

Straining to breathe in air heavy with silence, we sat staring as the camera continued to scan up and down the street that was imprinted with my father's childhood. Numerous houses were still smoldering after being hit. Paramedics ran left and right, retrieving bodies from under the debris and carrying away unmoving figures on stretchers. None of the sheets blanketing the bodies were completely white anymore, and most victims' faces were covered.

Before long, our home was filled with the unfamiliar sounds of Baba crying and Mama consoling him. Our happiness, our safe place, had been completely transformed.

"Inshallah kheir," Mama repeated quietly. "Allah knows best."

My sister and I sat there awkwardly, wiping away our own tears. I didn't know what Asmaa felt, but I couldn't handle seeing Baba break down like that. It was as if our house and all of Mokena had come crumbling down, and none of us could do anything about it.

We hadn't heard names of any of the casualties yet, but witnessing what seemed to be the death of my father's childhood was in and of itself difficult.

Later that night, I thought about my father's stories. He had a magical way of telling his memories as stories, and as I grew up, I had grown fonder of them. I thought about the time when his older brother made him carry his backpack to school, about the time he won a Charles Dickens classic for having read the most books, and about the one pair of school pants that he owned. I even thought about the time he was jailed for a few hours, for staying past curfew on the other side of the checkpoint. I felt saddened by the news report and it gave me chills when I reminded myself that those hadn't been just stories, but actual memories.

I found myself thinking about my own trip to Gaza, back in 1995, when things were safer. In the photos, the smiling faces of my aunts and uncles looked back at us: Amto Samira, Amto Mona, Amo Mohammed, Amo Osama, and Amo Ezz. I was just five years old at the time. Pictures showed me with long, curly hair, with Asmaa and Ahmed, who looked like twins, always cradled in someone's arms. It had been over a decade since we'd last seen our relatives, but we had spoken to them occasionally. From person to person, the phone would go around, before the prepaid card ran out.

"Here! They speak Arabic," Baba would exclaim proudly. "Ask them what they're studying! Mashallah, Saja is studying English in college now, and Ahmed is planning to be a doctor."

Sometimes we avoided being around when the phone calls happened—not because we didn't want to talk to whomever was on the other end of the line—but because our Arabic was not perfect.

"Who cares if you make a mistake, this may be the last time you ever hear their voice," my dad would sternly prod us. We never really understood why he would dramatize a phone call like that, but obviously, he knew better.

Most of all, I really loved hearing Tata Halima's voice on the other end of the line. My uncles and father had often told me that I had their mother's big brown eyes, her sensitive nature, and her complexion. Baba was often the first to rush to console me if I was upset, because he said I looked just like her when my eyes welled up with tears.

Within a couple of minutes on the phone, Tata Halima would pray for my success, my health, my future, my entry to heaven, and ease in my life. She would tell me she wished to see me and my siblings, she would remind me to take care of my parents and make me promise not to forget her. Then, she would weep. By the end of the phone call, we would all be reaching for tissues. Even Mohammed, who wasn't born when we went to Gaza, would become red in the face. He had a strong connection to her too. Some things were more powerful than latitude and longitude.

We sat at the edge of our seats for days as we continued to watch for updates. News reports continued to report, and additional atrocities continued to unfold.

AL JAZEERA, GAZA, JAN. 8, 2009—*In the last 48 hours, forces have escalated attacks on the Gaza Strip; intensified artillery shelling and aerial bombardment in populated areas has resulted in the apparent targeting of civilians. Ten Palestinian civilians in Jabalia Camp, including a woman and her daughters, and another two children were killed.*

My father continually scanned the channels, fearing that he would receive news of our relatives. It was strange to be subconsciously looking for something that you feared, but we were all glued to the TV. Our breakfasts, dinners, lunches, and social media feeds had become synonymous with news. It ate with us, sat with us, and rode in cars with us. I even dreamt about it sometimes. In our home, laughter became scarce, smiles were forced, and tensions were great.

We had no choice. The news was our main source of information, and because the electricity in Gaza had been out for a month, the news had become a one-way communication between my father and home. Unfortunately, it never provided us with any reassurance and only gave us more reason to worry, as attacks were reported on the same block as their home.

WASHINGTON POST, JERUSALEM, JAN. 17, 2009—*The UN Security Council on Thursday adopted a resolution calling for a cease-fire in the Gaza Strip, hours after the United Nations announced it would suspend humanitarian aid deliveries in the territory, citing Israeli attacks on its facilities and personnel.*

A cease-fire had been reached. Transitioning between dinnertime and coffee now included a family prayer in the living room, which we all attended. We prayed for change, safety, happiness, and peace.

My father called his family every day at different times, hoping he would be lucky enough to get through. Each time, we lingered around him, waiting to see if anyone picked up, or if there would be anything other than a busy signal at the other end. One day, for a brief moment, he flashed a hint of his familiar smile, and told us again about how one of his older brothers would bully him into carrying his backpack for him on their way to school. It was an old story, one that he had told many times, but we all laughed. There was hope in the innocence of that brief moment, before he heaved a deep sigh, and went back to staring off at the TV.

There was so much stress, worry, and fear in our home; yet it seemed that no one else knew what was happening. Math, English, and science classes went on as usual. Students laughed on their way between buildings, professors still penalized late work, and people complained about Blue Line delays. No one stopped to ask if everything was OK, no one talked about events halfway across the world; no one seemed to know anything other than what was going on in Chicago. Neighbors were upset that they couldn't wash their fancy cars, because there were new water restrictions in town. One day, Asmaa had even come home in tears, because her teacher had laughed at her and said that Palestine was not a country. I felt torn between acting like everything was OK and wanting to let others know about what was going on.

On what seemed to be an ordinary day of news-watching, table-setting, and dinner-eating, Baba's voice shattered the thick silence as Asmaa and I helped Mama clear off the table. Rushing to the family room, we all surrounded my father, eager for a breath of good news. Even Tata had left her usual place on the family-room couch to see what was going on in the living room.

"Alhamdulilah! Alhamdulilah!" Baba cried. Tata Halima's voice was audible on the line. She was sobbing, as she told the story of their neighbors who had been victims in the attacks. Houses on both sides of them had been hit, and the results were unbearable.

"They had five daughters, each one more beautiful than the other. Still blossoming flowers, and they all died. Not one of their innocent children are left," she wept.

In a moment of selfishness, someone else's tragedy had become our relief. This new feeling flowed through our home. It ate with us, sat with us, and rode in cars with us. We were not relieved that someone else was in mourning, but relieved that our relatives were safe and that stability would be back in our home. Nonetheless, it was short-lived. Immediately after that phone call, the entire situation worsened before it got better. Houses continued to be hit by missiles, whole families died in their sleep, and hundreds of children never reached their fifth birthday. In less than three weeks' time, almost 1,500 people had left this life for another.

Just a few years later, in 2014, there would be more than double the casualties, and the uprisings would come closer than ever before. From the proximity of the violence, my uncle Mohammed lost all the glass in the windows of his new home, and my uncle Osama's family room was struck while the entire family was gathered there, hoping to ride out the danger together.

While we have been lucky not to have suffered any casualties, all sides continue to live in fear. My father fears losing any of his brothers or sisters, and we fear that he should ever have to go through that pain. For now, my relatives are names, faces, and voices that I recognize, and people whom I hope and pray to meet again one day as an adult.

All we can do is continue to pray for change, safety, peace, and happiness. Keeping in mind the reality of the dangers "back home" has become a habit. And while my family has come closer together in terms of withstanding trying events, we have also learned that relief is not reliable. As long as the bad news, the grave news from the foreign region that we are most connected to continues, the claws of occupation find a way to scratch at our safe suburban front doors.

DURING THE REIGN OF VYTAUTAS THE GREAT

DAIVA MARKELIS

I wrote "During the Reign of Vytautas the Great" as a graduate student at the University of Illinois Chicago. I was studying the history of bilingual education in the United States, marveling at the ways immigrant parents passed down the language and traditions of their birthplace to their children. Lithuanian was my first language, and to ensure that my sister and I spoke it properly, my parents had us attend Lithuanian Saturday School. I was not at all happy about this as a girl, but today I feel very fortunate to speak Lithuanian, one of the oldest living languages in the world. Growing up in a Lithuanian household and community certainly didn't deter me from mastering English; today, as a professor of English, I frequently talk about the social, personal, and cognitive benefits of speaking two or more languages fluently.

EVERY SATURDAY MORNING, FOR SEVEN YEARS OF MY LIFE, WHILE other children were watching cartoons, I studied Lithuanian history and geography, literature and grammar, in the classrooms of St. Anthony's School. They seemed different on this day, these rooms, transformed from the orderly pristine spaces of the nuns, where during the week we sat, hands crossed, the girls in our prim green-and-white uniforms, the boys in navy pants and white shirts, to brighter, more chaotic chambers where little learning appeared to take place.

We didn't know enough, my sister and I, to protest this infringement of inalienable childhood pleasures—imagine, no Bugs Bunny. By the time we realized that most children did not have to wake up early Saturday morning and march off to school once again, it was too late. Not that our protests would have made a difference. We were told, again and again, how lucky we were to be able to attend a second school. We were "richer" than those poor *amerikonai* who spoke only one language, and mundane English at that.

At the beginning of each semester of Lithuanian Saturday School, we received notebooks in bright orange and lime green and mustard yellow with portraits of Maironis, Father of Lithuanian Poetry, and Vincas Kudirka, Freedom Fighter, on each cover—one notebook per subject. We drew fancy mustaches on Maironis, and otherwise defaced the notebooks. We made fun of the teachers, who had received their pedagogical training in Lithuania. We laughed at their fractured English, hurled spitballs at them, mangled their drawn-out Lithuanian names.

Among our victims was Ponia Motušienė, a short woman with perfect posture, which just accentuated her massive bosom, a chest so huge we wondered how it was able to stay in an upright position. "What about the laws of gravity?" we snickered every time she entered the room. Her colleague, Ponia Kliorienė, had inky black hair she wore in a huge bees' nest updo. We dropped the "ienė" ending from her name, substituting "ox," not because she was large or clumsy, but because the resulting Kliorox—Clorox!—was too tempting to resist. "Have you done the reading for Clorox's class?" we'd ask each other.

Some of us had Ponia Babrauskienė, who pronounced her *l*'s like *w*'s. Her speech impediment came most clearly into play the day the class was to read aloud Balys Sruoga's famous poem, "Supasi, supasi lapai nubudinti" (The Awakened Leaves Are Swaying, Swaying).

"Supasi, supasi *w*apai nubudinti," began Arvydas Žygas.

"It's not wapai," Babrauskienė corrected him. "It's wapai!"

"That's what I said, Supasi, supasi wapai nubudinti."

And then there was poor Ponas Zailskas, a good man, old-fashioned, courtly, but too proud and stubborn to wear the hearing aid he so desperately needed. We mouthed out answers to his questions about the dative case, shaping words with our lips. "Speak up," he'd say. We'd whisper back, "But we are speaking up," contorting our faces into manic imitations of speech.

And yet we learned. We conjugated verbs: *Aš matau, tu matai, jis/ji mato* (I see, you see, he/she sees). We wrote *diktantai* (dictation) on the board, fearing a sentence with too many *nosinés*, those squiggles appended to certain vowels to indicate nasality, literally translated as "handkerchiefs." We discussed with great seriousness the uses of the personal pronoun *tu* versus the formal *jūs*. We memorized poems, which we then had to recite on various public occasions—Lithuanian Independence Day, Mother's Day, the end of the school year. They were adult poems about death and heroism and the loss of freedom, about nature and God.

At Lithuanian Saturday School I learned a geography imbued with longing—Lithuania was a country of lush pine forests and golden dunes, a paradise on earth, forever embedded in amber. More important, I learned about the arbitrariness of borders, that a country can exist for one person and not for another—a lesson reinforced at home, where there were always maps, and a globe that my sister and I loved to twirl when my father wasn't around.

Depending on the politics of the mapmaker, Lithuania was either on the map, its borders penciled in with dashes, lines less certain than those that outlined France or Turkey, with the word *Lithuania* squeezed in (or sometimes, oh so wonderfully, *Lietuva*, the Lithuanian spelling), or it was missing, absent, obliterated by a large pink smear of color—the USSR.

At Lithuanian Saturday School I learned that words can be borders, imposed artificially, that "the Baltic States" were not a complete, unbreakable little set of countries—Lithuania, Latvia, Estonia—but a term conceived during the nineteenth century out of political expediency. Throughout the ages, Lithuania's history has been more firmly, closely linked with Catholic Poland's than with Lutheran Latvia's, although Lithuania's language, like Latvia's, is Baltic, not Slavic.

Lithuanian history, as taught by Juozas Kreivėnas, was my favorite subject. I learned (and still remember) that the Battle of Žalgiris (Tannenberg) was fought in 1410; the Lithuanian army mortally wounded the Teutonic

Knights. And I learned that the Treaty of Lublin, signed in 1569, which united Lithuania and Poland, made it impossible for a Lithuanian ever again to ascend the throne, though it allowed for the expansion of these two countries from the Baltic to the Black Sea. And most important, I learned that on February 16, 1918, Lithuania declared its independence from Russia and was able to act on this declaration to become a free nation for the first time in centuries, an independence that lasted until the Communist takeover in 1940 and would not be regained for another fifty-one years.

Kreivėnas was a heavy man whose gray suits were worn too thin for respectability and who, according to American standards, could have showered more frequently. We rarely made fun of him, though. We respected him; perhaps we even feared him a little. He made us believe that nothing was more important than what had transpired in the forests of Žalgiris more than five hundred years ago. Unless it was the conversion of the Lithuanian pagans, the last Europeans to accept Christianity, in the middle of the thirteenth century. Nothing was more interesting than the brave and wily Vytautas's attempts to be crowned king of Lithuania, nothing more tragic than the interception of the crown by the Poles on its way to Rome just days before his death.

"During the reign of Vytautas the Great," Kreivėnas would begin; we sat, entranced.

LONG AFTER I had graduated from Saturday School, I would visit Kreivėnas in his bungalow filled with books. He owned more books than anyone I knew. He kept them stacked in piles up to the ceiling, until the house could no longer contain them, then transformed his garage into a bookstore, where you could borrow and browse and even buy, for quarters, books printed in Vilnus on cheap paper, poorly bound.

There were people in our community who were suspicious of these books, suspicious of Kreivėnas himself. How to explain all that literature from Communist Lithuania when any correspondence was difficult; the latest dictionaries; the boring novels of proletarian life; the volumes of poetry that attempted and sometimes managed to circumvent the ruling order by playing with language—flattening words out so that they no longer meant what one thought they meant.

The attacks on Kreivėnas were a manifestation of a larger rift, one that threatened to tear apart the once sturdy cloth of the Lithuanian immigrant community, not just in Cicero, Illinois, but in Cleveland and Brockton and Brooklyn and Detroit. Opposing political ideologies had been a part of Lithuanian life since the nineteenth century, but they had been buried in the postwar years when more pressing concerns—finding a job, a place to live, a school to educate one's children—supplanted earlier divisions. More important, everyone was united in their hatred of the Soviets.

Then, sometime in the seventies, the thawing of the Cold War was met not with a unified sigh of relief, but a resurgence of the old quarrels. When the Lithuanian government opened its doors to the children of the immigrants in the form of month-long summer courses on the Lithuanian language, the arguments centered on whether one could visit Communist Lithuania and not become a Communist oneself. Those who believed in fostering connections to the occupied homeland were perceived as traitors by those who held to a "We won't go back until every Communist is dead" philosophy.

My parents belonged to the former group. My father, as head of the Cicero chapter of the Lithuanian Society, had spoken out about the need to support the young people who had chosen to travel to Lithuania.

"What the heck, I might even go with them," he said at a meeting to scattered applause and ominous murmurs.

On a bright Saturday morning in the middle of May sometime in the seventies, my mother ran up the two flights of stairs holding a pair of pruning shears like a weapon. She lunged into the kitchen where my father was finishing breakfast and my sister and I were arguing about whose turn it was to clean the bathroom: "Come look! Look what they've done!"

We scurried downstairs.

Giant slashes of bloody red paint covered our garage door; sections of the original brown peeked through, making our garage look like a giant Rauschenberg canvas.

We stared at our garage, my mother shaking, my father frowning. I felt a surge of illicit excitement. My parents, who complained about taxes, who subscribed to *Consumer Reports*, who had voted Republican in the last local election, were Communists!

Several weeks later my father came back from work to find a note written in Lithuanian attached to the doorknob of the front entrance to the house. He read it out loud to us before dinner:

"All you know how to do is hate and destroy, hate and destroy. Stop your hating and destroying before you tear apart the community, you slimy toad of a Communist."

There was no signature to the letter.

"It sure is poorly written," said my father, who had been a teacher of Lithuanian back in Aukštaitija: "Look, no comma after *griauti*!"

My mother was frightened, ready to call the police. My father looked at her and laughed. "No comma after *griauti*," he repeated several times, shaking his head. "No comma after *griauti*."

CHILDREN OF THE FIFTY-SIXERS

GROWING UP IN HUNGARIAN CHICAGO

REBECCA MAKKAI

Every city is really multiple cities, and in Chicago, many of those cities-within-the-city are ethnic enclaves. We see that sometimes neighborhood by neighborhood (Greektown, Chinatown, Devon Ave., etc.), but there are smaller pockets that aren't necessarily anchored by a physical neighborhood. There's no geographical Hungary-town (if there were, listen, we'd have the BEST food) but I grew up, nonetheless, in Hungarian Chicago. This was my best attempt to explain it. I'm quite often allergic to the second-person point of view, but for some reason this essay came out that way. Maybe because it felt like walking someone through my non-neighborhood-of-a-neighborhood, a guided tour.

L ET'S SAY THAT, LIKE SO MANY, YOU WERE BORN OUTSIDE THE BOR-ders of your own country. Or more specifically, you were born in Chicago in the middle of your father's fifty-year exile from his country. Say you're one of those children of the "Fifty-Sixers," the student revolutionaries who, after their rebellion was crushed (think Tiananmen Square, but with more statues of Lenin) ran across Hungary's borders and wound up months later, wearing refugee clothes, in Chicago, Cleveland, New York. The Fifty-Sixers were young—young enough to learn solid English, to make careers here, to have children here. Young enough when they arrived that most didn't head back after the Iron Curtain lifted. A few, like your father, are returning home only now.

If your family were French, or Russian, or Mexican, you'd grow up with at least a filmic impression of that place. But there are no movies, no children's books set there, no restaurants full of Hungarian food. Just the occasional Olympic swim team. (Technically you're Transylvanian— from the part of Hungary that's now trapped inside Romania—but you know that what you hear about that place is the cartoon version.) Your father won't bother teaching you the difficult and kinless language, because he doubts you or he will ever have the chance to return to the only place in the world where it's spoken. Your knowledge of Hungary is entirely limited to the parts of it that pass through Chicago. Fortunately, a lot of it passes through Chicago.

Here's how it usually happens: Someone has gotten out. They've obtained a travel visa with no intention of returning, or they've bribed someone, or they have, like your father, run over mine-laden farmlands in the middle of the night. They land in Chicago. It's 1982 or 1983 or 1985. And because you aren't in school that day, you're the one to ride with your father to O'Hare, to wait in the United terminal as the refugee steps off the plane, blinking and delirious. If it's 1987, you are thrilled to meet an adult who finds the new neon light tunnel from the C gates as amazing as you do, even if you and this quavering old man cannot understand each other in the slightest.

The refugee is astounded by your father's Volkswagen, which has air-conditioning. But you're still just on I-90. When the city itself comes into view—maybe the refugee got a good look from the plane, or maybe it was a cloudy day—you see it with his eyes. It's Xanadu. It's Olympus. It's the Emerald City.

Your father has plans. First: the observation deck of the Sears Tower. In retrospect, you'll wonder why more of these refugees didn't have heart attacks. Then Lake Shore Drive. Then up to the suburbs, where this man will spend a week or a month or a year living in your basement. On the way, your father makes sure to swing up Sheridan Road to show off those mansions with gates, the apex of capitalism. If it's a nice day, you'll go to the beach. But these people have seen lakes before. Hungary has a beautiful one.

Here's what they haven't seen: the produce section at Jewel. Which is why your father has saved it for the end of the tour. The Sears Tower might have been impressive, but this—*this*—is the culmination. One married couple can't believe it's real, thinks it's somehow been set up for their benefit, a Potemkin village of fruit. And although it's a produce section that would send a 2015 Chicagoan running for the farmers' market, even now you can see it as a spectacular thing. Mountains of lettuce, bananas not yet yellow, barrels of apples in five different colors. Strange, ugly things called avocados. Welcome to America.

Because enough of these people wind up in Chicago—thanks to your father and other helpful hosts—you grow up with pockets of Hungary all around you. There's the food: sweet noodles, goulashes to feed an army, plums wrapped in dough and boiled, salamis and sour cherry soup and salted duck fat spread on toast. When your father's cousin gets out, his wife sets up a ballet studio where the rigor of her classical, Communist training gives you, if not a lot of grace, at least good posture for life. (When your own daughters are old enough to start dance you'll try the watered-down version at the rec center, then quickly grand jeté them back to her studio.) And there's the music; you've grown up in a Chicago over which Georg Solti presides like a court composer, a Chicago with Bartók concerts sponsored by various Hungarian cultural groups. And you've grown up in a house with whole shelves of albums from expatriate musicians, ones who ran through the hills with cellos.

You've grown up with a Hungarian sheepdog, a puli named Pogácsa (after the addictive biscuits invariably set out as appetizers for guests) who is, like you, out of touch with his roots except in a few ways they manifest: his appearance, his instincts. When your parents have parties, he circles and bumps the guests until they're clustered into small groups. He is treating them, though he doesn't know it, like Hungarian sheep.

The night before your wedding, your father asks you—and for some reason, it seems a totally logical time to ask you this—if you consider yourself American. You answer yes, not because you feel like a baseball-loving Daughter of the American Revolution, but because to you, this is what it means to be American: to be both from here and from away, to belong also to a land you've never known, to look with perpetual wonder at the lemons in the grocery store. You are a daughter of a different revolution.

GROWING UP IN CHICAGO

TONY ROMANO

Chicago is made up of hundreds of distinct neighborhoods. Your Chicago is not quite my Chicago. You played kick the can, we played ringolevio. You played soccer, we played softball. You rooted for the White Sox, we rooted for the Cubs. In this sense, Chicago, to a kid, often feels like a quaint little town. Here's what growing up in Chicago felt like to me.

MY FATHER ARRIVED IN CHICAGO IN JANUARY 1958. HE SETTLED into an apartment, started working in a factory as a tailor for Hart Schaffner & Marx clothiers on Division Street, then sent for the rest of his family. My mother, my brother, and I arrived in June of 1958. I was a year old.

For thirteen years we lived on Ohio Street, a half-block away from St. Columbkille School on Marshfield Street and the adjoining church on Grand Avenue. Throughout those thirteen years, I don't recall venturing much beyond certain boundaries: Ashland and Damen from east to west, Chicago and Grand from north to south. My parents never owned a car, so we'd hop on the Grand Avenue bus and make our way to Lincoln Park Zoo on an occasional Sunday in the summer, where we'd eat homemade meatloaf sandwiches wrapped in oil-soaked wax paper. When I was seven, we spent several weeks in Italy, minus my father. And I worked with the neighborhood milkman when I was thirteen. But otherwise, my entire world existed within these fairly narrow confines.

Despite the fact that we had little money—so little my mom had to work nights at a factory in the neighborhood—and didn't go anywhere, I don't recall feeling deprived. Food was always plentiful, more than plentiful. The apartment, though small, never felt cramped. The only time I recall my security threatened was after we'd moved to a slightly bigger apartment two houses down. I came home from school and had forgotten and tried to barrel through the familiar back door. When it wouldn't budge, I peered inside to see it barren, which sent a shock of abandonment through me that I've never forgotten. After a few pounding heartbeats, I finally recalled where my family and all our stuff had gone.

The neighborhood provided its own security and riches. I'd usually be the first one outside with my bat and sixteen-inch softball, waiting for friends to join me. We'd play at the schoolyard, where we had spray-painted bases on the concrete. You'd have to hit the ball to left or left center because the school took up most of the field, but we didn't mind. We'd be out there every day until we couldn't see the ball. And there was never a single adult around to help us form teams or make calls on the field or to keep track of who had won or lost. We saw adults passing through, of course, on their way home from or going to work, but they never paid any mind to our world, and we certainly didn't pay much mind to theirs. I had no conception of Little League or Pee Wee football or any other organized sports.

If we didn't have enough players for a softball game, we'd play pinners on the side of the stairs, a game in which a "batter" tried to hit a curb with a rubber ball so that it would carom over fielders' heads. When we weren't playing softball or pinners, we'd play marbles—for keeps. Or we'd see who could spit the farthest. Often, we pitched pennies or quarters on sidewalk squares, then graduated to poker. We built cork-shooters out of sawed-off broomsticks, clothespins, and red produce rubber bands that shot flattened bottle caps hundreds of feet. It's a small miracle no one ended up in the hospital. We created puppet shows on the back porch of our apartment, the same place where I unraveled firecrackers and poured the powder into cardboard cylinders to make more spectacular fireworks. A few times we pulled down the school's fire escape; I still recall the rusty creaking of the ladder unfolding and stepping onto the wobbly steps.

When no friends were around, usually because they went to Lake Michigan (I rarely joined them as I didn't know how to swim and feared they'd throw me in), I busied myself reading on my front stoop, mainly comic books—*Superman, Batman, World's Finest*. Every Thursday the new comics would come out, and I'd have to scrounge the neighborhood for pop bottles, which were worth two cents each. I still recall the anticipation of seeing the new issues as I walked the three blocks to the far corner store, turning the wire rack, deciding which ones I could afford. I took great care with the comics I bought, never folding over the pages. Sometimes I'd spread the issues on the floor of my room or on my bed, just to take in the splash of colors. I must have had a collection of about a thousand comics. As a teenager, I started reading science fiction and mysteries and stored away my comics in the attic. Much to my dismay, and my heart still aches to think of this, my mother cleaned out the attic one day and threw out my entire collection. I have a vague recollection of my brother selling off a portion of the comics before this incident, but I'm not sure. Some of the comics were his, and he could have believed he was claiming his own.

At night we played elaborate rounds of ringolevio, where one team hid and the other would have to find, tag, and bring the hiders back to the jail at the school steps. If four people were captured, let's say, an uncaptured teammate could spring out and duck between guards to tag and free his entire team. I can still feel the ache in my chest from running too long. Other nights we played kick the can, caught lightning bugs and put them in jars, listened to both 45s and LPs on a battery-operated record player, walked to Battista's fish store for Italian lemonade, bought steaming hot dogs covered with fresh onions and chopped tomatoes from a man with a cart, stuck our ears close to streetlights to hear the buzz reverberating through the pole, and eavesdropped on adult conversations. This is the only fond memory I have of adults—men and women sitting around on lawn chairs or meeting at each other's houses for coffee and pastries. Their talk was loud, devoid of weighty matters—at least I can't recall much— but there was an intimacy and casualness to their talk that I still admire and miss. I feel as if I grew up with three languages: English, Italian, and Chicago. Most of the adults sitting on lawn chairs at night were fluent in all three tongues. *Hey, Wileyo, veni qua, tell me, you want two or tree sugar in your coffee?* When my novel came out, I imagined friends from the old neighborhood and even a few relatives remarked: "Hey, Antney, how did you write those sentences? You don't talk nothing like that." Sometimes I wonder the same. When I talk with people, my thought process and my very vocabulary is different than when I sit down to write. I suspect the difference has something to do with my fear of seeming pretentious, which would have made me a pariah in the old neighborhood and probably in my own house, where I didn't have much use for the private vocabulary and cadences I was creating during my reading time.

While much of this may sound idyllic, and it certainly still feels that way to me—vendors passing through our street on wooden carts selling lupini beans and sunflower seeds, tomatoes and watermelon, others peddling a sharpening tool for scissors and knives, calling the mothers to bring out their dull blades—the neighborhood included tensions. Gangs such as the Gaylords and the Latin Kings painted their emblems on sidewalks. One time I felt the foundation of our apartment quake from the vibration of a light pole being torn from its base and landing a few feet from our front door, all of which I discovered after rushing outside. Minutes earlier, a gang member had thrown a baseball bat into the windshield of a rival's car, which lost control and rammed into the pole. The driver stormed from his car unhurt, fire in his eyes.

One time a Puerto Rican family tried to move into our neighborhood, but moved out shortly after when a brick shattered their picture window. I never saw a Black person in our neighborhood until maybe 1968, though I knew that a "Black neighborhood" wasn't far away. After Martin Luther King Jr. was shot, I felt a visceral fear that riots would overtake our streets.

You'd think that we would have talked about some of these tensions at school, but St. Columbkille preferred to remain insulated from the worries of the outside world. We learned our multiplication tables and memorized our catechism lessons and recited our confessions, but we didn't talk about injustice or intolerance or anything remotely political. The one exception was my seventh-grade teacher, for whom we campaigned, handing out leaflets for his aldermanic aspirations. He was the cool teacher with the long hair that everyone liked.

How did this Chicago upbringing shape me? I'm not sure because I was always chronically shy as a boy, always on the periphery of the action. I feel as if I've been watching people my entire life. But the watching has been of Chicago, and I think the city has become part and parcel of my DNA. And through my observations, I've learned that you shouldn't throw things at other people or at other people's houses, regardless of who lives in those houses, but that this does happen. If you stand by and watch, the brick tossing will happen again. I've learned that people aren't going to give you things for free, but if you scrape, you're going to make a pretty good living. I've learned that attics, though quaint, are miserable storage spaces. I've learned that young people can negotiate this world fairly well on their own, that they don't need to rely on adults to call balls and strikes and to make everything right for them. I've learned to root for the underdog because in a city of big shoulders, high-rises dwarfing the many factories dotting the boulevards and avenues, not everyone is on equal footing, not everyone can prosper without a helping hand or a fighting chance.

THE VIEW FROM THE SOUTH SIDE, 1970

GEORGE SAUNDERS

I grew up in Oak Forest, a south suburb, after we moved there from Fifty-Fifth and California. So my whole childhood took place within that magnificent kingdom, Chicagoland. It was a rich experience—the city felt like a whole country, with countless zones and moods and hidden peoples and traditions, intercut with the wild Illinois woods that were the Forest Preserves, dotted by those ceremonial places of worship called "White Castle." In this piece, I just remember, or invent, a moment where I stand for a second at the front door of a long-defunct restaurant called Jardine's and look north toward Chicago, before going in and cleaning out the smorgasbord.

J ARDINE'S RESTAURANT SAT ON A HILL IN OAK FOREST, A SOUTH-
ern suburb. On a clear night you could see Chicago. Part of our Jardine's dining ritual was to pause at the door, have a look at the skyline.

There it was: small but bright, like a white fire in the Forest Preserve.

Comiskey Park was in there somewhere. Wrigley Field was there. Blackhawks jerseys, the most beautiful in sports, hung dignified in Chicago Stadium lockers. The major heroes of Chicago sport were there: Luis Aparicio, Bobby Hull, Dick Butkus. Also the minor: the Maki Brothers (Chico and Wayne), Jerry Sloan, Wilbur Wood, chubbiest pitcher in all of baseball, his knuckleball having rendered his physique irrelevant.

Mayor Daley was there, jowly, in his pajamas, nicer at home than at work.

My intellectual heroes were there: Studs Terkel; the columnist Mike Royko; his creation, Slats Grobnik, who I assumed was a real guy. My uncle John and his brothers were there, arguing politics like radicals out of Dostoevsky, only eating White Castles. The Old Town folk music scene was there: Steve Goodman, John Prine. Someday, when I could drive, I'd head downtown. Prine and Goodman would approach, go: *You play guitar?*

A little, I'd say.

Come with us, they'd say. *We need some fresh ideas. And you seem pretty cool.*

The Museum of Science and Industry was there: the Pickled Babies swam in their jars of green formaldehyde, even Full-Term, his head mushed down by the lid of his jar for all eternity; the talking mannequins of the Bell Telephone Exhibit waited creepily and silently for morning, when they could once again begin mechanically extolling the Virtues of Telephonic Communication.

Marquette Park was there, where crazy protesting Lithuanians had climbed into trees with flares the night Dr. King came to town. As Dad drove us through, I'd seen a guy reeling in a tree, face red-lit by his flare, fat branch between his legs, like an animatron in a ride called Race-Hatred Forest.

Grant Park was there, sanctified by the recent Convention protests. The lilac-covered wire fence in Gram's backyard was there. Fifty-Fifth Street was there, the ghost of General MacArthur driving along it in his ghost-car, on the way in from Midway. The Greek grocery was there, its gumball machine laced with plastic balls redeemable for candy bars. Uncle Bill and Aunt Anna's pipe-ceilinged basement apartment was there, on Mozart Street, where he'd studied the teachings of the Rosicrucians so devotedly that one night he accidentally astral-projected himself to the Palmer House, where he worked as a janitor. (Next day some of his coworkers swore they'd seen him, though in fact he'd never left his bed.)

The lake was there, heaving in the dark. The alewives were there, waiting to wash ashore.

Roses were there, clustered around fading Virgin Marys in crèches slightly askew. The Black Panthers were there, signaling secret meetings with African drums. The Nabisco plant was there, filling the night with the smell of vanilla. Lake Shore Drive was there, worrying me with its famous S-curve: When old enough to drive, would I be one of the dicks who drove into the lake?

Wide avenues of spreading oaks were there. Moss-covered park lagoons were there. Narrow gangways were there, smelling of wet brick. The Magikist lips were there, always kissing. A decommissioned DC-9 sat atop a restaurant on Cicero, so working South-Siders with no hope of vacationing anywhere but the Dells could have the experience of eating on a plane.

Porn showed in the grand old theaters; pigeons nested on the new Picasso statue; old babushkas sat alone, watching *The Munsters* on Channel 32; guys clomped down North Rush Street in early disco shoes. Harold Drumm was there, a boy who'd lost his arm in a trash compactor and haunted my dreams because, it had said in the *Chicago American*, he'd run home, arm in hand, calling for his mother.

Petersen Coal, where Dad worked, was there. The flophouse lobby where he'd been held at gunpoint by a crazed conspiracy theorist was there. Division Street was there, down which an angry heartbroken mob of Black high-school kids had marched the day of the King assassination, breaking out store windows with rocks and bricks, closing in on Dad's car when the Chicago cops intervened, firing their guns in the air. The famous racist Trent brothers were there—slumlords and customers of Petersen Coal—who'd mounted a machine gun in their office across from the Taylor Homes, anticipating the Uprising. They'd thrust delinquent Black tenants into basement boilers headfirst, and, when they felt it necessary, they'd shove the guy all the way in and walk off, leaving him to burn.

Chinatown was there, Greektown was there, the Ukrainian, Polish, Irish, and Mexican enclaves were there. Dad knew them all, down to the intersection where one ended and the other began.

We'd moved out too early. In truth I didn't know the city well at all. But someday I would. I'd move down there, live on Lake Shore Drive.

That would be my base of operations. Yes: someday that burning white fire would know me too. I'd move around it with confidence, taking cabs, tipping bartenders who knew me by name, hanging out with Royko, who'd see me as his protégé, the real thing, a true Chicago kid.

Why live there, people would ask me. Why not Paris? Why not New York?

Why, it is my city, I would reply. It contains everything one could ever desire.

But now it was time to eat.

The entire city could be blocked out with the thumb. That was part of the pre-Jardine's ritual: you held up your hand and blocked out Chicago with your thumb.

But because you were a kid, and Chicago was all you knew, it was in your heart, and stayed there forever, the yardstick against which the rest of the universe was judged.

ACKNOWLEDGMENTS

GROWING UP CHICAGO HAD ITS BEGINNINGS IN A SERIES OF CON-versations between David Schaafsma and Tony Grosch, a longtime faculty member in the Program in English Education at UIC, who wrote his dissertation at Northwestern University on Chicago novels and taught the immensely popular Chicago in Literature course. It was in luncheon talks with Tony at Tufano's (in Little Italy) and Nine Muses (in Greektown) that the idea of a book of writings emerging from Chicago neighborhoods was hatched.

Our first round of appreciation must be extended toward the talented and generous authors included in this anthology. We thank them for their patience and willingness to share their work with a new audience: readers whom we hope will find themselves in the outstanding works contained within. We are also thankful to all the authors who submitted stories. While we aimed to make this collection a widespread sampling of unique narratives, space limitations did not allow us to include them all.

Emil Ferris's evocative cover art has been a gift to this project. Its reference to Chicago's iconic Art Institute lions honors what we hope will be the enduring connections the anthology will make for our readers.

We are grateful to the many individuals who have each lent expertise, and an ear, to the growing vision of this book, including UIC's Luis Alberto Urrea, Cris Mazza, and Mustapha Kamal, Columbia College's Carmelo Esterrich, George Bailey, and Dominic Pacyga, and Northwestern's Bill Savage. Special thanks are extended to colleague Todd DeStigter and other faculty members of the Program in English Education at UIC who helped us to shape the vision of what this manuscript could become.

We would especially like to extend our appreciation to the University of Illinois Chicago, including four different heads of the Department of English: Walter Benn Michaels, Lennard Davis, Mark Canuel, and Lisa Freeman. We are grateful for the support from the reference department in the university's Richard J. Daley Library. We would like to thank UIC's Chancellor's Undergraduate Research Award program for funding undergraduate students to do research for and participate in the process of shaping the book, including Angela Duea, Jennifer Pontelli, Brenna Murphy, Madihah Sharif, Manylen Bunchen, Megan Gallardo, Quiahuitl Quezada, and Amanda Elfar. Scores of students in multiple classes helped us roadtest many of these stories, particularly in Dave's Young Adult Literature classes and Roxanne's seminar classes at Dominican University.

The broader vision of this collection is due in part to the several years of crucial work and unflagging commitment to this project from Salwa Halloway. Her dedication to the purposes of the project, and her insistence on its importance, was instrumental in its development.

Dave would like to thank his many friends who heard about and helped talk through this project over the years, and his family: Tara, Sam, Ben, Harry, Hank and Lyra, Shirley, Bob, Jim, Marilyn, Nancy, Rachel, Rosanne and Harold, and Todd.

Roxanne extends her appreciation to her family, especially: Greg, Michael, Hayley, Charlie, Eleanor, Christopher, Jennifer, Emmanuel, and Theo. She also thanks her friends, as well as associates and students at UIC, Dominican University, and North Central College, who provided support and valuable insights.

Lauren is especially grateful for Jeff, Matthew, Lucas, Sofia, Grace, and Ethel, along with her family and friends, who always have her back and believe in her no matter what. She thanks the students and colleagues in the Honors College and English Departments at UIC and in the Chicago Public Schools district, whom she values for their own stories and lived experiences. Finally, she appreciates the extraordinary people at StoryStudio Chicago, the Book Cellar, and the other wonderful organizations throughout the city that support the importance of storytelling and community every single day.

We salute Northwestern University Press for singling out this labor of love for publication. We feel honored to be part of the Second to None series that highlights its commitment to Chicago and aims to preserve and showcase the rich history, culture, and writings of the city. In particular we owe a debt of gratitude to the editorial and publishing teams at Northwestern University Press, who saw promise in the project and worked with us to bring it to you.

We respect and acknowledge the long history of Chicago writers, both famous and lesser known, whose collective works and words have inspired us all.

CONTRIBUTORS

Samira Ahmed is the *New York Times* best-selling author of *Love, Hate & Other Filters*; *Internment*; *Mad, Bad & Dangerous to Know*; and *Hollow Fires*. Ahmed was born in Bombay and grew up in Batavia, Illinois, in a house that smelled like fried onions, cardamom, and potpourri.

Dhana-Marie Branton is an award-winning playwright and essayist whose plays have been produced in Chicago and New York. A former fellow at the National Playwrights Conference at the Eugene O'Neill Theater Center, she earned her MFA in creative nonfiction. She is the artistic director of the writing collective Brainboat Literary and Film, which will release *Minors of the Universe* in 2022.

Anne Calcagno is the author of *Love Like a Dog*, which received the first-place New Generation Indie Book Award and a bronze Independent Book Publisher Award. Her story collection *Pray for Yourself* won the San Francisco Foundation Phelan Award, an NEA, and two Illinois Arts Council Artists Fellowships. Her fiction and nonfiction appear in numerous publications.

Ana Castillo is a poet, novelist, short-story writer, essayist, editor, playwright, translator, and independent scholar, whose extensive work includes eighteen books. She is editor of the zine *La Tolteca*, has held the Lund-Gill Chair at Dominican University, the first Sor Juana Inés de la Cruz Chair at DePaul University, the Martin Luther King Jr. Distinguished Visiting Scholar post at M.I.T., and was the poet-in-residence at

Westminster College. Her work includes an American Book Award for her first novel, *The Mixquiahuala Letters*, and the 2018 PEN Oakland Reginald Lockett Lifetime Achievement Award, honoring *Black Dove: Mamá, Mi'jo, and Me.*

Maxine Chernoff was born and raised in Chicago, where she taught in the City Colleges, at Columbia, AIC, and UIC. Her work includes sixteen books of poems, most recently *Camera*, and six works of fiction, all of which are set in Chicago. Her book of stories, *Signs of Devotion*, was a 1991 NYT Notable Book. She has won the Carl Sandburg Award, an NEA in Poetry, and the PEN Translation Award for her cotranslation of *The Selected Poems of Friedrich Hölderlin*. She is a professor in the San Francisco State University Creative Writing Program, which she chaired for twenty years.

M Shelly Conner is an assistant professor of creative writing and interim director of the MFA creative writing program at the University of Central Arkansas. Her multi-genre writings examine culture through a dapper-queer womanist lens and have appeared in *Crisis Magazine* and the *A.V. Club*, and on NBC News and *TheGrio*. Her debut novel is *everyman.*

Lauren DeJulio Bell teaches in the Honors College at the University of Illinois Chicago. She previously taught in the UIC English Department and the Chicago Public Schools district. She serves on the associate board of StoryStudio Chicago and leads a local project (*We Are All Chicago*), where she engages with the people of Chicago to foster civic engagement, community writing, and artistic endeavors.

Stuart Dybek is the author of *The Coast of Chicago* and five other books of fiction, as well as two books of poetry. His fiction, poetry, and nonfiction have appeared in *The New Yorker*, *Harper's*, *The Atlantic*, *Poetry*, and elsewhere. His writing has been widely translated and frequently anthologized, including work in both *Best American Fiction* and *Best American Poetry*.

Dybek's numerous awards include fellowships from the Guggenheim Foundation and the John D. and Catherine T. MacArthur Foundation.

Saja Elshareif was born and raised in the Chicago suburbs and has never lived anywhere else. With her husband and two young children, she currently lives in a southwest suburb of Chicago, where she is an English professor at the local community college.

Emil Ferris was born and raised in Chicago, spending much of her life in the Uptown neighborhood. A writer, artist, and designer, Ferris received her MFA from the Art Institute of Chicago. Her critically acclaimed graphic novel, *My Favorite Thing Is Monsters*, which stems from her fascination with creatures from other worlds and personal lived experiences, has been published in nine languages and honored with numerous awards (from the Eisner Award to the Fauve d'Or at the Angoulême International Comics Festival).

Jessie Ann Foley is the Printz Honor–winning author of the novels *The Carnival at Bray, Neighborhood Girls, Sorry for Your Loss, You Know I'm No Good*, and *Breda's Island*. Her work has been praised by *Kirkus Reviews, Booklist, YALSA, Bank Street*, and *Entertainment Weekly*, and has been featured on school and library recommended reading lists across the United States. Jessie lives with her family on the northwest side of Chicago, where she was born and raised.

Charles Johnson is a professor emeritus at the University of Washington and the author of twenty-two books. He is a novelist, philosopher, essayist, literary scholar, short-story writer, cartoonist and illustrator, an author of children's literature, and a screen- and tele-play writer. A MacArthur Fellow, Johnson received the 1990 National Book Award for his novel *Middle Passage*.

Rebecca Makkai is the Chicago-based author of the novel *The Great Believers* (a finalist for the 2018 National Book Award and the ALA Carnegie Medal), as well as *The Borrower* and *The Hundred-Year House*, and the collection *Music for Wartime*—four stories from which appeared in *The Best American Short Stories*. The recipient of a 2014 NEA Fellowship, Makkai has taught at the Tin House Writers' Conference and the Iowa Writers' Workshop and is on the MFA faculties of Sierra Nevada College and Northwestern University. She is the artistic director of StoryStudio Chicago.

Daiva Markelis is an English professor at Eastern Illinois University. Her work has appeared in the *New Ohio Review, American Literary Review, Cream City Review, Crab Orchard Review, Oyez*, and many others. She's a ranked tournament Scrabble player, loves to knit and quilt, and cheers for the White Sox.

James McManus is the author of eleven books of poetry, fiction, and fact, including *Positively Fifth Street* and *The Education of a Poker Player*. His work has appeared in *Harper's, Paris Review*, the *New York Times, The New Yorker, The Believer*, and in *Best American* anthologies of poetry, sports writing, political writing, and science and nature writing. He teaches at the School of the Art Institute of Chicago.

David Mura has written two memoirs, *Turning Japanese* and *Where the Body Meets Memory*. He is the author of *A Stranger's Journey: Race, Identity, and Narrative Craft in Writing* and a coeditor of the anthology *We Are Meant to Rise: Voices for Justice from Minneapolis to the World*.

Nnedi Okorafor is a Nigerian American author of African-based science fiction and fantasy. Her works include *Who Fears Death*, the Akata books, *Zahrah the Windseeker*, the Binti trilogy, and *Noor*. She also writes comics, including *Black Panther: Long Live the King, Wakanda Forever*, and the Shuri series. She is the winner of Nebula, Hugo, World Fantasy, and the Wole Soynika awards.

Christian Picciolini is the author of *White American Youth: My Descent into America's Most Violent Hate Movement—and How I Got Out* and *Breaking Hate: Confronting the New Culture of Extremism.* He is a former leader of the early American white-supremacist skinhead movement turned peace advocate, who has helped hundreds of people from around the world disengage from violence-based extremist ideologies.

Roxanne Pilat was born and raised in Chicago. A former journalist and corporate communications consultant, she is an adjunct associate professor at North Central College. Her work has been published in various journals, the *Chicago Tribune,* the *Chicago Sun-Times,* and in the anthology *Italian Women in Chicago.* She is a founding editor of the journal *Packingtown Review.*

Tony Romano is the author of the novel *Where My Body Ends and the World Begins.* He also wrote *When the World Was Young* and a story collection, *If You Eat, You Never Die,* which was selected as a finalist in the Associated Writing Program's annual fiction competition. Romano was named 2010 Illinois Author of the Year by the Illinois Association for Teachers of English and was recently awarded a Norman Mailer award for fiction.

Erika L. Sánchez is the daughter of Mexican immigrants. A poet, novelist, and essayist, she was most recently a Princeton Arts Fellow. *I Am Not Your Perfect Mexican Daughter* is her debut novel and was a National Book Award Finalist and a *New York Times* best seller.

George Saunders is the author of eleven books, most recently *A Swim in a Pond in the Rain,* a collection of essays about the Russian short story. He was raised in Oak Forest and teaches at Syracuse University.

David Schaafsma is a professor of English and director of the Program in English Education at the University of Illinois Chicago. The author of several books pertaining to teaching and learning in middle and high school classrooms, he is the editor of *Jane Addams in the Classroom* and coeditor of *Literacy and Democracy: Composition Studies and Literacy in Pursuit of Habitable Spaces; Further Conversations from the Students of Jay Robinson.*

Luis Alberto Urrea is a border boy by birth and a Chicagoan by choice. Author of The *Hummingbird's Daughter,* The *Devil's Highway,* and *The House of Broken Angels,* he received the Chicago Literary Hall of Fame's Fuller Award for Lifetime Achievement in 2021.

CREDITS

M Shelly Conner, "Finding My Femininity in Menswear." From *AfterEllen*, mediasite. Reprinted by permission of the author.

Stuart Dybek, "Vigil." *The Atlantic*, Fiction Issue, July 5, 2011. Copyright © 2011 by Stuart Dybek. Reprinted by permission of ICM Partners.

Stuart Dybek, "Death of the Rightfielder." From *The Coast of Chicago* (New York: Picador, 2004). Copyright © 1990 by Stuart Dybek. Reprinted by permission of Farrar, Straus, and Giroux.

Saja Elshareif, "Grave News." Copyright © 2022 by Saja Elshareif. Reprinted by permission of the author.

Emil Ferris, "Mothman." From Emil Ferris, *My Favorite Thing Is Monsters* (Seattle: Fantagraphics Books, 2017). Reprinted by permission of the author.

Jessie Ann Foley [Jessie Morrison], "Dillinger." *The Great Lakes Review* Vol. 1, No. 1 (Fall 2012). Reprinted by permission of the author.

Charles Johnson, "My Father's Pillow Talk." *Epoch Magazine*, 2014. Copyright 2014 by Charles Johnson. Reprinted by permission of the author.

Rebecca Makkai, "Children of the Fifty-Sixers: Growing Up in Hungarian Chicago." *Newcity*, mediasite, February 4, 2015. Reprinted by permission of the author.

Rebecca Makkai, "The Power and Limitations of Victim-Impact Statements." *The New Yorker*, June 8, 2016. Reprinted by permission of the author.

Daiva Markelis, "Chicago" and "During the Reign of Vytautas the Great." From Daiva Markelis, *White Field, Black Sheep: A Lithuanian-American Life* (Chicago: University of Chicago Press, 2010). Reprinted by permission of the University of Chicago Press.

Second to None

Harvey Young, series editor

Second to None: Chicago Stories
celebrates the authenticity of a
city brimming with rich narratives
and untold histories. Spotlighting
original, unique, and rarely explored
stories, Second to None unveils a
new and significant layer to Chicago's
big-shouldered literary landscape.